Electing Our Bishops

Electing Our Bishops

How the Catholic Church Should Choose Its Leaders

JOSEPH F. O'CALLAGHAN

A SHEED & WARD BOOK

ROWMAN & LITTLEFIELD PUBLISHERS, INC.

Lanham • Boulder • New York • Toronto • Plymouth, UK

A Sheed & Ward Book
ROWMAN & LITTLEFIELD PUBLISHERS, INC.

Published in the United States of America
by Rowman & Littlefield Publishers, Inc.
A wholly owned subsidary of The Rowman & Littlefield Publishing Group, Inc.
4501 Forbes Boulevard, Suite 200, Lanham, Maryland 20706
www.rowmanlittlefield.com

Estover Road
Plymouth PL6 7PY
United Kingdom

British Library Cataloguing in Publication Information Available

British Library Cataloguing in Publication Information Available

O'Callaghan, Joseph F.
  Electing our bishops: How the Catholic Church should choose its leaders /
Joseph F. O'Callaghan.
      p. cm.
  Includes bibliographical references and index.
  ISBN-13: 978-0-7425-5819-9 (cloth : alk. paper)
  ISBN-10: 0-7425-5819-3 (cloth : alk. paper)
  ISBN-13: 978-0-7425-5820-5 (pbk. : alk. paper)
  ISBN-10: 0-7425-5820-7 (pbk. : alk. paper)
  1. Catholic Church—Bishops—Appointment, call and election—History. I. Title.
  BX1905.O23 2007
  262'.122—dc22   2006034796

The one who is to be head over all should be elected by all.
No one should be made a bishop over the unwilling.
Pope Celestine I (422–432)

CONTENTS

Preface ix

Abbreviations xiii

CHAPTER 1
Bishop and People: A Bond of Trust 1

CHAPTER 2
Election of Bishops by Clergy and People in the Early Church 7

CHAPTER 3
Royal Nomination of Bishops in the Early Middle Ages 37

CHAPTER 4
To the Eve of the Protestant Reformation 65

CHAPTER 5
From the Protestant Reformation to Vatican II 85

CHAPTER 6
Contemporary Appointment of Bishops 119

CHAPTER 7
"Is He Worthy?" 153

Epilogue: Re-Membering a Dis-Membered Church 177

Select Bibliography 179

Index 185

About the Author 195

Preface

THE TERRIBLE MORAL FAILURE of the American bishops in handling the crisis of priestly sexual abuse has focused intense attention on the office of bishop. People ask: Who is our bishop? How did he get to be a bishop? How long will he be with us before he moves on to a larger and wealthier diocese? Inspired by Vatican II's call for collegiality between the bishops and the pope, a number of scholars raised the issue of the election of bishops by the clergy and people of the diocese. This was the practice in the Catholic Church in the first millennium but historical circumstances eroded popular participation in the process. Today bishops are routinely appointed by Rome without any significant consultation with the clergy and people whom they will serve. If the Church is to be renewed, not only in the United States, but also throughout the world, a return to the ancient tradition of popular election of bishops is imperative.

Before addressing the question of elections one must first look at the origin of the office of bishop. By the middle of the second century, bishops appeared as the leaders of the Christian community in each city or town and they also frequently gathered in synods or councils to resolve questions of belief and practice. In this day and age when we often hear that the Church is not a democracy, it may surprise some to learn that the clergy and people of the diocese assembled in a council elected their bishops. After Christianity became a legal religion in the Roman Empire in the fourth century, bishops achieved a greater public position and influence than before. Ambitious men viewed the office of bishop as a means to power, and some bishops found it convenient and desirable to remain in close contact with the imperial court. The emperor, and later, the kings who ruled western Europe during the Middle Ages, while paying lip service to the principle of election by clergy and people, intruded into the process by nominating the candidates. Determined to liberate the Church from secular control, eleventh-century reformers made the issue of free elections the capstone of their program.

Nevertheless, the role of both parish priests and ordinary lay folk in the election was greatly attenuated and eventually disappeared altogether. From the late twelfth century onward, the election was entrusted to the canons of the cathedral chapter, an elite body that was often closely associated with the nobility. The rank and file of priests were excluded, and ordinary people had no voice in the election, except perhaps to give consent by acclamation or in an even more ritualized manner in the ceremony of episcopal ordination. Although the emperor, the king, and some nobles might have a say, they were hardly representative of the people as a whole.

In the modern era concordats between the papacy and various European states, intended to assure the well-being of the Church, usually recognized the ruler's right to nominate or to object to a candidate on political grounds. The pope reserved the right to preclude the consecration of someone he deemed unacceptable. In the late nineteenth and twentieth centuries the papacy claimed the right to name the bishops in much of the world, an entitlement affirmed in the Code of Canon Law in 1917 and again in 1983.

On April 19, 2005, the whole world, through the medium of television, witnessed the external ceremonies attendant on the election of a bishop, namely, Pope Benedict XVI, bishop of Rome. Dating from the mid-eleventh century, the electoral process, carried out in secret by the cardinals, illustrates the manner in which bishops were elected throughout Europe from the High Middle Ages onward. Effectively barred from participation were the priests and people of Rome, to say nothing of Catholics worldwide, who, at a time when it seemed that nothing could be done without papal authorization, had a great stake in the outcome. The acclamation of the new pope by the crowd in St. Peter's Square is a vestige of the notion that the clergy and people should give their consent. The spectacle in Rome attests to the need for reform so that priests and people can give a truly effective consent to the choice of the person entrusted with their spiritual care.

Following this historical overview various proposals for broader participation by all the faithful in the process of selecting bishops will be assessed. I will also offer my own proposal for election by the clergy and people of the diocese. While reform of the electoral process is necessary, so is a change in the manner of episcopal leadership. In the concluding chapter I suggest several changes that ought to restore the confidence of the clergy and people in their bishop.

Drawing on the work of church historians, canon lawyers, and liturgists, I hope to provide an educational tool for the general Catholic public who know little if anything about the ancient tradition of the popular election of bishops and are inured to expect that their bishops will be appointed by the pope. A flurry of scholarly articles published in the 1970s and 1980s in journals such as *Concilium* and *The Jurist*, but not easily accessible to the people in the pews, drew attention to episcopal elections. In 1971 the Canon Law Society of America published a collection of essays entitled *The Choosing of Bishops*, and has otherwise attempted to keep the issue before the public; however, the extreme centralization of authority in the papacy has made discussion difficult, if not idle. Believing that the subject needs to be brought up to date, I have tried to create a historical synthesis based on narrative sources, conciliar documentation, liturgical texts, and the commentary of contemporary scholars. My hope is that this will initiate a conversation as well as further study of episcopal elections by parish and diocesan groups.

This study grew out of an attempt to define the third goal of Voice of the Faithful (VOTF), namely, to shape structural change in the Church. When the parishioners of St. John's Church in Wellesley, Massachusetts, organized Voice of the Faithful in the spring of 2002, they announced their mission to be "a prayerful voice, attentive to the Spirit, through which the faithful can actively participate in the governance and guidance of the Catholic Church." They adopted three goals: (1) to support survivors of sexual abuse, (2) to support priests of integrity, and (3) to shape structural change in the Church. Few Catholics would quarrel with the first two goals, but many have asked, "What do you mean by structural change?" In response to that question, members of Voice of the Faithful in the Diocese of Bridgeport, Connecticut, after studying *Lumen Gentium, The Dogmatic Constitution on the Church* promulgated by the Second Vatican Council, developed five proposals for structural change. The first proposal calls for the election of bishops by the clergy and people as an initial step toward renewal of the Church in this very troublous time.[1]

Although Voice of the Faithful provided the spur that set me on this research path, my book is not an official statement of VOTF's views and should not be construed as such. Responsibility for its content is my own.

I want to thank the members of VOTF in the Diocese of Bridgeport for their support and recognition of the need to renew our Church, especially the members of our Planning Committee for the Election of a

Bishop: Margaret Mooney, James Alvord, Jeanne Fogg, John Lee, Richard Maiberger, Robert Mulligan, Anne Pollack, Marie Rose, Daniel Sullivan, and Anthony Wiggins. I also owe a great debt of gratitude for their unwavering friendship and support to Margaret Hickey, Annette Maiberger, Sheila and Thomas Rietano, and Gloria Seymour.

In addition, I wish to express my warm appreciation to several scholars who gave me the benefit of their wise counsel. Msgr. Robert Trisco, editor emeritus of *The Catholic Historical Review*, carefully read my manuscript in its entirety, as did Professor John J. Burkhard, OFM Conv., of the Washington Theological Union, and Professor Paul Lakeland of Fairfield University. Msgr. Thomas Green, professor of canon law at Catholic University, and Richard R. Gaillardetz, professor of Catholic studies at the University of Toledo, read chapters 1, 6, and 7. My readers and I did not always agree, but I have given their comments and suggestions careful consideration; some I adopted, and others I did not. Final responsibility for the text is mine alone. I am also grateful to Robert Blair Kaiser, the distinguished journalist.

Scripture texts in this work are taken from the New American Bible with Revised New Testament and Revised Psalms © 1991, 1986, 1970 Confraternity of Christian Doctrine, Washington, DC, and are used by permission of the copyright owner. All Rights Reserved. No part of the New American Bible may be reproduced in any form without permission in writing from the copyright owner.

Since my baptism seventy-eight years ago I have loved and served the Catholic Church. At this time when our Church is ailing and old ways and structures no longer seem capable of meeting new challenges, I believe that every Catholic must offer his or her gifts to renew the Body of Christ. This book is intended as a small contribution to that effort. If it encourages discussion about the right of the community to elect its leaders, it will have served its purpose.

Notes

1. See *Counsel and Consent as Christian Virtues: Five Proposals for Structural Change in the Catholic Church*, at www.votfbpt.org/proposal.

Abbreviations

ANF	*Ante-Nicene Fathers*
CCSL	*Corpus Christianorum, Series Latina*
CD	*Christus Dominus. Decree on the Pastoral Office of Bishops in the Church*
CLSA	Canon Law Society of America
CSEL	*Corpus Scriptorum Ecclesiasticorum Latinorum*
LG	*Lumen Gentium. The Dogmatic Constitution on the Church*
MGH	*Monumenta Germaniae Historica*
NPNF	*Nicene and Post-Nicene Fathers*
NRB Report	*A Report on the Crisis in the Catholic Church in the United States. The National Review Board for the Protection of Children and Young People Established by the United States Conference of Catholic Bishops.* Washington, DC: USCCB 2004.
PCLSA	*Proceedings of the Canon Law Society of America*
PG	*Pastores Gregis*: John Paul II's Postsynodal Exhortation
PL	Jacques Paul Migne, *Patrologia Latina*
USCCB	United States Conference of Catholic Bishops

Bishop and People
A Bond of Trust

1

T HE OFFICE OF BISHOP is a noble one. The primary teacher of the faithful, charged with the task of preaching the Gospel with authenticity, the bishop bears a grave responsibility for the spiritual comfort of the priests and people of his diocese. He is their shepherd or leader, directing them on the road to holiness through the priestly ministry of the sacraments, and guarding them against evil. Over the centuries many bishops have attained a high measure of personal sanctity and are rightly venerated by the Church, but some noted scoundrels have also occupied the episcopal throne.

For most Catholics the bishop is a remote figure who is rarely visible in parishes. They may see him at the annual celebration of the sacrament of confirmation or during his pastoral visit every two or three years. Some parishioners may even have the opportunity to shake his hand and say hello during a perfunctory parish visit, usually lasting only a few hours, but few are ever able to engage him in intimate conversation. Some may see his picture in the newspaper or in the parish offices dressed either in his black suit with a gold cross hanging on his chest or garbed in chasuble and miter with his pastoral staff or crosier in his hand. They may read his column in the diocesan newspaper or possibly hear him on a radio talk show or see him on television. On occasion he may appear at a public forum to respond to questions, but some, in the vein of Gen. Charles de Gaulle, have been known to respond only to written questions submitted in advance.

The traditional notion of the bishop as shepherd, who knows his flock and who is known by them, is strained in this day and age when bishops are responsible for the care of hundreds of thousands or even millions of souls in their dioceses or archdioceses. In spite of the vast distance that separates the bishop from the everyday parishioner, bishops have enjoyed the respect and confidence of their people until comparatively recently. A bond of trust that seemed unshakable linked the bishop and the faithful whose spiritual well-being is his principal care.

In our day that bond has been severely damaged and in some instances has been ruptured entirely. The scandal of priestly sexual abuse that gained world-wide attention in the last few years has not only cast suspicion on all priests, but it has also harmed the bishops, so many of whom have been revealed as covering up and protecting priestly predators. While scrambling to set things right again, the bishops have been faced with insistent demands from the laity that they live by the principles of accountability and transparency, that is, that they be held answerable for their actions to the people and also in civil courts, and that they be open in explaining how they have expended millions of dollars in contributions by the faithful to settle cases of priestly sexual abuse. This self-inflicted wound will not be cured easily. More than likely another generation or two will have to pass before bishops are again held in the esteem that they enjoyed prior to the great shame of our time.

The Office of Bishop: Ideal and Reality

The ideal to which every bishop should aspire is presented with especial clarity in two texts of the Second Vatican Council, namely, chapter 3 of *Lumen Gentium, The Dogmatic Constitution on the Church*, and *Christus Dominus, The Decree on the Pastoral Office of Bishops in the Church*. Pope John Paul II's apostolic exhortation *Pastores Gregis*, issued in 2003, reiterated that ideal.[1] As successors to the apostles, the bishops, by their ordination, receive the Holy Spirit and are commissioned to continue the work of preaching the word of God, presiding at the liturgy, and governing the churches entrusted to their care. Just as the apostles under the headship of Peter were said to form a college, so too the bishops together with the pope as Peter's vicar are held to constitute a college. Collegiality is expressed especially when the bishops gather in ecumenical councils and synods and in the participation of neighboring bishops in episcopal ordinations. Whereas each bishop has responsibility for his particular church, the entire college of bishops, in union with the pope, is jointly responsible for the whole Church. The bishops, according to these texts, must always act in conjunction with the pope, but he, as Christ's Vicar with supreme and universal authority over the Church, can act independently. The bishops, however, are not papal vicars.

In proclaiming the Gospel, one of his principal duties, the bishop is expected to uphold the dignity and value of the human person and the stability of the family, and to propose principles for the resolution of societal problems such as economic injustice and military conflict. Rather than live in isolation from society, he should initiate and carry on a courteous and humble dialogue with others in the community. Both father and pastor, he should be a servant to his people, "a good shepherd who knows his sheep and whose sheep know him, . . . a true father who excels in his love and solicitude for all, to whose divinely conferred authority all readily submit"(*CD* 16). Displaying a particular affection for his priests, as his sons and friends, he must always be willing to listen to them, to engage them regularly in dialogue, and to show compassion toward those who fail in their vocation. In order to lead his people to holiness, he should be conversant with their needs and the circumstances of their daily lives. Recognizing their right and duty to collaborate in building up the Body of Christ, he ought to welcome their participation in the work of the Church. While the faithful are reminded to cling to their bishop, "he should not refuse to listen to his subjects whose welfare he promotes as of his very own children and whom he urges to collaborate readily with him" (*LG* 27).

Christus Dominus also took up the issue of episcopal elections and resignations; the bishop's right to appoint the clergy and his obligation to provide sufficient priests to care for the faithful; the restructuring of diocesan boundaries; the convocation of diocesan synods; and the establishment of diocesan pastoral councils and national episcopal conferences. Some of these topics are discussed later in this volume.

The ideal described above is wonderful in many ways, but its implementation is often inadequate. The principle of collegiality was exciting when it was first broached because it suggested that the model of Church government as an absolute monarchy would be modified. In accordance with the council, Popes Paul VI and John Paul II convened several synods "representative of the whole episcopate" (*CD* 5), but it soon became clear that the topic and the agenda were developed in Rome; that the bishops summoned to participate had little impact on the outcome; and that whatever decisions were taken were only advisory to the pope. Given the excessive centralization of power in Rome during John Paul II's pontificate, there has been little discussion of collegiality in recent years.

Although the council emphasized that bishops are not vicars of the pope (*LG* 27), today they are often perceived by some in exactly that way, as subordinates or branch managers presiding over administrative subdivisions of a multinational corporation whose headquarters is in Rome. Many bishops, unfortunately, act as though their only obligation is to the pope and the Roman curia. They seem content to be seen as mere functionaries executing directives from Rome, rather than as successors of the apostles, endowed with the capacity for independent thought in caring for their own particular churches and for the Church as a whole. The generation of American bishops in the immediate aftermath of Vatican II displayed an independence of mind when, after wide consultation with the faithful, they drew up major pastoral letters on the economy and on war and peace. Their efforts to do the same on the place of women in the Church foundered, however, in part because of interference from Rome, and these bishops have since given up any attempt to issue another pastoral letter.

Nor have the bishops taken any serious steps to engage the faithful in the governance of the Church, despite John Paul II's admonition in September 2004, summoning them "to create better structures of participation, consultation, and shared responsibilities."[2] Too many bishops seem still to think of their people in the language of *Lumen Gentium* 27, whose unfortunate use of the term "their subjects" is reminiscent of the feudal relationship of lords and serfs. The document's reference to the people of the diocese as children implies a "father knows best" mentality that fails to acknowledge that the majority of the faithful are adults endowed with an intelligence and wisdom that could be put to the service of the Church.

Most grievously the efforts of the bishops to provide sufficient priests to serve the faithful have failed as the Church faces the prospect of an aging priesthood, a shortage of replacements for those who die or retire, and the consequent abandonment of the Eucharist in favor of communion services in the absence of a priest, and the clustering and closing of parishes. The bishops assembled from the whole world in the Synod on the Eucharist in October 2005 touched on some of these problems but failed to take any firm action.

The gravest failure of the American bishops in the second half of the twentieth century is their handling of the crisis of priestly sexual abuse. Their terrible betrayal of trust renders it most difficult for the faithful to respond positively to Vatican II's summons to "submit to their bishops' decision, made in the name of Christ, in matters of faith and morals and to adhere to it with a ready and respectful allegiance of mind" (*LG* 25).

In its report in 2004, the National Review Board (NRB), appointed by the United States Conference of Catholic Bishops to inquire into that ignominious chapter in the history of the Church, made clear how far the bishops had departed from the ideal set forth by the Second Vatican Council. Witnesses questioned by the NRB stressed the need to review the process of selecting bishops. Too often the choice was limited to a narrow pool of candidates, most of whom were former curial officials, seminary rectors and professors, and diocesan officials. Many newly appointed bishops had minimal pastoral experience in parishes; some tended to approach their responsibility with "a management mindset" rather than a pastoral one, and often paid more attention to administrative concerns than to "the human needs" of their people. As a consequence of the transfer of bishops from see to see, a new bishop frequently received little or no information about problem priests. A restriction of episcopal transfers, it was suggested, could assist a bishop in developing and retaining strong connections to the local clergy and people. Moreover, priests who spoke their minds were seldom chosen as bishops, and bishops who did so were not likely to be made archbishops or cardinals. "The predictable result was that priests and bishops did not speak out when that is exactly what the situation demanded." Witnesses stressed the need to broaden the search for suitable candidates for the office of bishop and urged that "greater involvement by the laity in the selection of bishops could help to ensure that future bishops are pastors, prophets, and men of honor and not mere management functionaries.[3]

The National Review Board's devastating critique prompts this look at the history of episcopal elections and the possibility of reestablishing an electoral process in which all the faithful can participate. The principle that the bishop should be chosen by the clergy and people of the diocese was established in the earliest times, but underwent modification over the centuries as kings and emperors attempted to control the elections. The current practice in the Latin Church of papal appointment of bishops, without any real input by either the clergy or the people of the diocese, is a comparatively recent development, first formally affirmed in the Code of Canon Law promulgated in 1917 (c. 329.2).

A return to the ancient and hallowed Catholic tradition of allowing clergy and people to elect as bishop someone they know and recognize as worthy of the office will do much to restore the trust between bishops and the faithful that has been so eroded.

Notes

1. Austin Flannery, OP, ed., *Vatican Council II: The Conciliar and Post-Conciliar Documents*, 2 vols., (Northport, NY: Costello Publishing, 1996), 1:350–425 (*Lumen Gentium*), 564–89 (*Christus Dominus*). See the text of *Pastores Gregis* at www.vatican.va.

2. For the text see www.vatican.va; Tom Rachman, "Pope Talks with U.S. Bishops about Scandal," *Austin American-Statesman*, September 11, 2004.

3. *A Report on the Crisis in the Catholic Church in the United States.* The National Review Board for the Protection of Children and Young People Established by the United States Conference of Catholic Bishops (Washington, DC: USCCB 2004), 127–29.

Election of Bishops by Clergy and   2
People in the Early Church

ANY CATHOLICS, INCLUDING SOME BISHOPS who ought to know better, seem to think that the way the Church exists and functions today is exactly the way it has always been and that indeed Jesus set it up that way. As Francine Cardman remarked: "Thinking historically about the church is not the first instinct of Roman Catholic ecclesiology. The 'default mode' is to think dogmatically and imagine the church as an unchanging, divinely willed institution that has always looked the way it looks now."[1] With reference to that attitude, James Hennesey, the noted Jesuit historian, observed: "When a sentence begins, 'For two thousand years, the church has . . .' it is amazing how often it ends with a false conclusion."[2] The Church exists in historical time and place, evolving over the centuries and borrowing ideas of governance and administration from secular society. Biblical scholars have demonstrated that Jesus intended to reform Israel and expected his disciples to continue that work after his death. The fount and origin of the Christian faith, Jesus did not found a new church nor did he provide his disciples with an organizational chart for such an institution.

The Church that we know today is the result of historical development following Jesus's death. The first Christians (called Nazarenes by their opponents), rather than thinking of themselves as members of a new church, hoped to continue their lives as members of the Jewish community and to attend the synagogue. The Gospel stories describe the followers of Jesus as disciples, that is, men and women who were being taught by him. He was their Teacher and Master. He alone was the High Priest. Prominent among them were the Twelve whom Jesus selected to represent the Twelve Tribes of Israel and thus the whole people of Israel (Lk 22:30; Mt 19:28). After the death of Jesus the Twelve are properly called apostles because they were sent by him to preach the Gospel. However, there were other apostles besides the Twelve, St. Paul most notably, and his companion Barnabas (Acts 20:17–18; 1 Tim. 3, 8, 13). Mary Magdalen has been hailed as the apostle to the apostles because she met the risen Christ and was commissioned by him to tell the others that he had risen from the dead. The term *apostle* died out with the death of the first generation, as no one in the second generation could claim to have seen Jesus and to have been commissioned by him.[3]

The hostility between the new Jewish Christians and their Jewish brethren in Jerusalem and the admission of Gentiles into the Christian community, largely through the preaching of St. Paul and St. Peter, resulted in a gradual rupture between Judaism and Christianity. The decision of the Council of Jerusalem in AD 51 not to require Gentile converts to submit to Jewish law hastened the process of separation (Acts 15:2). The expulsion of the Christians from the synagogue and the destruction of the temple at Jerusalem in AD 70 permanently severed the Christian community from its Jewish roots. No longer identified with the Jewish synagogue, the Christians began to develop a self-conscious awareness of being a different community, a new and distinct religious movement, an *ecclesia*, an assembly, a church (Acts 5:11, 8:1).[4]

Evolution of Ministry in the Early Church

In origin the Church was a community, without distinction between the ordained and nonordained (the clergy and laity of a later date), guided by the Twelve and the other apostles such as St. Paul. As this Church developed, a variety of ministries to serve the needs of the community came into being.[5] Even during the lifetimes of the Twelve the Christian community recognized the need for leaders who would assume responsibility for a multiplicity of tasks. St. Paul (1 Cor. 12:8–10, 28; Rom. 12:5–8; Eph. 4:11) mentions some of the charismatic ministries: teachers, prophets, miracle workers, healers, interpreters of tongues, and administrators.[6] Paul does not tell us how these persons were acknowledged as ministers of the Church, but there are some examples from Acts that suggest how that occurred.

Following the resurrection and ascension of Jesus, Peter spoke to the assembled disciples about the need to replace Judas as one of the Twelve:

> It is necessary that one of the men who accompanied us the whole time the Lord Jesus came and went among us beginning from the baptism of John until the day on which he was taken up from us, become with us a

witness to his resurrection. So they proposed two, Joseph called Barsabbas, who was also known as Justus, and Matthias. Then they prayed: "You, Lord, who know the hearts of all, show which one of these two you have chosen to take the place in this apostolic ministry from which Judas turned away to go to his own place." Then they gave lots to them, and the lot fell upon Matthias, and he was counted with the eleven apostles. (Acts 1:21–26)

We do not know how the two candidates were first proposed. Perhaps someone suggested Barsabbas and someone else Matthias. Nor do we know how "lots" were drawn; perhaps the disciples threw stones on the ground. However that may have been, this is an early example of an election of a minister of the Church. In the later ritual for the making of a bishop the same procedure of calling on God's guidance was followed and the one elected was believed to be God's candidate.

In like manner, when the need for assistants became apparent, the Twelve summoned the community of disciples and said, "Select from among you seven reputable men, filled with the Spirit and wisdom, whom we shall appoint to this task." So they selected seven men and the apostles "prayed and laid hands on them." The seven, whom later history would describe as deacons, were chosen by the whole community to take care of the material wants of widows among the Greek Christians (Acts 6:1–8). Again we do not know the details of the process, but it is another example of an election. In this and the preceding instance we must ask whether the disciples who participated in these elections included women as well as men. The laying on of hands was a rite of commissioning that later became part of the liturgy for the ordination of a bishop.

The choices of Matthias and of the seven are examples of ecclesial democracy, which, according to Patrick Granfield, "is not a new thing in the Church. It has its roots deep in Christian tradition. Evidence of democratic elements in the open system which is the Church appears primarily in the selection of office-holders."[7]

Over time the offices of priest and bishop would become the most important in the Christian community, absorbing many of the earlier ministries. The terms overseer or bishop (*episcopos*) and elder, presbyter, or priest (*presbyteros*) are used interchangeably in the Acts of the Apostles (20:17–29) and other New Testament texts to mean those in charge of a particular church. The Pastoral Epistles to Timothy and Titus, traditionally attributed to St. Paul, but probably written by another toward the latter part of the first century, set forth qualifications for presbyters and bishops, but used those terms interchangeably. The First Epistle to Timothy, reflecting the patriarchal ideal of the Roman paterfamilias, proclaims:

Whoever aspires to the office of bishop desires a noble task. Therefore, a bishop must be irreproachable, married only once, temperate, self-controlled, decent, hospitable, able to teach, not a drunkard, not aggressive but gentle, not contentious, not a lover of money. He must manage his own household well, keeping his children under control with perfect dignity; for if a man does not know how to manage his own household, how can he take care of the church of God? He should not be a recent convert, so that he may not become conceited and thus incur the devil's punishment. He must also have a good reputation among outsiders so that he may not fall into disgrace, the devil's trap. (1 Tim. 3:1–7; also 5:17–19)

This passage from the First Letter to Timothy was incorporated into the later liturgies for the ordination of a bishop. In slightly different language the Epistle to Titus (1:5–9) counsels:

Appoint presbyters in every town . . . on condition that a man be blameless, married only once, with believing children who are not accused of licentiousness or rebellious. For a bishop as God's steward must be blameless, not arrogant, not irritable, not a drunkard, not aggressive, not greedy for sordid gain, but hospitable, a lover of goodness, temperate, just, holy, and self-controlled, holding fast to the true message as taught so that he will be able both to exhort with sound doctrine and to refute opponents.

The First Letter of Peter (I Peter 5:1–4), more than likely by the hand of another and dating from the end of the first century, refers to Peter as a presbyter and stresses the responsibilities of a presbyter:

So I exhort the presbyters among you, as a fellow presbyter and witness to the sufferings of Christ. . . . Tend the flock of God in your midst, not by constraint but willingly, as God would have it, not for shameful profit but eagerly. Do not lord it over those assigned to you, but be examples to the flock. And when the Chief Shepherd is revealed you will receive the unfading crown of glory. Likewise you younger members, be subject to the presbyters. And all of you clothe yourselves with humility in your dealings with one another.

In these and other references it is apparent that the words *episcopos* and *presbyteros* were used to describe the same function of overseeing or leading. Apparently in imitation of the Jewish synagogue a body of elders or presbyters/bishops seems to have been given responsibility for leading the community. There is no evidence in the New Testament of a single bishop governing a diocese. It is indeed an anachronism to refer to any of the apostles as a bishop. As the Christian community spread about the Mediterranean world, local churches emerged in different cities and towns. Each church believed that it was authorized by Jesus to preach the Good News and to designate persons to lead the community in the breaking of the bread. Thus, for example, the "church in Jerusalem . . . sent Barnabas to Antioch" to minister to the large number of new converts there (Acts 11:22). When the question of the admission of Gentiles into the community arose, "it was decided that Paul, Barnabas, and some of the others should go up to Jerusalem to the apostles and presbyters about this question. They were sent on their journey by the church. . . . They were welcomed by the church, as well as by the apostles and the presbyters." Once the issue was resolved, "then the apostles and presbyters, in agreement with the whole church, decided to choose representatives, and to send them to Antioch with Paul and Barnabas" (Acts 15:2–4, 22). In these circumstances the community at Antioch determined to send Paul and Barnabas to Jerusalem; then the church at Jerusalem, under the leadership of the apostles and elders, chose representatives to return to Antioch.[8]

These local churches were especially focused on stressing that they taught as Jesus did and as did the apostles or missionaries who first implanted the seed of Christianity among them. In that sense particular churches were apostolic, and apostolicity was their essential characteristic. In time this concept, formulated as apostolic succession, meant that a particular community or *ecclesia* was founded by one of the apostles (not necessarily one of the twelve) and that it continued to teach and to preach the same Gospel as its founder. Only later did the idea of apostolic succession come to be linked with the transfer of leadership from one bishop to another.[9]

The idea of apostolic succession, that is, that the apostles chose persons to succeed them, is first expressed in the First Letter of Clement of Rome to the Corinthians, usually dated about AD 95. Entitled "From the Church of God Which Sojourns at Rome, to the Church of God Sojourning at Corinth," the letter emphasizes that Jesus chose the apostles who, in turn, "appointed the first-fruits [of their labors], having first proved them by the Spirit, to be bishops and deacons of those who should afterwards believe" (chap. 42). This is the notion of apostolic succession, a hallmark of Catholic belief concerning the office of bishop. The letter was written because young men ousted older presbyters who were "appointed by them [the apostles] or afterwards by other eminent men with the consent of the whole Church" (chap. 44). Objection was made, not to the right of the people of Corinth to remove their leaders, but to the fact that the presbyters forced out were without fault. The use of both terms, bishop and presbyter, reflects the ambiguity of the first century and does not indicate that a single bishop governed the church at Corinth at that time. How the entire Christian community at Corinth gave consent to the commissioning of bishops or presbyters was not stated, but consent was essential. The letter, often cited as an example of the exercise of the Roman primacy, is better understood as a fraternal exhortation from one church to another.[10]

Origin of the Office of Bishop

The first clear reference to the office of bishop, as we understand that term, comes from the letters of Ignatius, bishop of Antioch in Syria, who died around 107. Addressing himself to five churches in Asia Minor (Philadelphia, Smyrna, Ephesus, Magnesia, Tralles) and to St. Polycarp, bishop of Smyrna, he addressed each bishop by name and spoke of the priests and deacons assisting him. "Do all things with a divine harmony, while your bishop presides in the place of God, and your presbyters in the place of the assembly of the apostles, along with your deacons, who are most dear to me, and are entrusted with the ministry of Jesus Christ" (Magnesians 6). The hierarchical structure of bishops, priests, and deacons with which we are familiar appeared at least in these churches in Asia Minor.[11]

Worried about discord in the community, Ignatius emphasized that as the bishop reflects the mind of Christ, so the faithful should act in accord with the bishop and not oppose him (Eph. 3–5). All should respect the bishop just as they respect God's authority and defer to him so that unity may be preserved (Magnesians 3; Trallians 2). "Be ye subject to the bishop and to one another as Jesus Christ to the Father . . . that so there may be a union both fleshly and spiritual" (Magnesians 13; Smyrnaeans 8–9). The bishop's office exists for the good of the entire community and so all should follow him like sheep (Philadelphians 2). Ignatius stressed that the faithful should be united to their bishop and should avoid schism. The unity of the bishop and his community was likened to the unity of Christ and the Church, which in turn was compared to the union of husband and wife. This developed later into the idea that the bishop was wedded to his see, a union symbolized by the ring he wore. Consequently, he should not abandon his flock for another. While emphasizing the unity of the Church under the bishop, and counseling him to allow nothing to be done without his consent, Ignatius also stressed the importance of involving the community by holding frequent meetings and seeking out everyone by name (To Polycarp, 4).[12]

In his letter to the church of Rome, Ignatius did not mention the bishop, priests, or deacons. Perhaps that was due to his ignorance of the bishop's name, though that seems unlikely. It is more probable that he did not do so because the monarchical episcopate developing in Asia Minor had not yet been established in Rome.[13]

Although the Roman letter to the Corinthians cited above and written a few years before Ignatius suffered martyrdom does not identify its author, tradition attributes it to Clement, whose name is included in later lists of the bishops of Rome. However, just as the attribution of that letter to Clement is doubtful, even more so is the description of him as bishop of Rome. In order to emphasize that authentic teaching had been handed on from apostolic times, Irenaeus, bishop of Lyon in what is now southern France (d. 202), declared that Peter and Paul, after founding the church of Rome, handed over the office of bishop to Linus. Irenaeus then gave a list of succeeding bishops down to his own time.[14] Despite Irenaeus, it is generally believed today that the church in Rome, until about the middle of the second century, was administered by a council of elders or presbyters rather than by a single bishop. As there was a Christian community in Rome before either Peter or Paul arrived there, neither could be described as the first bishop of Rome. Paul addressed his letter to the Romans (around AD 56–58) "to all the beloved of God in Rome, called to be holy" (Rom. 1:7). He made no reference to a bishop, and when he extended his greetings to the faithful at Rome he did not mention Peter or Linus.

That the church at Rome was governed by a council of elders or presbyters rather than a bishop is suggested by a passage from *The Shepherd of Hermas*, written in the city in the second quarter of the second century: "You shall read this in the city with the presbyters who are in charge of the Church." Anicetus (154–166), who was visited by Polycarp, bishop of Smyrna (martyred in 155), is regarded as the first person to function as a monarchical bishop in Rome. In that sense it is erroneous to portray Peter as the first bishop of Rome. In his *Ecclesiastical History*, Eusebius, bishop of Caesarea in Asia Minor (d. 338), lists the bishops from different sees in order to demonstrate the transmission of authentic teaching from the time of the apostles. It is noteworthy, however, that he recorded Linus as the first bishop of Rome and Peter as the first bishop of Antioch. His anachronistic description of them as bishops reflects the governmental structure of his own time rather than that of the first century.[15]

The office of bishop developed over time to meet the needs of the Church in particular times and regions. Thus the monarchical episcopate appears around the end of the first century in Asia Minor, as evidenced by Ignatius's letters, but we have to wait until the middle of the second century for clear evidence of the acceptance of rule by a single bishop in other parts of the Christian world. The office of bishop obviously served and continues to serve a useful purpose, but like other aspects of the institutional structure of the Church, it was not established by Jesus Christ and so can be altered to suit new needs. What is important is not to uphold the institutional structure, but rather the faith as taught by Jesus. Institutions are means to facilitate that, but they are nothing more than means.

Episcopal Election in Early Texts

Several early texts emphasize the principle of episcopal election. *The Didache or The Teaching of the Twelve Apostles*, dating from the second century, states: "You must, then, elect for yourselves bishops and deacons who are a credit to the Lord, men who are gentle, generous, faithful, and well tried." The Greek word *cheirotonesate*, translated as "elect," derives from the custom of electing magistrates by a show of hands by the citizens. The use of the plural "bishops" suggests that the community for which the text was written was not ruled by a single bishop but by several overseers.[16]

Writing around AD 215, St. Hippolytus of Rome, in his *Apostolic Tradition* (2–3), comments: "Let the bishop be ordained as we appointed above, having been elected by all the people. When he has been named and found pleasing to all, let the people come together with the presbyters, and any bishops who are present on the Lord's day. When all give their consent they lay hands on him, and the presbytery stands in silence." All prayed silently that the Holy Spirit would come upon the bishop-elect. One of the bishops, laying his hand on him, called upon God, who had chosen this man "for oversight," to enable him to act without reproach. The words of Hippolytus illustrate the two stages in the process of making a bishop that will be evident for many centuries, namely, election and ordination, or consecration. First the people chose the bishop, and then the entire community of people, priests, and bishops gathered on a Sunday and again gave their consent. Ordination followed, as the bishops laid hands upon the elect, praying and affirming that God had chosen him. Inasmuch as *The Apostolic Tradition* appeared in translation in several Eastern languages, it is possible that election by the clergy and people was characteristic of the churches in Egypt and Syria as well as Rome.[17]

The history of the bishops of Rome in the third century may exemplify that of other sees during a time of intermittent persecution. Hippolytus, having been elected in opposition to Callistus I (217–222) and thus regarded as the first antipope, was exiled to Sardinia together with Pontian (230–235), who abdicated apparently because he believed he would not be able to carry out his responsibilities. During the Decian persecution, the Roman see remained vacant for more than a year before Cornelius (251–253) was elected. Because of persecution, almost two years elapsed before the election of Dionysius (260–268), and more than three and a half years before the election of Marcellus (306–308).[18]

In the meantime, St. Cyprian, bishop of Carthage in North Africa (248–258), one of the major figures in the early theological development of the Church, gave further testimony concerning popular election of bishops. According to his biographer, Cyprian was elected "by the judgment of God and the favor of the people."[19] As only four years had elapsed since his conversion and his admission to the priesthood, some objected to his election, as he himself acknowledged. Addressing his congregation, he declared that the people, "with so much love and eagerness," had made him their bishop and that the actions of his opponents were "against your vote (*suffragium*) and God's judgment" (ep. 43.1). He referred again to his election "by the vote [*suffragium*] of all the people" (ep. 59.6).[20]

Cyprian was insistent that all the faithful, ordained and nonordained, as well as nearby bishops, in obedience to divine authority, should take part in the election: "We see that this comes from divine authority, namely, that the priest [bishop] should be chosen in the presence of the people before the eyes of all, and that he should be approved as worthy and suitable by public judgment and testimony" (ep. 67.4). As evidence of divine authority, he cited the example of Moses's investing Aaron's son Eleazar as priest and continued:

> God commands a priest to be appointed before the entire assembly; that is, he instructs and shows that the ordination of priests should not be carried out without the knowledge of the people standing by, so that in the presence of the people both the crimes of the wicked may be laid bare and the merits of the good may be declared, and the ordination, examined by the suffrage and judgment of all, may be just and legitimate. (ep. 67.4)

Cyprian found additional evidence of divine authority for the popular election of a bishop in the selection by all the assembled disciples of Matthias to replace Judas (Acts 1:15–26). This was done "that no unworthy person might creep into the ministry of the altar or to the priestly office" (ep. 67.4). Thus when a bishop was to be ordained, the community should adhere to a practice derived from "divine tradition and apostolic observance, which is also maintained among us, and in almost all the provinces" (ep. 67.5). Cyprian summed up this practice:

> For the correct celebration of ordinations all the neighboring bishops of the same province should assemble with the people for whom the leader is ordained, and the bishop should be chosen in the presence of the people, who know most thoroughly the life of each person, and have scrutinized the actions and conduct of each one. (ep. 67.5)

He concluded by noting that this practice was observed in the election of Sabinus, a Spanish bishop: "By the vote [*suffragium*] of the whole brotherhood and by the judgment of the bishops who had assembled in their presence, and who had written letters to you concerning him, the episcopate was conferred upon him and hands were imposed on him" (ep. 67.5). Cyprian held that the people, abiding by the commandments and fearing God, should separate themselves from a sinful bishop especially because they "have the power either of choosing worthy priests and of rejecting unworthy ones" (ep. 67.3).[21] He also stressed that the process outlined above was followed in the election of Cornelius (251–253) as bishop of Rome: "Cornelius was made bishop by the judgment of God and of His Christ, by the testimony of almost all the clergy, by the vote [*suffragium*] of the people who were then present, and by the college of mature priests and good men" (ep. 55.8).[22]

In sum, the right of all the faithful to participate in the election of the bishop rests on God's own authority and the custom followed from the time of the apostles. By its presence and participation, the community could testify to the character and habits of the candidate, rejecting the wicked and declaring worthy of election the one distinguished for learning, holiness, and virtue. Confirming that the election was validly conducted, the provincial bishops would give their consent to it, and, by the laying on of hands, ordain the one chosen by the whole people. As the people have the power to choose worthy bishops and to reject the unworthy, Cyprian reminded them not to associate with a wicked prelate.

Drawing on Cyprian's letters, Patrick Granfield outlined the electoral process. At a time when Christians were still permitted to assemble, the community of the ordained and nonordained and bishops from neighboring dioceses gathered to choose a bishop "under the eyes of all." Reiterating that the assembly was public and not held in secret, Cyprian spoke of the "public judgment and testimony." His reference to the "suffrage and judgment of all" suggests unanimity in the final decision. Mention of the "suffrage of the entire brotherhood" may imply that women were not included in the assembly. Given the fact that the Church was under persecution, the number of adult male Christians likely to participate in the election of the bishop was not great, perhaps only about 100 to 200. The process apparently entailed three stages, namely, testimony (*testimonium*), vote (*suffragium*), and judgment (*iudicium*). The first step was to listen to the testimony of the clergy and the laity, as well as the neighboring bishops, who knew the likely candidate or candidates and could speak about their qualifications or lack thereof. This was necessary so that "no unworthy person may creep into the ministry of the altar." Next came the vote, or suffrage. It has been

suggested that Cyprian's use of the term *suffragium* (vote) recalls the Roman custom whereby the citizens gathered in a local assembly (*comitia*)
and voted by inscribing names on wax tablets. However, that custom may
have been obsolete by the middle of the third century. Whether the vote
was written, or taken by a show of hands, or by a voice vote we simply do
not know. The relatively small number of participants would not preclude
the counting of hands or heads. In any case, Cyprian's language leaves no
doubt that the clergy and people had a decisive role in the election. The
nineteenth-century church historian F. X. Funk concluded that there can
be "no doubt that the congregation had not only a right to suggest but a
right to elect in the full sense of the word." The final step in the process
was judgment (*iudicium*), whereby the whole assembly, clergy, people, and
bishops confirmed their choice (*suffragium*). Whatever objections may have
been raised in the previous voting stage, they were now set aside as the
candidate received the unanimous acceptance of the community. People,
clergy, and bishops ultimately collaborated in "the judgment of God," because, as Cyprian put it, "God is the one who makes bishops."[23]

The process delineated by Cyprian was common in Africa, Spain, Rome,
and "almost all the provinces." In those areas the election of bishops by clergy
and people was a well-established custom, though it is possible that in some
places differing procedures were in use. Cyprian's contemporary, Origen of
Alexandria, Egypt (d. ca. 254), notes that when the bishop was ordained "the
presence of the people is also required that all may know and be certain that
from all the people one is chosen for the priesthood who is more excellent,
who is more wise, who is more holy, who is more eminent in every virtue."
Nearly two centuries later the custom may have changed: St. Jerome (d.
ca. 420), tells us that the priests chose the bishop. Granfield comments that
"Cyprian's consistency in recognizing the popular voice in the election of
bishops is particularly remarkable when compared with his teaching on the
elevated status of the episcopacy. . . . No other early Christian writer, before
or after Cyprian, has so championed the cause of community participation
and has given us more details concerning the elective procedure." At a time
when the Church was under severe persecution, Cyprian "felt impelled to
employ the traditional and tested practice of electing bishops in order to
preserve the stability and unity of the Church."[24]

Episcopal Elections in the Christian Roman Empire

During the first three centuries when the Church was a persecuted minority found mainly in the cities, its adherents were comparatively few. Thus it
is probable that, depending on the size of the city, the electors numbered

only in the hundreds. After Emperor Constantine published the Edict of Milan in 313 granting religious freedom to Christians, and subsequent Christian emperors extended further legal benefits, ultimately denying religious liberty to pagans, the Christian population increased substantially, swelling the number of potential electors. Popular election continued to be the norm, but the preservation of an orderly electoral process and the elimination of actions that could result in the choice of unworthy candidates became a matter of increasing concern. Ambitious persons, many of them new converts, saw the office of bishop as an opportunity for power and influence. To that end some bishops attached themselves to the imperial court. Convinced, moreover, that the secular ruler had a duty to foster and protect true religion, the bishops turned increasingly to the emperor to resolve crises within the Church. Imperial intrusion into ecclesiastical affairs ultimately created many difficulties for the Church.

Some examples of episcopal elections drawn from letters and narrative sources depict the excitement and commotion, and even the disorder, that occasionally occurred. The silence concerning most elections is perhaps testimony to the routine and reasonably tranquil nature of the process. Given our common humanity over the centuries, we should not be surprised to discover that at times elections took on some aspects of a modern political campaign, as rival candidates were proposed. Witness the speculation that preceded the election of Pope Benedict XVI.

Signs believed to be divinely inspired sometimes influenced the people's choice. For example, Eusebius of Caesarea, the first church historian, suggests divine intervention in the election of Pope Fabian (236–250). During the assembly to elect a new bishop, the names of several notable persons were mentioned, but no one thought of Fabian. However, when a dove suddenly flew down and settled on his head, the whole assembly, recalling the descent of the Holy Spirit on Jesus, took this as a sign of God's will and unanimously declared that Fabian was worthy and seated him on the bishop's throne.[25]

The Arian heresy that divided the Christian people in many areas also contributed to conflicts between competitors for the episcopal office. Thus, Athanasius, the champion of orthodoxy against Arianism, was elected bishop of Alexandria in 328, "by the suffrage of all the people," in conformity with the wishes of his predecessor. The people acclaimed him and the bishops gave their approval. At his ordination the people repeated, "Athanasius! Athanasius! He is a good Christian. He is an ascetic. He is a real bishop." Nevertheless, his opponents harassed him for many years, as is noted below.[26]

Gregory of Nazianzus (d. 389) tells a story about the uproar concerning the election of the bishop of Caesarea. The people were of different minds, each group "with its own candidate, as is usual in such cases," but at length they all agreed that one of the chief citizens, though unbaptized, was the best choice. Aided by a troop of soldiers, they presented him to the assembled bishops and demanded that he be ordained. However, when the emperor learned of this he became angry, and the provincial governor, a political opponent of the new bishop, demanded that the ordaining bishops declare the election invalid. A bishop "of an unimportant and suffragan see" replied that the governor had no right to interfere and declared that "we have one Censor of all our actions. . . . He will review the present consecration which we have legitimately performed according to His will." Commenting on the confusion arising when a succeeding bishop had to be chosen, Gregory suggested that the election should be left to "that select and most pure portion of the people whose business is in the sanctuary and the Nazarites among us," rather than to the rich and powerful "or the violent and unreasonable portion of the people, and especially the most corrupt of them." In effect he seems to propose that the election be reserved for the clergy, to the exclusion of the unruly and disorderly people.[27]

After the death of the bishop of Constantinople in 398, controversy over the choice of a successor was resolved when all agreed on John Chrysostom (d. 407), an eloquent priest of Antioch. "John was adjudged worthy, in word and in deed, by all the subjects of the Roman Empire. . . . The clergy and people were unanimous in electing him; their choice was approved by the emperor, who also sent the embassy which should conduct him [from Antioch]; and, to confer greater solemnity on his ordination, a council was convened." We are told that if the people of Antioch had realized that they were losing John, "they would probably have excited a sedition, and have inflicted injury on others, or subjected themselves to acts of violence, rather than have suffered John to be taken from them." Although the patriarch of Alexandria proposed another candidate, he yielded, perhaps compelled by the emperor.[28]

Popular pressure sometimes was needed to overcome the reluctance of a potential bishop. In Gaul around 372 the people of Tours sought out the hermit St. Martin to make him their bishop. Induced to leave his hermitage, he was taken "practically as a prisoner" to Tours, where a great multitude, convinced that he was the most suitable person to be their bishop, had assembled. Displaying an attitude more appropriate to aristocrats than followers of Jesus, a few bishops, however, demurred, commenting that Martin was a "despicable individual and quite unfit to be a bishop, what with his insignificant appearance, his sordid garments and his disgraceful hair." The people laughed at these objections and Martin was duly chosen. In 449 St. Germanus of Auxerre was also elected by the clergy, nobility, townspeople, and country people.[29]

The election of St. Ambrose as bishop of Milan illustrates the spontaneity that might occur and was thought to manifest the will of God. Following the death of the Arian bishop in 373, a great tumult arose when the clergy gathered to choose a successor. When Ambrose, a catechumen and civil governor of the province, endeavored to restore order as crowds milled about, a child's voice was heard crying out, "Ambrose for bishop." The crowd took up the cry and demanded that the clergy accept him. Despite his efforts to avoid election, the people prevailed and within the course of a week he was baptized and ordained as a priest and a bishop. Once bishop, Ambrose himself intervened in Vercelli, where disputing factions impeded the election of a new bishop. Reminding the people that even though the previous bishop was not well known at the time of his election, "justly did he turn out so great a man, whom the whole Church elected, justly was it believed that he whom all had demanded was elected by the judgment of God." So Ambrose urged the people to come together and elect a bishop in concord.[30]

As is well known, in 393 a council of bishops, clergy, and lay folk elected St. Augustine, whose conversion was inspired by Ambrose's sermons, as coadjutor to Bishop Valerius of Hippo in North Africa. Augustine later acknowledged that he occupied the episcopal see during the lifetime of his predecessor, "which I did not know was forbidden by the Council." Bishop Severus of Milevi also designated his successor, but his failure to advise the people, though he had informed the clergy, prompted some "ambitious or contentious parties" to disturb the peace. Nevertheless, the people ultimately acquiesced. In 426 Augustine, lest his expected successor be exposed to censure, proposed that the presbyter Eraclius be elected by an assembly of two bishops and seven presbyters, "while the clergy and a large congregation of laymen stood by." Acclaiming Eraclius as "worthy and just," the people repeatedly shouted, "To God be thanks! To Christ be praises!" It was agreed, however, that he should not be ordained until after Augustine's death. As a safeguard against any future dispute, notaries recorded the proceedings and Augustine required the assembly to "show your assent by some acclamations." Once they did so, "the record of your consent and of your acclamations was read aloud to you" and he asked as many as possible to subscribe their names.[31]

These examples are sufficient to convey something of the spirit and circumstances of an episcopal election in the Christian Roman Empire.

Conciliar Legislation

In time, provincial and ecumenical councils or synods, spurred by questions arising in the course of the electoral process, enacted regulatory canons. The nearly annual convocation of provincial and local councils, and the less frequent ecumenical councils, to respond to challenges to church order, electing bishops, judging accused bishops, and even deposing them, illustrates the conciliar nature of church government in the first millennium. Provincial councils or synods—the words are often used interchangeably—were assemblies of the bishops of a given province; ecumenical councils were convened by the Christian emperors and were often attended not only by bishops from many provinces but also by the emperor and his court. The Church of the early centuries was a conciliar church, not a papal one, in the sense that authority was understood to rest in these assemblies rather than solely in the bishop of Rome.[32]

Among the principal councils legislating on episcopal elections are the following. The councils of Arles in southern Gaul (314) and Ancyra, the ancient capital of Galatia, now Ankara in Turkey (314), both convoked at the command of Emperor Constantine, were plenary assemblies of the bishops of Gaul and Asia Minor respectively. The Council of Antioch, the ancient metropolis of Syria (341), which brought together nearly 100 eastern bishops, enacted a lengthy series of canons concerning bishops that were later sanctioned by the Council of Chalcedon (c. 1) in 451. The continuing conflict concerning Athanasius, bishop of Alexandria and principal opponent of Arianism, prompted Emperor Constans to summon some 170 bishops from both East and West to the Council of Sardica, now Sofia, the capital of Bulgaria (343/344). The Council of Laodicea (now Lattakiyeh, on the coast of Lebanon) is usually dated between 343 and 381. In 419 the Council of Carthage, attended by 217 bishops from several provinces in North Africa, including Augustine of Hippo, promulgated an extensive list of canons.[33]

The Council of Nicaea summoned by Constantine in 325 and attended by 318 bishops, chiefly from the East, is counted as the First Ecumenical Council. The Second Ecumenical Council, held at Constantinople (381), and the Fourth Ecumenical Council of Chalcedon (451) were also convened by the emperors and attended mainly by Eastern bishops. Like Nicaea, their principal business was to respond to the Christological issues spawned by the Arian heresy and to pronounce clearly on the nature of Jesus Christ.[34]

Although most of these councils were regional in character, the gradual dissemination of their canons throughout the Christian world helped to develop a consensus concerning the office of bishop and the electoral process. Some of the canons eventually were incorporated into medieval canonical collections whence they found their way into the modern Code of Canon Law.[35]

The Apostolic Constitutions, purporting to be the work of the apostles themselves but actually originating in Syria around the end of the fourth century, and *The Apostolic Canons* (the eighth book of the *Constitutions*) included and expanded upon the earlier conciliar legislation. How well known these texts were is uncertain, but aside from the original Syriac version, Greek and Latin translations suggest a reasonably wide distribution.[36]

The canons cited reflect the Church's efforts to deal with the many questions that arose over time in the process of making a bishop, for example: what are the qualifications of a bishop; who should elect the bishop; who should ordain him; what are his responsibilities; may he transfer to another see; may he resign; and can he be deposed?

Concern about the understanding and depth of commitment to the faith likely prompted Nicaea I's decision (c. 2; based on 1 Timothy 3:6–7) to bar recent converts from ordination as priests or bishops (Laodicea, cc. 3, 5; *Apostolic Canons*, c. 80). The Roman concept of a *cursus honorum*, that is, an orderly progression from one office to another, led to a ban on making a rich man or a professional advocate a bishop until he had first served in the lesser offices of lector, deacon, and presbyter for a term of years. By his doing so the people would come to know his reputation and character and his worthiness for the episcopate (Sardica, c. 10). Before ordination a bishop was expected to know the canons, lest he "might afterwards repent of having through ignorance acted contrary to law." In addition, he ought not to be ordained until all the members of his family and his household were Christians (Carthage, cc. 18, 36).

The Apostolic Constitutions, often reiterating ideas found in the letters to Timothy and Titus, offers an elaborate description of the qualities expected in a bishop. Above all he should be without reproach and at least fifty years of age, an assumption that he would be "past youthful disorders." Well educated or at least firmly grounded in the scriptures, he should frequently meditate on them in order to interpret them carefully. If someone over fifty could not be found in a small see, then a younger person esteemed as worthy by his neighbors was acceptable. "The husband of one wife," just as he was her only husband, the bishop should educate his children in the faith and govern his own household well. A humble man of loving temper, he ought to be frugal, temperate, and sober, not given to wine; prudent, resolute in his duty, gentle, and patient; not a brawler; not greedy or covetous or susceptible to bribes; not subservient to the rich and powerful or disdaining the poor; merciful and generous, especially to widows and strangers; not entangled in worldly affairs; not litigious or ambitious; not a liar or dissembler, but a man of honest speech, not speaking ill of others or listening to calumny. Endowed with authority, he must not be silent but should rebuke offenders, yet also show mercy to penitents. As a guide and watchman, a good shepherd, and a friend to all, he should be ready to serve and minister to the people committed to his care, loving them as his children. His conduct should be blameless, so that the people might honor, love, and revere him, and imitate his example (bk. 2, chaps. 1–3, 5–6, 9, 11–12, 14–15, 17–18, 20).

The Apostolic Canons excluded from the office of bishop anyone who was twice married, or married to a widow, a divorcée, a prostitute, a serving maid, an actress, or to two sisters or a niece, or who kept concubines. A man castrated during persecution was eligible, but if he mutilated himself he was not. The deaf and blind could not be bishops because they would be unable to carry out their responsibilities; however, if a man had lost only one eye or was lame he could be chosen (cc. 17–19, 21–23, 77–78).

The canons emphasized the necessity of confirmation and ordination by the metropolitan and provincial bishops. To guard against future quarrels, Arles forbade a single bishop to select another and required that seven or at least three bishops be present at the election (c. 20). Nicaea I (c. 4) determined that if not all the provincial bishops could take part in the ordination, at least three should do so, the others giving written consent. The metropolitan had the responsibility of confirming the proceedings (Antioch, c. 19; Sardica, c. 6; Laodicea, c. 12; Carthage, cc. 13, 49–50; *Apostolic Constitutions*, bk. 8, chap. 27). As some metropolitans delayed episcopal ordinations, apparently to enjoy the revenues of the vacant see, the Council of Chalcedon in 451 required that a bishop be ordained within three months, and that in the meantime the diocesan steward should hold "the income of the widowed church" (c. 25). This may be the earliest use of the term "widowed church," which implies the spiritual marriage of the bishop and his see.

The Council of Laodicea stipulated, however, that "the election of those about to be ordained to the priesthood [both priests and bishops] is not to be referred to the people" (c. 13). The council fathers apparently did not intend to eliminate the laity from any role in the election, but rather to guard against a tumultuous crowd that might impede a free process. The people gathered in St. Peter's Square at the funeral of Pope John Paul II clamoring for instant sainthood ("Santo Subito" or "Saint Now") is an example of this sort of occurrence. Those who ordained the bishop had to give him their signed, written testimony of the event, so that issues of precedence could be resolved (Carthage, cc. 86, 89). The *Apostolic Canons*, while demanding that a bishop be deposed and excommunicated if he obtained his dignity through simony or with the help of the temporal powers, allowed the re-ordination of a bishop who had previously been ordained by heretics (cc. 1, 29–30, 68). Reception of the new bishop by the people was clearly essential. If he failed to go to the diocese for which he was ordained, "through no fault of his own," but "because of the rejection of the people," he was still to "enjoy his rank and ministry" but should not "disturb the affairs of the Church which he joins" (Antioch, c. 18).

The Council of Antioch, rather than Nicaea I, as Augustine mistakenly believed, prohibited a bishop, "even at the close of life," to name his successor. Church law required "that a bishop must not be appointed otherwise than by a synod and with the judgment of the bishops, who have the authority to promote the man who is worthy" (c. 23). The possibility that the office of bishop might become hereditary prompted the *Apostolic Canons* to forbid bishops to ordain their sons or relatives to the episcopacy (c. 66).

As a consequence of the persecutions, some bishops and priests abandoned their churches, seeking refuge in other dioceses and sometimes challenging the ecclesiastical leaders there. As this disturbed the good order of the Church, the Council of Arles, perhaps referring to priests rather than bishops, required clerics to remain in the churches for which they were ordained (cc. 2, 21). However, the Council of Ancyra reproached wandering bishops who interfered in other sees and ordered their suspension and excommunication. They could return to their former place among the priests, but if they conspired against the bishops, they would be expelled from the presbyterate (c. 18).

Repeating the decrees of Arles and Ancyra, the Nicene fathers also prohibited bishops, priests, and deacons from transferring from city to city (c. 15). If a bishop, lacking a see of his own, seized a vacant bishopric without the approbation of a full synod presided over by the metropolitan, he would be ejected "even if all the people over whom he has usurped jurisdiction should choose him." Each bishop was obliged "to remain in the Church to which he was allotted by God from the beginning and [he] shall not be translated from it" (Antioch, cc. 16, 21). One of the distinguished churchmen of his day, Bishop Hosius of Córdoba, castigated bishops who moved from small cities to larger ones, and noticed that no bishop wanted to leave a large city for a smaller one. "Such persons," he said, "are inflamed with excessive covetousness and are only serving ambition in order to have the repute of possessing greater authority" (Sardica, c. 1). Cardinal Bernard

Gantin of the Congregation of Bishops echoed these sentiments in the twentieth century.[37] Toward the close of the fourth century, the Second Ecumenical Council of Constantinople (c. 2) prohibited a bishop once ordained for a particular church to move elsewhere or to intrude in the activities of his fellow bishops or to spend excessive time outside his own diocese (Carthage, cc. 48, 53–55, 71, 120, 123).

Although each bishop had authority in his own diocese, he was not permitted to take any extraordinary action without the metropolitan who had precedence over him. Each bishop had the right to ordain presbyters and deacons, but he was admonished not to visit or to ordain priests in other dioceses without being invited by the metropolitan and provincial bishops (Antioch, cc. 9, 13, 22). Nor was a bishop allowed to travel overseas without the metropolitan's consent. If a bishop failed to take up his ministry, or neglected to instruct the people in "the way of godliness," he would be excommunicated. Bishops were forbidden to engage in worldly business or public affairs, to serve in the army, or to lend money at interest. As the bishop and his family were expected to be beyond reproach, his sons would not be given their independence until he was certain of their moral habits; they were also forbidden to attend secular spectacles or to marry pagans or heretics (Carthage, cc. 5, 15–16, 21, 23, 35; *Apostolic Canons*, 6, 36, 44, 58, 81, 83).

The bishop was not only entrusted with the spiritual care of the congregation but, with the assistance and consent of the presbyters and deacons, he was also responsible for the administration of church property. As his private property and that of the diocese were to be kept separate, he could bequeath his own goods to whomever he wished. He was entitled to take what he needed from diocesan funds, but if he took more than necessary or misappropriated to his personal use the resources of the Church or allowed his priests or personal servants and relatives to do so, he would be subject to correction by the provincial synod (Antioch, cc. 24–25; *Apostolic Canons*, 38, 40–41).

From time to time bishops might resign due to old age or infirmity. Otherwise a council might depose a bishop on the grounds of heresy, indiscipline, invalid election, fornication, perjury, theft, or assault (*Apostolic Canons*, 27). Two examples may be cited by way of illustration. In 311 in North Africa, where the Donatist heresy was still strong, Caecilianus was "elected [bishop of Carthage] by the vote (*suffragium*) of all the people"; however, one of his consecrators, Felix of Aptonga, was accused of being a *traditor*, that is, one who, during the recent persecution, handed over the liturgical books to imperial officials for burning. A synod of bishops of the province of Numidia deposed Caecilianus, but the Council of Rome in 313, acting on Constantine's prompting, accepted him as a true bishop. The Council of Arles, held in southern Gaul in 314, again at the instance of the emperor, confirmed that decision. What is noteworthy here is that the Donatists appealed to the emperor to resolve an internal dispute within the Church. Though Constantine did not judge the matter himself, he appointed the bishops who did.[38] About twenty years later the enemies of Athanasius, bishop of Alexandria, brought about his deposition at the Council of Tyre in 336, and the emperor forced him into exile. The decision of the Council of Antioch in 341 denying the possibility of restoration to a bishop, who, though deposed by a synod, continued to exercise his ministry, is thought to have been directed against him. The same penalty was applied to a bishop deposed by a synod who appealed to the emperor (cc. 4, 12).

If a bishop was accused his case should be heard by twelve bishops (Carthage, cc. 12, 19). Should the provincial bishops disagree in weighing accusations against one of their number, the metropolitan was instructed to summon bishops from the neighboring province to participate in the judgment; but a unanimous verdict of the provincial bishops could not be reviewed again. On pain of deposition, disgruntled bishops were forbidden to carry their problems to the imperial court without the written consent of the metropolitan and the provincial bishops. If a bishop then dared "to trouble the ears of the Emperor," rather than submit his case to review by a greater synod, he would lose forever any possibility of being restored to his bishopric (Antioch, cc. 11–12, 14–15). If a bishop believed that he had been wrongly judged, the Council of Sardica allowed him to appeal to the bishop of Rome so that "the case may be retried by the bishops of the neighbouring provinces and let him appoint arbiters" (c. 3). This canon has traditionally been cited as evidence of papal primacy. Once deposed, if a bishop continued to meddle in the affairs of his church, he would be excommunicated (*Apostolic Canons*, 28).

Papal Pronouncements on the Election of Bishops

The election of the bishops of Rome was comparable to that of bishops elsewhere in that the clergy and people participated. From time to time rival candidates jousted for support and occasionally the emperor intervened in favor of one or another. A majority of the faithful, for example, elected Damasus I (366–384), but some priests, deacons, and "holy people" chose another candidate. When Siricius (384–398) was elected, Emperor Valentinian I acknowledged that the faithful had chosen a good man. A controversy arose when Boniface I (418–422) was elected, causing Emperor Theodosius II to intervene ultimately in his favor and to declare that the bishop of Rome should be elected by the consent of all the clergy and people of the city. In 422 Boniface asserted that any attempt to prevent the clergy, nobility, and people from participating in the election was contrary to the laws of the Church.[39]

In the fifth century, when the empire was beginning to be overrun by the Germanic tribes, two popes strongly reaffirmed the tradition of election by clergy and people. Pope Celestine I (422–432) stated emphatically: "The one who is to be head over all should be elected by all." This is another way of stating the Roman law principle: "What touches all should be approved by all (*quod omnes tangit ab omnibus debet approbari*)." Celestine added: "No one should be made a bishop over the unwilling; the consent and desire of the clergy, the people and the order is required."[40] Celestine's use of the word "order" has prompted various interpretations. Some think it refers to the nobility, others to the order of bishops, and still others to the city magistrates or the civil authority. If it means the civil authority, that would seem to grant the secular power a significant role in episcopal elections. The emperor appears to have had the right to approve the election of the bishops of Constantinople and of Rome, the new and old imperial capitals.[41]

Repeating the principle that "the one who is to preside over all should be elected by all," Pope Leo I, the Great (440–461), declared that "the approval of the clergy, the testimony of those held in honor, the consent of the order and the people" was necessary (ep. 10.6). Furthermore, he insisted that no one should be made a bishop unless he was "elected by the clergy, demanded by the people, and consecrated by the provincial bishops with the judgment of the metropolitan" (ep. 167.3). Thomas Reese comments that, "This was a checks-and-balances system that would have been admired by the authors of the *Federalist Papers*." The bishop had to be acceptable to the clergy and people. Anyone who was unwanted and unasked for should not be ordained, lest the people, not being allowed to have the one they desire, should despise and hate a bishop forced on them (ep. 14.5). Should a dispute arise, the pope proposed that the metropolitan decide the election in favor of the one who had the greater merit. Leo I was also aware that popular disorder might impede a valid election and reprimanded the African bishops for having allowed intriguers and a riotous populace to dictate the outcome of an election (ep. 12).[42] Summarizing this development, Legrand comments: "In the early period, when the Christian community was free to organize its own life itself, it insisted upon respect for the practice of election, through the mouthpiece of its bishops and popes, who are also saints."[43]

The Liturgy of Episcopal Election and Ordination

The process of making a bishop during the early centuries, as Sharon McMillan notes, involved two steps, namely, election and ordination. The election of Matthias and then of the seven by the community and the laying on of hands by the Apostles illustrates the process.[44] In like manner *The Apostolic Tradition* (chap. 2:1–2) of St. Hippolytus required the election of the bishop by all the people; when he was ordained both clergy and people affirmed that they had indeed chosen him. Following that, one of the bishops and presbyters laid hands on his head and prayed over him.

The canons do not shed much light on the electoral process, but references to examination and testimony in *The Apostolic Constitutions* reflect the practice of Cyprian's time, namely, that before ordination a bishop had to be examined as to his knowledge of Christian teaching, especially the scriptures, and the community had to testify to his upright character and his worthiness. A preliminary inquiry may have taken place before the people gathered with their priests and the neighboring bishops in church on Sunday. The chief bishop inquired whether the person "chosen by the whole people" was the one whom they wished to rule over them. Once they gave consent, he solicited testimony concerning the candidate's worthiness. Three times he asked the entire assembly whether the candidate was indeed a man without blemish. If they concurred, he asked for their vote. After it was given and silence was established, the bishops, standing at the altar surrounded by the priests, proceeded to ordain the bishop-elect (bk. 8, chap. 4).

As the deacons placed the book of the Gospels over his head, the principal bishop, together with two others, called on God to send down the Holy Spirit so

> that this thy servant, whom Thou hast chosen to the holy office of Thy bishop, may discharge the duty of a high priest to Thee, and minister to Thee unblameably night and day; that he may appease Thee unceasingly, and present to Thee the gifts of Thy holy Church, and in the spirit of the high-priesthood have power to remit sins according to Thy commandment, to give lots according to Thy injunction, to loose every bond according to the power which Thou hast given to the apostles, and be well-pleasing to Thee. (bk. 8, chap. 5)

As the newly ordained bishop was seated on his throne, apart from the other bishops, all gave him the kiss of peace. Following the liturgy of the word, he gave the homily and the mass then proceeded in the usual manner.[45]

Once Christianity became a legal religion the imperial authorities determined that bishops had to have their proper place in the social strata of the Roman Empire. The liturgist Theodor Klauser observes that bishops were accorded many of the privileges and insignia of the highest-ranking imperial dignitaries (the *illustres*). Notable insignia included the *lorum*, or pallium, a type of scarf worn about the neck; the *mappula*, or maniple, a napkin usually worn on the sleeve; *campagi*, or special shoes; the *camalau-cum*, a hat, the forerunner of the later miter; and perhaps a gold ring. St. Augustine speaks of the bishop's ring (ep.127.59). The bishop also had a throne of specific height and shape and the honor of being accompanied by candles and incense and of receiving a kiss on his hand. The bishop of Rome, whose dignity was nearly equivalent to that of the emperor, could have his portrait displayed in churches. A choir would greet him on his entry into church and those who served him were required to genuflect before him and kiss his foot. Some bishops were reluctant to make much of this, but others believed that the public display of their status would enhance their authority. In later centuries, especially in the eleventh and twelfth, efforts were made to endow these insignia with a spiritual meaning. Klauser concludes that this episcopal panoply could distract the congregation from the essence of the liturgy. Given the secular, indeed the pagan, origin of episcopal insignia, one may ask whether there is justification for their continued use.[46]

Development of a Territorial Structure

A brief comment about the development of dioceses and provinces mentioned in the preceding pages will be helpful. In the early years small communities of people, comparable in numbers to a modern parish, gathered in a particular place, usually a city, around the one they had chosen as bishop; as he was known to them, so he knew them. The idea that a bishop was bound to a particular community restrained wandering bishops and led to the development of a territorial structure. As the Church adapted to its own purposes the imperial territorial administration, the bishop's jurisdiction extended to the entire municipality, with the city proper (*civitas*) and the rural territory dependent on it. The word *parochia* used to designate the bishopric was in time replaced by the imperial term *diocese*. The bishopric was also called the see (*sedes*), the bishop's seat. From about the fourth century, as the community grew, parishes were established in urban and rural areas. Bishoprics were grouped in provinces, that is, the civil provinces of the Roman Empire. The head of the province was the bishop of the provincial capital or metropolis; he was called the metropolitan bishop (as he is still in the Greek Church), and from the sixth century in the Latin West, he was known as the archbishop.

As the ecclesiastical province consisted of several dioceses, the metropolitan or archbishop had jurisdiction over his suffragans, or provincial bishops, and was expected to summon them to a provincial council or synod once or twice each year. He also presided at the election of his suffragans and ordained and installed them. No one who became bishop without the approval of the metropolitan should be recognized (Nicaea I, cc. 5–6). Bishops, as we have seen, often assembled in provincial councils to resolve issues of discipline and teaching, reprimanding and even deposing negligent bishops (Carthage, cc. 18, 39, 52, 76, 95). The Council of Sardica in 343 allowed a bishop deposed by a provincial council to appeal to the bishop of Rome, who, if he found the appeal worthy, could appoint several bishops of the neighboring province to settle the issue (c. 3).

The First Council of Nicaea in 325 acknowledged that bishops of the greatest and most prosperous cities in the Roman world, namely, Alexandria in Egypt, Antioch in Syria, and Rome, had a superior jurisdiction extending over several provinces. On that account they were called patriarchs. Their preeminence thus was founded on the prominence of their sees and did not derive from apostolic foundation. The council also affirmed that Jerusalem should be honored but should not impinge on the rights of the metropolitan bishop of Caesarea Philippi (cc. 6–7); in other words, Jerusalem came to be recognized as a patriarchal see, but did not have jurisdiction over a civil province or group of provinces. While confirming the preeminence of Antioch, Alexandria, and Rome, the Second Ecumenical Council of Constantinople in 381 declared: "The bishop of Constantinople shall have the prerogative of honor after the bishop of Rome, because Constantinople is New Rome" (cc. 2–3). That statement recognized that the bishop of Rome enjoyed a primacy of honor because Rome was the ancient imperial capital; but the bishop of the new imperial capital was entitled to rank second to the bishop of Rome. The Fourth Ecumenical Council of Chalcedon in 451 emphasized that Constantinople should rank equally with Old Rome (c. 28). These canons concerning papal primacy are at the root of the separation of the Greek and Latin churches that continues today.[47]

This territorial organization of the Church continues into our own time. In the United States, there are thirty-one ecclesiastical provinces; sometimes a province is coterminous with a state. The archbishop of New York, for example, heads a province including the bishoprics of Brooklyn, Rockville Centre, Albany, Syracuse, Rochester, Buffalo, and Ogdensburg. On the other hand, the archbishop of Boston presides over a province including the dioceses of Worcester, Springfield, and Fall River, but also Burlington, Vermont; Manchester, New Hampshire; and Portland, Maine.

In Connecticut the archbishop of Hartford counts among his suffragans the bishops of Norwich and Bridgeport, but also Providence, Rhode Island.

The territorial structure of the Church evolved as historical circumstances required and is not the result of divine action or institution. Consequently it can be altered as needed. Indeed, Pope Gregory VII acknowledged as much in the eleventh century when he asserted that the bishop of Rome alone could create, suppress, or unite dioceses (*Dictatus Papae*, 7). Just as the diocese is not an administrative subdivision of the universal Church, so too parishes are not simply administrative units of the diocese. Dioceses and parishes are an "integral manifestation of the Body of Christ in a particular place." They are charged with proclaiming the Gospel, worshipping God in the liturgy, and serving all humanity in God's name (*LG* 26).

Recapitulation

To recapitulate what has been said, the Christian community early recognized the need for leaders or ministers as the choice of Matthias and the seven reveals. Leadership of local churches by groups of presbyters or bishops—terms used interchangeably—gradually gave way to the monarchical episcopate that appeared at least in Asia Minor at the end of the first century. Texts such as *The Didache* of the second century and the early third-century *Apostolic Tradition* of Hippolytus of Rome testify to the election and ordination of bishops. In the middle of the third century, Cyprian of Carthage emphasized that, by virtue of divine authority, the bishop should be elected by all the faithful and that the provincial bishops, after consenting to the election, should ordain the one elected. The inspiration of the Holy Spirit sometimes prompted a spontaneous election, as in the instance of St. Ambrose. Though some elections were contentious, most were probably without incident. The fourth-century popes Celestine I and Leo I insisted on the right of the faithful to elect their own bishop and condemned any attempt to impose someone without their consent.

Church councils, while reiterating the principle of election by clergy and people, began to regulate the process, which seems to have entailed three stages, namely, testimony concerning the candidate's character, vote by the participants, and judgment or confirmation of the election by everyone. The candidate's worthiness was assessed by an examination of his knowledge of scripture and the laws of the Church and by the testimony of the clergy and people as to the honesty of his life. Among those excluded from consideration were persons new to the faith who were obliged to wait for an indeterminate period and to serve in the lower offices of the Church before they could aspire to the episcopacy.

Although it has been suggested that under the direction of the metropolitan and the provincial bishops, the clergy nominated candidates for the office of bishop and the laity gave consent, the sources do not indicate such a neat procedure. Surely priests may have proposed candidates, but so too might have the provincial bishops and the laity. After testimony was heard, priests and people were asked to vote. It may be that variant procedures were followed across the Mediterranean through the first three or four hundred years. As the process became more formalized, the procedures used in civil elections may have been adopted. Individual votes may have been recorded on tablets, or the vote may have been taken by a show of hands or by counting heads, or by asking all in favor to say "aye." Otherwise the community might give consent simply by the acclamation "worthy." The one chosen had to be accepted by both the provincial bishops and the metropolitan. A unanimous choice obviously was desirable and was taken as a sign of God's favor. Defeated candidates often withdrew, but disputed elections could also lead to schism. Notaries drew up a written record of the proceedings.[48]

Ordination by at least three bishops became the established norm. Placing their hands on the newly elected bishop's head, bishops and priests prayed over him. In the very earliest times the entire body of the faithful may also have done so. Once ordained for a particular church, the bishop was forbidden to move elsewhere or to infringe upon the activities of his fellow bishops or to spend excessive time outside his own diocese (Constantinople I, 381, c. 2). This suggests that some overly ambitious bishops hoped to exercise power and influence on a larger stage. Bishops were also forbidden to designate their successors or to treat the bishopric as a heritable estate.

The venue for the election was likely the principal church in the city. Limitations of space would impose constraints on the number of electors. A crowd assembled outside the church might voice its approval or disapproval, but those inside likely determined the outcome. In the very beginning when Christian communities were quite small, everyone, both men and women, probably participated in the choice of ministers, whose offices were not yet clearly defined. As the number of Christians increased, the influence of Roman patriarchy in all likelihood led to the exclusion of women, so that from the second century onward only men had a role in the election. By the fourth century, as the office of bishop became more prominent, and a significant increase in the Christian population occurred, there were attempts to effectively exclude ordinary laymen such as laborers and craftsmen, as possible causes of turmoil, and to restrict the electors to persons of wealth and quality.

In Benson's judgment, "a proper election needs not only the will of the clergy, but also of the more eminent laymen and of the common people." The laity wielded a "constitutive power" in the election. Buckley comments: "Despite the heightened clericalization of the process, however, it is important to underline that in the first millennium the local church—the laity together with the local clergy and bishops—had or was expected to have, in one way or another, a decisive voice in the selection of its bishop." Pointing to the evidence from east and west of episcopal elections by the clergy and people, Granfield concludes: "The democratic ideals of majoritarianism and decentralization were incorporated into Church government. . . . The involvement of the laity and clergy reflected the ancient legal maxim: *Quod omnes tangit, ab omnibus approbetur* [What touches all should be approved by all]."[49]

Notes

1. Donald W. Wuerl, then bishop of Pittsburgh, "Reflections on Governance and Accountability in the Church," in *Governance, Accountability, and the Future of the Catholic Church*, ed. Francis Oakley and Bruce Russett (New York: Continuum, 2004), 13–24; Francine Cardman, "Myth, History and the Beginnings of the Church," in Oakley and Russett, *Governance*, 33–48.

2. James Hennesey, SJ, "The Ecclesiology of the Local Church: A Historian's Look," *Thought: A Review of Culture and Idea* 66 (1991): 368–75, esp. 374.

3. Raymond Brown, *The Churches the Apostles Left Behind* (New York: Paulist Press, 1984); Daniel Harrington, *The Church according to the New Testament: What the Wisdom and Witness of Early Christianity Teaches Us Today* (Franklin, WI: Sheed & Ward, 2001), esp. 19–22.

4. Thomas Bokenkotter, *A Concise History of the Catholic Church*, rev. ed. (New York: Doubleday Image Books, 1990), 7–27; Henry Chadwick, *The Early Church* (Baltimore: Penguin, 1967), 9–31.

5. Carolyn Osiek, RSCJ, "Who Did What in the Church in the New Testament," in *Lay Ministry in the Catholic Church: Visioning Church Ministry through the Wisdom of the Past*, ed. Richard W. Miller II (Liguori, MO: Liguori, 2005), 1–12.

6. Harrington, *The Church*, chap. 5.

7. Patrick Granfield, *Ecclesial Cybernetics: A Systems Analysis of Authority and Decision-Making in the Catholic Church with a Plea for Shared Responsibility* (New York: Macmillan, 1973), 139, 144–47.

8. Raymond E. Brown, *Priest and Bishop: Biblical Reflections* (Mahwah, NJ: Paulist Press, 1970); Edward Schillebeeckx, *Ministry: Leadership in the Community of Jesus Christ* (New York: Crossroad, 1984), 1–38; Richard McBrien, *Ministry* (San Francisco: Harper & Row, 1987), 27–33.

9. Francis A. Sullivan, SJ, *From Apostles to Bishops: The Development of the Episcopacy in the Early Church* (New York: Newman Press, 2001), 17–80; John J. Burkhard, *Apostolicity, Then and Now: An Ecumenical Church in a Post-Modern World* (Collegeville, MN: Liturgical Press, 2004).

10. "The First Epistle of Clement to the Corinthians," *ANF* 1:16–17; Cyril C. Richardson, *Early Christian Fathers* (New York: Macmillan, 1970), 43–73; Sullivan, *Apostles*, 91–102; Granfield, *Cybernetics*, 149–50.

11. "The Epistles of Ignatius," *ANF* 1:61.

12. "The Epistles of Ignatius," *ANF* 1:50–51, 60, 64–65, 66–67, 80, 93–96; Richardson, *Fathers*, 87–120. In his letter to the Philippians about AD 150, Polycarp, bishop of Smyrna, associated his presbyters with him and described their functions of caring for the sick, widows, and orphans with compassion and mercy; Richardson, *Fathers*, 131–37; Sullivan, *Apostles*, 103–25; Granfield, *Cybernetics*, 150.

13. "The Epistles of Ignatius," *ANF* 1:73–78.

14. Irenaeus, "Against Heresies," *ANF* 1:415–17, bk. 3, chaps. 3–4; Richardson, *Fathers*, 372–74; Cardman, "Myth," 38–41; Sullivan, *Apostles*, 141–53.

15. Joseph M.-F. Marique, trans., "The Shepherd of Hermas," in *The Fathers of the Church: The Apostolic Fathers*, ed. Ludwig Schopp (New York: CIMA, 1947), 240 (Vision 2:4); Eusebius, *The History of the Church from Christ to Constantine*, trans. G. A. Williamson (Baltimore: Penguin, 1965), 233, bk. 5, chap. 24; Sullivan, *Apostles*, 132–37; Richard McBrien, *Lives of the Popes: The Pontiffs from St. Peter to John Paul II* (San Francisco: HarperSanFrancisco, 1997), 39, says Pius I (ca. 142–ca. 155) was the first "single, or sole, Bishop of Rome."

16. "The Teaching of the Twelve Apostles, Commonly Called the Didache," in Richardson, *Fathers*, 178; Sullivan, *Apostles*, 81–90; Everett Ferguson, "Election to Church Office," in *Encyclopedia of Early Christianity*, ed. Everett Ferguson, 2nd ed., 2 vols. (New York: Garland Publishing, 1997), 1:366–67; Granfield, *Cybernetics*, 149.

17. Hippolytus, *On the Apostolic Tradition*, trans. Alistair Stewart-Sykes (Crestwood, NY: St. Vladimir's Seminary Press, 2001), 56–64; Paul F. Bradshaw, *Ordination Rites of the Ancient Churches of East and West* (New York: Pueblo, 1990), 107–12; Sharon L. McMillan, *Episcopal Ordination and Ecclesial Consensus* (Collegeville, MN: Liturgical Press, 2005), 3–5; Sullivan, *Apostles*, 172–82; Peter Stockmeier, "The Election of Bishops by Clergy and People in the Early Church," in *Electing Our Own Bishops*, *Concilium* 137, ed. Peter Huizing and Knut Walf (New York: Seabury Press, 1980), 2–4; Michael Buckley, SJ, "Resources for Reform from the First Millennium," in *Common Calling: The Laity and Governance of the Catholic Church*, ed. Stephen J. Pope (Washington, DC: Georgetown University Press, 2004), 72; Cardman, "Myth," 33–38.

18. McBrien, *Lives*, 45, 47, 51.

19. Pontius, *Vita S. Cypriani*, chap. 5, PL 3:1545; Pontius, *The Life and Passion of Cyprian, Bishop and Martyr*, ANF 5:269.

20. Cyprian, *Epistolae*, 43, 59, CSEL 3:591, 673; G. W. Clarke, trans., *Letters of St. Cyprian of Carthage*, , 4 vols., Ancient Christian Writers 43, 44, 46, 47 (New York: Newman Press, 1984–1989), 2:61, 3:71, 4:23–24, ep. 43:1–2, 59:6, 67.5; Sullivan, *Apostles*, 192–216.

21. Cyprian, *Epistolae*, 67, CSEL 3:735–43; Clarke, *Letters of St. Cyprian*, 4:23–24, ep. 67; Francis A. Sullivan, SJ, "St. Cyprian on the Role of the Laity in Decision Making in the Early Church," in Pope, *Common Calling*, 40.

22. Cyprian, *Epistolae*, 55, *CSEL* 3:629; Clarke, *Letters of St. Cyprian*, 3:38, ep. 55; Thomas F. O'Meara, "Emergence and Decline of Popular Voice in the Selection of Bishops," in *The Choosing of Bishops*, ed. William W. Bassett (Hartford, CT: The Canon Law Society of America, 1971), 26; Sullivan, "St. Cyprian," 39–49; Peter Stockmeier, "Congregation and Episcopal Office in the Ancient Church," in *Bishops and People*, ed. and trans. Leonard Swidler and Arlene Swidler (Philadelphia: Westminster Press, 1970), 48–60; L. John Topel, SJ, "Ways the Church Selected Its Bishops," *America*, September 2, 1972, 118–21.

23. Patrick Granfield, "Episcopal Elections in Cyprian: Clerical and Lay Participation," *Theological Studies* 37 (1976): 42–49; Francis Xavier Funk, "Die Bischofswahl im christlichen Altertum und im Anfang des Mittelalters," *Kirchengeschichtliche Abhandlungen und Untersuchungen* 1 (1897): 23–29, cited by Stockmeier, "Election of Bishops," 5–6; Buckley, "Resources," 72; Yves Congar, *Lay People in the Church: A Study for a Theology of Laity* (Westminster, MD: Newman Press, 1965), 244.

24. Origen, *Homilies on Leviticus*, trans. Gary Wayne Barkley (Washington, DC: Catholic University of America Press, 1990), 120, Hom. 6.3; Jerome, *Epistolae*, 146.1, *CSEL* 3:739, and *Letters*, *NPNF*, ser. 2, 6:288–89, letter 146; Granfield, "Episcopal Elections in Cyprian," 41–42, 44–45; Sullivan, *Apostles*, 183–95.

25. Eusebius, *History*, 267–68, bk. 6, chap. 29.

26. Sozomen, *The Ecclesiastical History of Sozomen, Comprising a History of the Church from A.D. 324 to A.D. 440*, *NPNF*, ser. 2, 2:269–70, bk. 2, chap. 17; Athanasius, *Apologia contra Arianos*, *NPNF*, ser. 2, 4:103, chap. 6.

27. Gregory of Nazianzus, *Oration 18, On the Death of His Father*, *NPNF*, ser. 2, 7:265–66, chaps. 33–35.

28. Sozomen, *History*, *NPNF*, ser. 2, 2:399–400, bk. 8, chap. 2; Socrates, *The Ecclesiastical History of Socrates*, *NPNF*, ser. 2, 2:138, bk. 6, chap. 2; Stockmeier, "Election of Bishops," 8; Buckley, "Resources," 72–73.

29. Sulpicius Severus, "The Life of St. Martin, Bishop of Tours," in *The Western Fathers, Being the Lives of Martin of Tours, Ambrose, Augustine of Hippo, Honoratus of Arles, and Germanus of Auxerre*, ed. F. R. Hoare (New York: Harper Torchbooks, 1965), 22–23, chap. 9; Constantius of Lyon, "The Life of St. Germanus of Auxerre," in Hoare, *Western Fathers*, 287, chap. 2.

30. Paulinus the Deacon, "The Life of St. Ambrose," in Hoare, *Western Fathers*, 152–53, chap. 6; Socrates, *History*, *NPNF* ser. 2, 2:113–14, bk. 4, chap. 30; "The Letters of St. Ambrose," *NPNF*, ser. 2, 10:457, letter 63.

31. Possidius, "The Life of St. Augustine," in Hoare, *Western Fathers*, 197–98, 202–3, chap. 4, 8; *PL* 32:39–40; *The Letters of St. Augustine*, *NPNF*, ser. 1, 1:568–70, letter 213.

32. Cardman, "Myth," 43–47; Granfield, *Cybernetics*, 151–52.

33. For the texts see Henry Percival, ed., *The Seven Ecumenical Councils, NPNF* ser. 2, 14:63–75 (Ancyra), 103–21 (Antioch), 123–60 (Laodicea), 411–36 (Sardica), 437–511 (Carthage); Stockmeier, "Election of Bishops," 7; J. E. Lynch, "Co-Responsibility in the First Five Centuries: Presbyteral Colleges and the Election of Bishops," in *Who Decides for the Church? Studies in Co-Responsibility*, ed. James A. Coriden, (Hartford, CT: Canon Law Society of America, 1971), 14–53, esp. 36–52.

34. Norman Tanner, *Decrees of the Ecumenical Councils*, 2 vols. (London: Sheed & Ward; Washington, DC: Georgetown University Press, 1990); Christopher Bellitto, *The General Councils: A History of the Twenty-One Church Councils from Nicaea to Vatican II* (Mahwah, NJ: Paulist Press, 2002).

35. Yves Congar, "Reception as an Ecclesiological Reality," in *Election and Consensus in the Church, Concilium* 77, ed. Giuseppe Alberigo and Anton Weiler (New York: Herder and Herder, 1972), 43–68.

36. *The Apostolic Constitutions, ANF* 7:396–413.

37. John Allen, "Ratzinger Weighs In on Careerism of Bishops," *National Catholic Reporter*, July 30, 1999.

38. Optatus of Mileve, *De Schismate Donatistarum, CSEL* 34.2.407, bk. 1, chap. 18; Eusebius, *History*, 404–6, bk. 10, chap. 5.

39. *Collectio Avellana, Epistolae*, 4, 14, *CSEL* 35:47–48, 59–84; Ammianus Marcellinus, *Res Gestae*, bk. 27, chap. 3:12–15, in *Ammianus Marcellinus*, 3 vols. (Cambridge, MA: Harvard University Press, 1939), 3:19–21; Boniface I, *Epistolae*, 12, *PL* 20:772–74; Lynch, "Coresponsibility," 46–47; McBrien, *Lives*, 62–65, 68–69.

40. Celestine I, *Epistolae*, 4.5, *PL* 50:434–35: "Nullus invitis detur episcopus. Cleri, plebis et ordinis consensus ac desiderium requiratur." Jean Gaudemet, "Bishops: From Election to Nomination," in Huizing and Walf, *Electing Our Own Bishops*, 11.

41. Joseph Lécuyer, "The Bishop and the People in the Rite of Episcopal Consecration," in Huizing and Walf, *Electing Our Own Bishops*, 45, n. 6; McBrien, *Lives*, 69–71.

42. Leo I, *Epistolae*, 10.6, 12, 14.5–6, 167, *PL* 54:634, 673, 1203–4; *The Letters and Sermons of Leo the Great, NPNF*, ser. 2, 12:11, 12–15, 18–19, 109–13, letters 10, 12, 14, 167; Thomas Reese, SJ, "The Impact of the Sexual Abuse Crisis," in Oakley and Russett, *Governance*, 149.

43. Hervé-Marie Legrand, "Theology and the Election of Bishops in the Early Church," in Alberigo and Weiler, *Election and Consensus*, 34; Stockmeier, "Election of Bishops," 7; Leonard Swidler, *Toward a Catholic Constitution* (New York: Crossroad, 1996), 111–13; O'Meara, "Emergence," 28; McBrien, *Lives*, 75–77.

44. McMillan, *Episcopal Ordination*, 3–6.

45. *The Apostolic Constitutions, ANF* 7:481–83.

46. Theodor Klauser, *A Short History of the Western Liturgy: An Account and Some Reflections* (Oxford: Oxford University Press, 1979), 32–37.

47. Tanner, *Decrees*, 1:8–9, 31–32, 99–100.

48. Günter Biemer, "Election of Bishops as a New Desideratum in Church Practice," in Swidler and Swidler, *Bishops and People*, 38–53; Ferguson, "Election to Church Office," 367.

49. Robert L. Benson, *The Bishop-Elect: A Study in Medieval Ecclesiastical Office* (Princeton, NJ: Princeton University Press, 1968), 24–25, 33, 36; Buckley, "Resources," 73; Granfield, *Cybernetics*, 156.

Royal Nomination of Bishops in the Early Middle Ages

3

T HE TRANSFORMATION OF THE POLITICAL and social milieu of the Roman Empire as a consequence of the Germanic invasions impacted the process of making bishops. From the fifth century onward several Germanic tribes overran the empire, establishing new kingdoms in the former imperial provinces of Italy, Spain, Gaul, and Britain. The Roman Empire, now described as the Byzantine Empire, was reduced to the eastern Mediterranean and some parts of northern Italy. The empire suffered further losses in the seventh and eighth centuries as the Muslims established Islamic rule throughout the Middle East and the southern shore of the Mediterranean from Egypt to Morocco and in much of the Iberian Peninsula.

The inability of the Byzantine emperors to provide effective protection against the Lombards, who threatened to overrun Italy, prompted the bishops of Rome to seek alliance with the Franks who dominated Gaul. By crowning Charlemagne emperor in 800 the pope turned away from Constantinople, but raised up a rival for the leadership of Christian society in the West. As the Carolingian empire disintegrated in the late ninth century, feudalism, based on the personal bonds of homage and fealty between lord and vassal, emerged as a characteristic mode of political organization in much of the West and soon entangled the Church. The tenth-century revival of the Western empire, now limited mainly to greater Germany and northern Italy, renewed tensions between emperors and popes as they vied for supremacy in Christendom. The struggle centered on control of episcopal elections.

Episcopal Elections in the Byzantine Empire

During this period of roughly six hundred years the election of bishops underwent significant modification in both East and West. The growing wealth of the Church attracted the attention of emperors and kings who endeavored to influence the choice of bishops. As secular rulers gained greater control over elections, the involvement of the lower clergy and the rank and file of the laity was curtailed, if not entirely ended.

In the East the Byzantine emperor dominated the Church. The bishops acknowledged him as divinely appointed not only to exercise authority in secular matters, but also to foster the spiritual well-being of the people. Just as the Arian heresy had prompted the convocation of the First Council of Nicaea, the continuing Christological disputes in the sixth and seventh centuries led at times to schism and irregularities in episcopal succession. Although the emperor customarily nominated the patriarch of Constantinople and other bishops, who were then elected by a synod of bishops, the consent of the clergy and people was still viewed as a necessary formality. Thus, in 520 Epiphanius informed the pope that he had been chosen as patriarch of Constantinople by the emperor and the nobility, "with the consent of the priests, monks, and people." Pope Agapetus I (535–536) also acknowledged that the election of Menas as patriarch of Constantinople was approved by the emperor with the consent of the clergy and people.[1]

In the sixth century Emperor Justinian I restricted participation in episcopal elections to the clergy and nobility, to the exclusion of ordinary laypeople. The metropolitan would choose the most suitable candidate of the three nominated by the clergy and nobles. The clergy and people were eliminated entirely in the seventh century as the provincial bishops reserved the right of election to themselves. Bishops, usually drawn from the ranks of celibate monks, were elected for life and considered to be married to their sees, so that translation to another diocese was prohibited. Those who displeased the emperor were easily deposed and replaced by others more amenable to direction. The emperor also claimed the right to confirm a newly elected bishop of Rome; authority to do so was given to the exarch of Ravenna, the imperial representative in northeastern Italy. Until 668 the emperors often demanded large sums of money in return for confirmation.[2]

Both the pope and a general council upheld the principle of episcopal election during the Iconoclastic controversy sparked by the emperor's decision to remove images in churches and public buildings. Pope Gregory II (715–731) admonished Leo III, who styled himself as emperor and bishop, not to intrude in the election of bishops: "For just as the pontiff does not have the power to intervene in the palace and to confer royal dignities, so the emperor does not have the right to intervene in the Church and to bring about the elections of the clergy."[3]

imposed their own candidates, often selling the office to the highest bidder, including laymen.[14]

Numerous councils held in the Merovingian realm in the sixth and seventh centuries reasserted the right of the clergy and people to elect their bishop, but also acknowledged royal intervention. Repeating Celestine I's statement that "no one who is unwanted by the citizens should be ordained," and Pope Leo I's admonition that "the one who is to rule over all should be elected by all," the councils condemned the use of threats, bribery, and intrigue. Should the clergy and citizens bow to the pressure of powerful persons in giving consent, the bishop, who, in effect, gained office through force, would be deposed. No candidate could be imposed by royal command contrary to the desire of the metropolitan and the provincial bishops. This was not so much a rejection of the royal right of nomination as a restriction. King Chlothar II confirmed the canons of the Council of Paris in 614 providing for free, popular election, but emphasized that if the one elected were worthy, especially if he were nominated by the king, he should be ordained at the royal command.[15] According to the *Formularies* of Marculf, a late seventh-century text, the king, on receiving notice of a bishop's death, consulted his bishops and nobles, named a new bishop, ordered the provincial bishops to consecrate him, and informed the people of the appointment.[16]

In Spain the majority of the Hispano-Roman population remained faithful to the Orthodox faith, although the Visigoths adhered to Arianism. The canons relative to the office of bishop enacted by the ecumenical councils and oriental synods were adopted by the Second Council of Braga held in 572 under the presidency of Martin, archbishop of Braga. Thus, no bishop was permitted to appoint his successor. After the death of a bishop, all the provincial bishops, meeting in council, would examine the worthiness of a candidate for the episcopacy in terms of his preaching, faith, and spiritual life. If some bishops were impeded by distance, at least three had to be attend the council; but all, whether absent or not, had to give consent. The metropolitan, whose attendance was necessary for the validity of the election, would ordain the bishop-elect. Although it would seem that the council reserved the election to the bishops, it is likely the clergy and people still played a role, though their candidate had to be approved by his prospective colleagues. The council also prohibited any bishop, out of ambition, to move from a smaller see to a greater one; rather, according to the ancient canons, he was obliged to remain in the place where God ordained him to serve. Should a bishop, lacking a diocese of his own (perhaps because of exile or expulsion), intrude himself into another, deceiving the people into demanding him for bishop, he would be removed. All the acts and appointments and ordinations of the intruder would be invalid. Priests and deacons were similarly forbidden to move from the churches for which they were ordained (cc. 1–9).[17]

After the conversion of King Recared in 587, relations between the Church and the monarchy developed more harmoniously. Not quite fifty years later the Fourth Council of Toledo (633), whose authority extended throughout the kingdom, regulated the election of bishops. Complaining that some sought the episcopacy out of ambition, intrigue, bribery, or even by committing crimes, the council denied election to a whole class of persons, namely, convicted criminals; those branded as infamous; public penitents; heretics; those who were self-mutilated, married for the second time, or married to widows, abandoned women, or women no longer virgins; men living with concubines; slaves; neophytes; soldiers; litigants; the illiterate; anyone under thirty years of age, or who had not passed through various ecclesiastical ranks; anyone seeking to gain the office by bribery, or who was appointed by the previous bishop. The council affirmed the traditional custom: "In future no one should be bishop except the one whom the clergy and the people of the city elect, under the authority of the metropolitan and with the assent of the bishops of the province." If there were no impediments and the candidate's life and doctrine were commendable, only then, according to the decrees of synods, "with the will of all the clergy and citizens," should he be ordained by the metropolitan and all the provincial bishops, or at least three of them; those who were absent were obliged to send their written consent. The ordination should take place on a Sunday in a place designated by the metropolitan. The metropolitan should be ordained by all the provincial bishops in the provincial capital. Should anyone gain office contrary to this decree, he and those who ordained him would lose their offices. If a bishop were restored to his see, after being deposed unjustly, he would again receive the signs of his office, namely, the stole (*orarium*), staff, and ring (cc. 19, 28).[18] Later councils condemned the practice of simony in ecclesiastical appointments. In spite of these conciliar enactments the king nominated the bishops.

Isidore, archbishop of Seville (d. 636), the most distinguished scholar of Visigothic Spain, reiterated the canons of the Fourth Council of Toledo. The bishop had to be at least thirty years of age and grounded in the faith; not a neophyte; a virgin or married only once; upright and honest; and knowledgeable in the scriptures and canons so that he could instruct the people committed to his charge. All, or at least three, of the provincial bishops should ordain him through the imposition of hands. During the ceremony he received the staff to enable him to govern and correct the people and the ring as a "sign of the pontifical honor and as a sign of secrets." This is probably the earliest reference to the episcopal crosier and ring as symbols of the bishop's status, but in mentioning them, Isidore does not refer to the crosier as a shepherd's staff nor does he suggest that the ring symbolizes the bishop's marriage to his diocese.[19]

The Carolingian Empire

The political structure of much of western Europe changed in the eighth century as the Carolingians supplanted the Merovingian dynasty in Gaul and extended their rule into Germany and Italy. In 722 Pope Gregory II ordained as a missionary bishop to the pagans in Germany St. Boniface, who swore the oath required of suffragan bishops of the Roman see. Ten years later, in recognition of Boniface's success, the pope sent him the pallium and raised him to the status of archbishop, but without a fixed see. In effect, rather than being elected by the people to whom he was sent, Boniface was deputed by the pope, who also instructed him to establish suffragan bishoprics as needed.

Boniface's letters depicted the sorry state of the church in the kingdom of the Franks. Many bishoprics were in the hands of greedy laymen, appointed so they could enjoy the revenues, or they were headed by adulterous clerical carousers, who were equally at home on the field of battle or in the hunt. The church lacked a clear provincial organization and there were no archbishops, nor had any councils been held in the previous eighty years. The canons were ignored and the clergy were poorly educated, scarcely knowing Latin, the language of the liturgy. "To restore the laws of God and of the Church corrupted in the time of previous leaders," the bishops assembled in the so-called *Concilium Germanicum* in 743 decreed that councils should be held every year (c. 1). In 747 Boniface repeated that directive and obliged the bishops to summon their clergy to inform them of conciliar decrees, which, lest anyone forget, were to be read annually. Just as metropolitans were responsible for the conduct of their bishops, so each bishop was commanded to visit his diocese annually to confirm the spiritual life of his priests and people.[20]

During the next generation the alliance between the papacy and the Carolingian kings altered the Frankish church significantly. Responding to an appeal from Pope Stephen II (752–757), King Pepin destroyed the Lombard kingdom in northern Italy and conferred on the pope a substantial territory extending from Rome eastward across the peninsula. The Donation of Pepin, which occurred in 754, became the cornerstone of the Papal

States that existed until the late nineteenth century. In addition to spiritual authority, the pope, now for the first time as an independent monarch, wielded political power over a significant portion of Italy. In 800 Pope Leo III (795–816) crowned Pepin's son Charlemagne as Roman emperor, thereby ending papal allegiance to the emperor in Constantinople. From then on Charlemagne and his immediate successors ruled Gaul, much of Germany, and northern Italy.[21]

Charlemagne accepted the principle of election by clergy and people, and indeed granted several charters to bishoprics guaranteeing free elections. Nevertheless, he named the bishops, relatives or friends or former members of his household, with little inclination to a spiritual life, and treated them as imperial functionaries. One favored bishop was given more than one diocese. At times bishoprics were left vacant for extended periods while Charlemagne enjoyed their revenues.[22]

With the intention of bringing order to the Church, Charlemagne summoned the Synod of Herstal in 779 and established twenty-one ecclesiastical provinces, each headed by a metropolitan or archbishop. The metropolitans were admonished to correct whatever needed correction in the ministry of their suffragans, and the authority of bishops over their clergy was affirmed (cc. 1, 4). In the past some persons, named to bishoprics so they could enjoy the income, had not bothered to be ordained, and thus were bishops in name only. To amend this the synod required them to be ordained without delay (c. 2). Reforms proposed by the Synod of Frankfort in 794 were more extensive. Bishops were forbidden to transfer from one diocese to another or to be absent from their sees for longer than three weeks; priests and deacons were also required to reside in their churches (cc. 7, 41). The property of deceased bishops was to remain in the church's domain, rather than pass into the hands of the bishop's relatives. Bishops were required to inform themselves about the canons (cc. 20, 53) and to instruct their people, so that "in God's house there will always be found men who are worthy to be chosen according to the canons" (c. 29). Bishops were admonished to do justice and priests were reminded of their obligation to obey their bishops (cc. 6, 30, 38–39). No bishop was to be ordained in a small town or village (c. 22). The synod acknowledged the right of appeal from a decision of the bishop to the metropolitan and provincial bishops and a final appeal to the king. Most bishops were likely members of the aristocracy, but the stipulation that a slave could not be made a bishop without his lord's consent indicated the possibility that slaves might be advanced to this office (c. 23). Those who were quickly accommodated themselves to the comfortable life of the aristocracy.[23]

Following the death of Charlemagne the empire eventually dissolved into several kingdoms, most prominently those of the West Franks (modern France) and the East Franks (Germany). As quarrels among Charlemagne's descendants tore society apart, the Church fell victim to the disorders of the day. The Synod of Thionville in 844 (c. 2) protested that dioceses had been left vacant because of rivalries among the Carolingian princes and demanded that they be filled promptly in accordance with the canons. Declaring that the people were endangered for lack of a leader, the Synod of Meaux in 845 urged the king, as a temporary expedient, to quickly fill a vacant see (c. 2).[24] The king could not be ignored. Not only was he a powerful political figure, but he was also believed to have a near priestly character that entailed his responsibility for the spiritual welfare of his people. Consequently, the bishops endeavored to find a proper role for him in episcopal elections. Thus the Synod of Valence in 855 reiterated the right of the clergy and people to elect the bishop; but the election could not take place until the king first authorized it. This principle, the *licentia eligendi*, known later as the *congé d'élire*, or permission to elect, became a fixed rule throughout Europe in succeeding centuries. The synod also stressed that even if the king nominated a bishop, his qualifications should be investigated and the clergy and people would still be free to elect a more appropriate candidate. Nevertheless, the king could insist on his choice.[25]

Two outstanding churchmen of the late ninth century, Archbishop Hincmar of Rheims and Pope Nicholas I (858–867), clashed over the episcopal office. When Hincmar in 862 deposed one of his suffragans, he appealed to the pope. Arguing that in disciplinary matters an archbishop could act independently, Hincmar denied the papal right to interfere, but Nicholas I contended that only the pope could depose a bishop. He extended papal influence by insisting that Rome should intervene if a bishop moved to another see, or if an election was disputed as irregular, or if the metropolitan objected. Nicholas I also spoke out against royal interference in the naming of bishops. Yet he ordered the bishops to warn King Lothar to depose an unworthy bishop and to allow the "clergy and people of that church to choose a bishop for themselves according to canonical prescriptions." When the Council of Fismes in 881, under Hincmar's leadership, found that the bishop of Beauvais, elected by the clergy and people at the instance of the king, was unworthy, King Charles the Bald demurred. He insisted that when he authorized an election, the person he nominated should be chosen, because he could give church property to whomever he wished. The bishopric, in effect, was a proprietary church that the king could bestow as he pleased.[26]

Early Medieval Liturgical Texts

Sharon McMillan has demonstrated how liturgical texts reflect the gradual transformation of the manner of making a bishop. The twofold process of election and ordination found in early medieval texts for the ordination of a bishop was modified over the centuries to eliminate any reference to the electoral phase.[27]

The eighth-century *Ordo Romanus XXXIV*, the earliest Roman text for the ordination of a bishop, described the two stages of election and ordination. After the death of the bishop the people of the city (a term that evidently included both clergy and laity) chose a new bishop. The priests, clergy, and people drew up an electoral decree and presented it together with letters of petition to the bishop of Rome, asking him, as metropolitan of the province, to ordain the bishop-elect. Priests and people brought their bishop to Rome, where the archdeacon, on the pope's command, examined him. The bishop-elect, in reply, swore on the gospels that he was not guilty of the four capital sins. The next day in the presence of the people the pope himself addressed several ritual questions to one of the priests speaking on behalf of the community that elected the bishop. In response the priest asked the pope to "grant us a patron," that is, a bishop, and affirmed that the elect, who had served the local church for so many years as a priest or deacon, was present. If he came from another church, he had to present dimissorial letters from his bishop, authorizing him to transfer from one diocese to another. In a reminiscence of the First Epistle to Timothy, the pope asked if the elect was married and had taken care of his household. The priest-spokesman stated that because the bishop-elect possessed the virtues of "chastity, hospitality, goodness, and all good things that are pleasing to God," the people had elected him. After determining that the elect had made no promise to anyone and knew that simony was contrary to the canons, the pope ordered the decree of election to be read aloud.

Following this the pope questioned the bishop-elect in the same manner, but also asked what scriptural books were read in his church and whether he knew the canons. The pope reminded him of the proper times for ordinations and warned him not to ordain bigamists or members of the municipal council. Fourth-century Roman law forbade the ordination of the latter, lest certain municipal functions and responsibilities be neglected. Once the examination was finished and the electoral petition was read again, the pope, commenting that "because the votes of all agree upon you," ordered the bishop-elect to fast and to return on the next day to be ordained.

During Sunday mass the First Epistle to Timothy was read. While the gradual was sung, the bishop-elect, vested in dalmatic, chasuble, and distinctive footwear (*campagi*), was brought in. The pope prayed: "The clergy and people of such and such city have consented, with their neighboring sees, and have elected for themselves such a one, the deacon, or presbyter, to be consecrated bishop. Therefore let us pray for this man, that God and our lord Jesus Christ may grant to him the episcopal chair to rule his church and all the people." After the Kyrie and the litany, the pope blessed him, gave him the kiss of peace, and commanded him to take his seat among the bishops. The mass then continued to the end.[28]

The tenth-century Romano-Germanic Pontifical (*PRG*) provided the formula of the decree of election to be signed by the clergy and people; their petition to the metropolitan to ordain the bishop-elect; and the appropriate form for the signatures of the metropolitan and provincial bishops whose consent was necessary (chaps. 56–57). After the examination, which included the bishop-elect's promise of fidelity to the metropolitan, it was stipulated that he might be ordained "with the consent of the clerics and laity and the assembly of the bishops of the entire province and especially by the authority or presence of the metropolitan." Later recensions here repeated Celestine I's admonition: "No bishop may be imposed on the unwilling; the consent and desire of the clergy, people, and order is required." At least three bishops, as established by the First Council of Nicaea (c. 4), were needed for consecration.

Once the bishop-elect was presented, the metropolitan prayed the opening exhortation (*Servanda est*) taken from the *Missale Francorum*, an amalgam of Roman and Gallican elements dating from the eighth century. As the previous bishop had died, the ancient custom of the Church required the election of the worthiest successor through whose continuous vigilance the Church might grow ever stronger. After emphasizing the qualities essential to a good shepherd, the consecrating bishop noted that "with the testimony of the presbyters and of the whole clergy and with the counsel of the citizens and of those assembled, we believe that the reverend N. should be elected." A man of honorable birth, good morals, faithful, merciful, humble, just, peaceful, charitable, and steadfast, he possessed "all the good things that are to be desired in priests." The consecrator concluded by summoning the assembly to "acclaim this man, elected by the testimony of good works, as most worthy of the priesthood, crying out your praises together and say: 'He is worthy.'"[29]

Incorporated into later texts, this prayer emphasized that the clergy and people of the diocese elected as bishop the one they considered most worthy. Acknowledging their choice and agreeing with it, the metropolitan bishop asked the congregation to give their consent a second time by proclaiming: "He is worthy." That language is reminiscent of the example cited from the time of St. Augustine.

In the Romano-Germanic Pontifical, after the Kyrie and the litany, two bishops placed the Gospel book between the bishop-elect's neck and shoulders while the metropolitan said a blessing and the bishops laid hands on him. Anointing the bishop and saying the prayer of ordination, the metropolitan gave him the staff and ring. Later editions of the text state that immediately after his election the bishop-elect was vested and seated in his *cathedra*, or chair. McMillan remarks that this act signified that he had taken possession of his diocese and that even before consecration he was now a bishop. These editions also include prayers for vesting the bishop in sandals, gloves, and dalmatic.[30]

The process of making a bishop as described in these texts consisted of three stages, namely, election, examination, and ordination. First the clergy and people of the diocese elected a bishop and received the consent of the provincial bishops. A written decree of election and supporting recommendations were presented to the metropolitan. Next came the examination to determine whether the bishop-elect was sufficiently grounded in the essentials of the faith. In Rome the archdeacon conducted the examination and on the next day the pope, as metropolitan, asked essentially the same questions and had the electoral decree read aloud. Confirming that the elect had received the votes of everyone, the metropolitan summoned him to appear for ordination on the next day, that is, on Sunday. During the third stage of ordination the metropolitan acknowledged that the clergy and people of the see, with the consent of the provincial bishops, had elected their bishop. The ordination prayer was said, and in the later texts, the new bishop was anointed. After praying over him the pope ordered him to be seated with the other bishops. The fact of the election with the consent of the clergy and people and the provincial bishops was recognized in the second and third stages of examination and ordination.

Papal Elections

As the Carolingian empire disintegrated, secular rulers thoroughly dominated the Church; clerical morality deteriorated; raiding bands of Norsemen plundered churches and church property; and the Muslims threatened Rome itself. For some time the Roman nobility controlled papal elections. In 769 the Roman Synod summoned by Pope Stephen III (768–772), victorious over two rivals, stipulated that only the cardinal priests and deacons of Rome (persons attached to particular churches in the city) should have the right to vote. Laymen were excluded from any direct participation in the election, although they might acclaim the one chosen by the clergy. Under

Nicholas I the Roman Synod of 861, while emphasizing the traditional role of the clergy, restored the right of participation to the Roman nobility.[31]

Whereas in the past the Byzantine emperor had reserved the right to confirm the papal election prior to ordination, the Western emperor Louis the Pious in 816 guaranteed the freedom of papal elections, requiring only notification after ordination. Disturbances in Rome, however, led to more direct imperial involvement. In 824 the emperor's son Lothar required the Romans to elect their bishops according to ancient rules, that is, without the exclusion of laymen as set forth in the decree of 769. All had to swear allegiance to the emperor: "I will not consent . . . that the election of a Pontiff to this Roman See should be made otherwise than canonically and legally; and that he who shall be elected with my consent shall not be consecrated Pontiff until he shall have taken this oath in the presence of the Emperor's inspector and of the people."[32] The constitution provided for canonical election, but the bishop-elect had to be confirmed by the emperor before ordination.

A most disturbing chapter in the history of papal elections occurred after the death of Pope Formosus (891–896). His successor, Stephen VI (896–897), put the deceased pope on trial before the Roman Synod. The body of Formosus, which had been in the grave for nine months, was exhumed, dressed in pontifical garments, and propped up on a throne with a deacon standing nearby to respond in his name. The Synod of the Corpse, as it came to be known, charged Formosus with having transferred from the see of Porto to Rome, contrary to the canons. That being the case, he was posthumously declared deposed and his ordinations while pope were invalidated. His body was stripped of its garments and thrown into an unmarked grave, but the Roman mob seized it and threw it into the Tiber. The principal beneficiary of this was Stephen VI, who was guilty himself of transferring from another see; Formosus had ordained him bishop of Anagni. Due to Stephen's declaring Formosus's ordinations invalid, there was no canonical impediment to Stephen's being bishop of Rome. During a rebellion later in the year, Stephen was thrown into prison and strangled. The body of Formosus was fished out of the river and given honorable burial. Sergius III (904–911), however, reopened the process against Formosus, nullifying his ordinations, because he had ordained Sergius as bishop of Ceri.[33] This squalid story emphasizes the idea that a bishop was elected to serve the people of one diocese and should not transfer to another.

Bishops as Feudal Princes

Throughout its history the Church has adapted itself to contemporary political structures and adopted customs that seemed appropriate. From

the seventh century onward, bishops, chiefly because of the great possessions they controlled, ranked with nobles as counselors to the king. As the
Carolingian empire crumbled, bishops became fully absorbed into feudal
society as vassals of kings and emperors, and their offices were regarded in
much the same way as fiefs given to secular lords. Free election thus became
a casualty as monarchs appointed the bishops.

When a see fell vacant, the ruler, in accordance with feudal custom,
took possession of it and collected its revenues until a successor was named,
a right that came to be known as the *jus regale*. As the wealth of the Church
was the gift of kings, so kings believed that they were entitled to use it as
they wished. The *jus spolii*, or right to the spoils, allowed the monarch to
seize the personal property of a deceased bishop. The election took place
once the ruler, while reserving his right of appointment, authorized it.
Election by clergy and people was thereby reduced to a formulaic consent
to his nominee. If rulers claimed the right of appointment, they also did
not hesitate to depose bishops who displeased them.

After election the bishop pledged homage and fealty to his lord, the king
or emperor, who invested him with his office by giving him his pastoral staff
and ring. The deliverance of these symbols of the bishop's spiritual authority
came to be known as *lay investiture*. As a vassal holding his office as a fief, the
bishop owed both military and court service to the ruler. Thus it was not un-
common for bishops to go off to war with their complement of troops and
even to engage in battle, though numerous church councils explicitly condemned the shedding of blood by clerics. Many bishops, more notable for
their political and military skills, could best be described as warrior bishops.

The king's right to name the bishops was recognized by Pope John X
(914–929) in 921 in a letter protesting the ordination of a bishop "without
election by the clergy or the consent of the people. . . . Ancient custom
requires that no one shall confer a diocese on a cleric except the king, who
has received the scepter from God." In another letter the pope repeated:
"Ancient custom and the noble rank of the monarchy decreed that no
one should consecrate a bishop without the king's authority."[34] Later in
the century the German King Otto I, crowned emperor by Pope John
XII (955–964) in 962, reasserted imperial control over papal elections. He
renewed the Constitution of Lothar of 824, which required the bishop-
elect of Rome to take an oath of fidelity to the imperial legate prior to
ordination. In the next year the Roman Synod deposed the pope because
he had incurred the emperor's wrath. In subsequent years, depending on
the interest or power of the emperor, the Roman nobility again controlled
elections to the papacy.[35]

The intrusion of kings and emperors into the electoral process led to a major struggle in the eleventh and twelfth centuries as the Church endeavored to reassert the right of free election without secular interference. Two distinguished prelates described the reality of the situation early in the eleventh century. Fulbert, bishop of Chartres, queried: "How can one speak of election where a person is imposed by the prince, so that neither clergy nor people, let alone bishops, can envisage any other candidates?" About thirty years later Cardinal Humbert of Silva Candida remarked: "In the election of bishops, kings come before primates and metropolitans. . . . The roles are reversed."[36] The difficulty of distinguishing the spiritual and temporal functions of the bishop resulted in conflict between the papacy and empire. As reformers pointed to the incongruity of a layman's conferring spiritual authority on a bishop, lay investiture became a major source of contention.

Reformers also charged that episcopal elections were corrupted by simony, a word derived from Simon Magus, a magician of sorts, who offered money to St. Peter and the others if they shared with him what he perceived to be their magical powers (Acts 8:9–25). When the king named a bishop he often exacted a price, which could be construed as simony, or payment, for the office, but in feudal terms it was comparable to a relief, a contribution made by a new vassal to his lord upon being invested with his fief. The bishop could argue that he was simply paying a relief and not purchasing the office, but that distinction was obscure. The king usually named persons who had demonstrated their fidelity to him and would likely continue to do so, or he invested wealthy candidates, expecting to receive substantial payments from them in return for appointment. Insisting on a return to the old rules of election by clergy and people, Cardinal Humbert condemned simony as heresy and strenuously opposed investiture by laymen and especially the use of spiritual insignia for that purpose.[37]

The culmination of imperial domination over episcopal elections was nowhere more clearly exhibited than in the Synod of Sutri outside Rome in 1046. There Emperor Henry III, despite some protest, deposed three claimants and subsequently appointed three Germans in succession as bishops of Rome. The last of his nominees, Leo IX (1049–1054), refused to be consecrated until the Roman clergy and people acclaimed him in the usual manner. A reforming pope, he traveled to France and Germany, holding councils and insisting on canonical elections. The Council of Rheims in 1049, for example, decreed "that no one should be advanced to the rule of a church without election by clergy and people" (c. 1).[38]

The Papal Electoral Decree of 1059

A major step toward the liberation of the papacy from control by the emperor or the Roman nobility occurred in 1059 when the Roman Synod convened by Pope Nicholas II (1058–1061) enacted a decree regulating papal elections. The seven cardinal bishops governing the suburbicarian dioceses dependent on Rome as the metropolitan see (Ostia; Porto; Sabina; Santa Rufina, or Silva Candida; Albano; Praeneste, or Palestrina; Tusculum, or Frascati) took the lead in the election. They were expected to choose someone from the Roman clergy, but if there were no suitable candidate they could look elsewhere. The election would be held in Rome but if that were impossible they could move elsewhere. Once the cardinal bishops agreed on a candidate they would inform the other cardinal priests and deacons (attached to the twenty-eight title churches in Rome) and present the bishop-elect to the populace, who would give consent by acclamation. Next the bishop-elect would be ordained and the emperor would be notified. By implication his disapproval would be of no effect. The seven cardinal bishops exercised the role of a metropolitan bishop and the principle of decision making by the *sanior pars*, the wiser group, rather than the *maior pars*, or majority, was emphasized. Nicholas II's decree effectively created the College of Cardinals as a body whose primary function was to elect the bishop of Rome. The participation of the laity was reduced to acclaiming the candidate chosen by the cardinals. As their power and influence increased they came to be regarded as princes of the Church; happily, that terminology fell into desuetude after Vatican II. In an attempt to condemn the practice of lay investiture, the synod prohibited any cleric from receiving a church from the hand of a layman (c. 6). To guarantee free elections Nicholas II made an alliance with the Normans of southern Italy, conferring that region on them to hold as a fief of the papacy.[39]

When a disputed election occurred following the death of Nicholas II, the imperial government ordered the rival candidates to withdraw to their dioceses until the emperor could make a decision. The decision was in favor of Pope Alexander II (1061–1073), but by acknowledging the right of the imperial court to resolve the schism, he undermined the very concept of the electoral decree of 1059.[40]

Gregory VII and the Condemnation of Lay Investiture

The electoral decree of 1059 was not entirely observed in the election of Hildebrand, who assumed the name Gregory VII (1073–1085). Before the cardinals had an opportunity to convene, the Roman people demanded the election of Hildebrand, the most influential cleric during the pontificate of Alexander II. Thus some were later to suggest that the election was invalid. In his first letters announcing his election Gregory VII emphasized that he had not sought the office but had bowed to the popular will. The official record of his election stated:

> We, the cardinals . . . acolytes, subdeacons, deacons, and presbyters in the presence of venerable bishops and abbots supported by priests and monks, and amid the acclamations of vast crowds of both sexes and of various ranks, assembled in the church of St. Peter *ad Vincula*, do choose for our pastor and supreme pontiff a man of piety, eminent for learning . . . famed for love of justice and equity . . . and according to the words of the Apostle [cf. 1 Timothy] of good character, of pure life, modest, sober, chaste, given to hospitality, ruling well his own house . . . namely Archdeacon Hildebrand, whom we choose to be and to be called now and forever, Gregory, Pope and *Apostolicus*. "Do you agree?" "We agree!" "Do you desire him?" "We desire him!" "Do you approve him?" "We approve him!"[41]

By this threefold acclamation the mass of the Roman faithful consented to the election. In our time, however, the people are not asked whether they agree, desire, or approve.

Gregory VII's initial intention seems to have been to continue his predecessor's moral reform program and to work closely with the emperor to achieve that goal. German opposition to his demand that married priests be denied the right to administer the sacraments prompted the pope to adopt stronger measures. Thus in February 1075 in the Roman Synod he condemned lay investiture, prohibiting anyone from receiving a bishopric from an emperor or other secular ruler. Whoever did so would be excommunicated and would be required to resign.[42]

As vassals holding fiefs from the emperor and exercising political authority in his name, bishops were, in effect, officers of state. If the emperor gave up his right of investiture and consented to free election, he would not be able to decide on politically suitable candidates and the existing political and governmental system would collapse.

This decree provoked a strong reaction from Emperor Henry IV, who promptly ignored the papal prohibition and appointed three bishops to sees in northern Italy. Admonished by the pope, Henry IV persuaded the German bishops in the Synod of Worms in January 1076 to depose the pope. In a letter full of bile Henry accused Gregory of treading the bishops underfoot and called on him to step down from the papal throne that he had usurped. In February Gregory, in turn, deposed Henry and released his subjects from their oath of allegiance. Threatened with revolt in Germany, a chastened

Henry came to Canossa in Tuscany in January 1077 seeking reconciliation. Despite that, a civil war ensued in Germany and continued until 1080 when the pope excommunicated Henry again. At that time the pope noted that the usual means of making bishops was by the election of the clergy and people. Nevertheless, Henry IV did not submit, but rather convened the Synod of Brixen that deposed Gregory again and elected an antipope. As Henry's forces advanced on Rome, Gregory appealed to the Normans, who rescued him and took him to Salerno where he died in 1085.[43]

In his *Dictatus Papae*, or *Dictate of the Pope*, drawn up in March 1075, Gregory VII laid down several principles concerning bishops. Only the pope, for example, without convening a synod, could depose or reinstate bishops; his legate took precedence in a council and could depose bishops (art. 3–4, 25); the pope could transfer bishops from see to see in case of necessity (art. 13); and he alone could establish new bishoprics or divide or unite them (art. 7). Nevertheless, he did not assert a right to name bishops. These, and other rules intended to enhance the authority of the pope, passed into later collections of canon law.[44]

The War of Investitures

The period of thirty years following the death of Gregory VII is known as the war of investitures as popes, emperors, and kings fought over the royal and imperial right to name the bishops and to invest them with their offices. Urban II (1088–1099) prohibited investiture with spiritual (the episcopal staff and ring) and temporal insignia such as a standard. No bishop was permitted to do homage or swear fealty to any layman; nor could a bishop invest anyone with a clerical office if that person had taken an oath to a layman.[45]

Nevertheless, Emperor Henry V insisted on the full right of investiture. Speaking on his behalf in 1107, the archbishop of Trier outlined the procedure followed in previous episcopal elections. Once a see became vacant and the emperor approved the nominee, the people, gathered in a public assembly, asked that the candidate be elected; the clergy elected him, and the emperor consented to the election. This was done without simony and in accordance with canon law. After the bishop was consecrated, he was invested with the ring and the staff by the emperor to whom he pledged homage and fealty. Only in this way could the bishop be entrusted with cities, castles, and other items pertaining to the emperor. The bishop of Piacenza, speaking for Pope Paschal II (1099–1118), responded that Jesus Christ had liberated the Church and that it should not be enslaved again. By allowing the emperor to control episcopal elections, the Church would be made his slave. The emperor usurped God's rights when he invested the bishop with his staff and ring. When the bishop pledged fealty and placed his hands, sanctified by the Lord's blood, in the bloodstained hands of the emperor, his priestly ordination and anointing were degraded.[46]

After many threats Paschal II opened negotiations with the emperor and concluded the so-called Concordat of Sutri in 1111. The pope acknowledged that many bishops and abbots were preoccupied with secular affairs, frequently attending the imperial court and performing military service. As royal ministers holding cities, revenues, and properties pertaining to the emperor, they could not be ordained until they first received investiture from him. Denouncing this intolerable custom, the pope declared that the Church would surrender all rights to imperial revenues and appurtenances acquired since the time of Charlemagne. Liberated from worldly affairs, the bishops, no longer absent from their churches while on the emperor's service, would be able to care for their people. By renouncing all temporal possessions in the empire, the Church would be free of imperial control and the emperor would have no reason to insist on the investiture of bishops. It was a radical solution, but the German and Lombard bishops refused to accept it, as they had no wish to be reduced to poverty and apostolic simplicity. The reformers also objected that church property was given to the patron saint of a church and could not be alienated. Much to his dismay Paschal II was denounced in the Roman synod as a thief and a heretic.

Henry V also refused to abandon his rights. When the pope declined to crown him as emperor he seized Paschal and compelled him to revoke the Concordat. Under pressure, the pope conceded to the emperor the right to invest bishops with the staff and ring, but without simony or violence. Following investiture, the metropolitan and provincial bishops would ordain the bishop-elect. If the clergy and people elected anyone without the emperor's consent, this person could not be ordained. Recalling that past emperors had enriched and protected the churches in their realm, the pope also acknowledged that the emperor would restrain popular dissension that might arise during an election. In effect, by refusing to invest the bishop-elect the emperor could bar him from office.[47] After the emperor's departure, Paschal II argued that he had yielded to force and offered to abdicate. Together with him, the Roman Synod rejected the privilege extorted by Henry V.

The Concordat of Worms, 1122

Both sides to this dispute eventually recognized the necessity of reaching an accommodation. Thus Pope Callistus II (1119–1124) and Henry V concluded the Concordat of Worms in 1122. The pope agreed that in Germany episcopal elections should be free, without violence or simony, and held in the emperor's presence. In case of a disputed election, the emperor, with the counsel of the metropolitan and provincial bishops, could assist and give consent to the best candidate. After the election the emperor would invest the bishop-elect with the scepter, thus conferring temporal authority upon him as an imperial vassal. Finally, the bishop-elect would be ordained. By his very presence the emperor was in a position to influence the election, but he could also withhold temporal investiture of a candidate of whom he did not approve. In return for these concessions, the emperor yielded all claims to investiture with the ring and staff and guaranteed free canonical elections and ordinations and pledged to restore confiscated church property. In the other imperial territories of Italy and Burgundy, the election would be free, but the emperor need not be present. The bishop-elect would be consecrated and would receive temporal investiture by the emperor or his representative within six months. In this instance the clergy had a greater freedom of choice.[48]

The Concordat of Worms distinguished between a bishop's two functions. On the one hand he was a shepherd charged with the spiritual guidance of his flock. Once elected, he would be ordained and invested by his metropolitan with the spiritual insignia of his office, namely, his pastoral staff and ring. Yet, as the bishop was also a feudal vassal holding extensive lands as fiefs, the emperor claimed the right to receive an act of homage, an oath of allegiance, and, using a standard or scepter, to invest him with the temporal authority attached to his office.

Early in the new year the First Lateran Council convened by Callistus II, the first general council held in western Europe, ratified the Concordat of Worms by insisting on the canonical election and consecration of bishops. "No one may consecrate as a bishop someone who is not canonically elected. If anyone should presume to do this, let both consecrator and consecrated be deposed beyond hope of restoration" (c. 3). The council also upheld the bishop's responsibility for the care of souls (c. 4); condemned simony (c. 1); and excluded laymen from ecclesiastical administration and the usurpation of church property (c. 8).[49]

The problem of lay investiture was resolved in England in much the same way as in the empire. After his conquest in 1066 William the Conqueror replaced Anglo-Saxon bishops with Normans, who as royal vassals were obligated to attend the king's court and provide troops for his army. Bishops were not allowed to leave the realm and the decrees of national councils were not binding without royal consent. William II allowed bishoprics to fall vacant so he could seize their revenues. Fearful of dying, in 1093 he appointed Anselm of Bec, the noted theologian, as archbishop of Canterbury, but quarreled with him and drove him into exile. In his coronation charter of 1100 Henry I promised that the Church would be free and not subject to spoliation during episcopal vacancies. Recalling Anselm, in 1107, after some controversy, they reached an agreement known as the Concordat of London. The king, for his part, gave up the right of investiture using the spiritual symbols of the staff and ring, while Anselm acknowledged that the bishop could do homage and fealty to the king. As the future revealed, it was the custom to hold a free election in the presence of the king, who, after receiving an oath of fealty from the bishop-elect, would invest him with the temporalities of his see, using a secular symbol. Following that the bishop-elect would be duly consecrated and invested with his staff and ring. Despite the Concordat the English kings continued to control the Church, appointing the bishops as they wished.[50]

In France, according to Hugh of Fleury, once the king granted permission, an election by the clergy and people was held and the king consented to the ordination of the bishop-elect. However, if the election was not in accord with the canons and the bishop-elect was blameworthy, neither the king nor the people should accept him. After confirming the election, the king received an oath of fidelity from the bishop-elect and conferred temporal authority by investing him with secular insignia. The metropolitan and provincial bishops consecrated him, giving him the ring and staff as signs of his responsibility for the spiritual care of his people.[51] The king also retained the *jus regale*, the right to take possession of a bishopric during a vacancy and dispose of its revenues.

Recapitulation

The independence of the Church had been steadily undermined since the fourth century when Christians, recently emerging from terrible persecution, welcomed Constantine's concession of religious freedom and subsequently accepted financial, military, and administrative privileges. The entanglement of the Church in the business of government was especially evident in the making of bishops. In the Byzantine Empire an episcopal synod, excluding the ordinary clergy and laity, elected bishops, but the emperor designated the candidates. In western Europe the barbarian kings asserted a similar prerogative, although Gregory the Great emphasized the popular right of election with the consent of the metropolitan and the provincial bishops. Church councils in Merovingian Gaul reiterated this principle, but kings named the bishops, whose quality, as Gregory of Tours testified, was deplorable. In Spain the summaries of previous canonical legislation by the Second Council of Braga in 572 and the Fourth Council of Toledo in 633 influenced the composition of later canonical collections.

Several synods convened by Charlemagne confirmed the right of the faithful to elect their bishops, opposed their transfer, and condemned absenteeism. However, he treated bishops as imperial functionaries, entrusting them with civil jurisdiction and military obligations. As his empire dissolved, later councils, while reaffirming popular election, accepted the king's right to authorize the election and to nominate the candidate. In Rome the electors and the bishop-elect had to swear allegiance to the emperor who confirmed the election, and, by implication, could reject it. Expanding papal authority, Nicholas I claimed the right to intervene in depositions, irregular elections, and transfers. Roman liturgical texts circulating throughout Europe depicted the process of election, examination, and ordination.

Insisting on free elections, eleventh-century reformers challenged the imposition of candidates by secular rulers and condemned the growing practice of simony. The electoral decree of 1059, intent on eliminating the influence of the Roman nobility and the emperor, entrusted the election of the pope to the cardinals. The struggle over lay investiture touched off by Gregory VII ultimately focused on the use of the pastoral staff and ring as the instruments of investing a bishop. Reformers objected that when a secular ruler handed those symbols to the bishop it seemed that he was conferring a spiritual authority that was not his to give. The Concordat of Worms in 1122, ratified by Lateran I in the following year, resolved the dispute by distinguishing between the bishop's spiritual and temporal powers. Henceforth the archbishop conferred the staff and ring and the monarch used a scepter or standard. In theory, episcopal elections by clergy and people were still free, but in fact the royal or imperial right to nominate the bishops remained intact. In that sense the reformers' goal of an independent Church was not achieved. So long as the union of church and state was believed necessary for the good of society, ecclesiastical independence was never a possibility. The consequences for the whole body of the faithful were unfortunate.

Notes

1. Letter of the Synod of Constantinople to Pope Hormisdas, *PL* 63:483–85; Agapetus I, *Epistolae*, *PL* 66:47–50; Antonio Rosmini, *The Five Wounds of the Church*, trans. Denis Cleary (Leominster, MA: Fowler Wright Books, 1987), chap. 4, pt. 1, art. 78. See the text at www.rosmini-in-english.org/fivewounds; Richard McBrien, *Lives of the Popes: The Pontiffs from St. Peter to John Paul II* (San Francisco: HarperSanFrancisco, 1997), 90.

2. See Justinian's Novels 123, chap. 1, and 137, chap. 2, in S. P. Scott, *The Civil Law*, 17 vols. (Cincinnati: Central Trust Co., 1932), 17:82, 154; Henri Grégoire, "The Byzantine Church," in *Byzantium: An Introduction to East Roman Civilization*, ed. N. H. Baynes and R. St. L. B. Moss (Oxford: Clarendon Press, 1961), 128–29;

Francis Xavier Funk, *A Manual of Church History*, trans. P. Perciballi and W. H. Kent, 2 vols. (London: Burns, Oates and Washbourne, 1938), 1:184.

3. Gregory II, *Epistolae*, 13, *PL* 89:522–24; Brian Tierney, *The Crisis of Church and State* (Englewood Cliffs, NJ: Prentice Hall, 1964), 13–14, 19–20; McBrien, *Lives*, 80–82, 118–19.

4. Norman Tanner, *Decrees of the Ecumenical Councils*, 2 vols. (London: Sheed & Ward; Washington, DC: Georgetown University Press, 1990), 1:139–40.

5. Tanner, *Decrees*, 1:170, 173, 175, 176–77, 180–81, 182–83.

6. Ladislas Orsy, SJ, "The Papacy for an Ecumenical Age: A Response to Avery Dulles," *America*, October 21, 2000, 9–15, esp. 12.

7. Louis Duchesne, ed., *Liber Pontificalis*, 2nd ed., 3 vols. (Paris: E. Boccard, 1955–1957), 1:260–68; Raymond Davis, trans., *The Book of Pontiffs (Liber Pontificalis)* (Liverpool: Liverpool University Press, 2000), 45–48; "Acta synodorum Romae habitarum a. 499, 501, 502," *MGH Auctores Antiquissimi*, 12:402–5, 426–32, 444, 448–51; McBrien, *Lives*, 83–85.

8. For the form letters see John Eidenschink, *The Election of Bishops in the Letters of Gregory the Great* (Washington, DC: Catholic University of America Press, 1945), 22–29.

9. *The Letters of Gregory the Great*, bk. 3, ep. 22; bk. 5, ep. 17; bk. 7, ep. 19, *NPNF*, ser. 2, 12:128, 166, 218; Eidenschink, *The Election of Bishops*, 47–53.

10. *The Book of Pastoral Rule*, pt. 2, chap. 1, *NPNF*, ser. 2, 12:9; McBrien, *Lives*, 96–98.

11. Prosper of Aquitaine, *Chronicon*, *PL* 51:594–95, and *Liber Contra Collatorem*, 21, *PL* 51:271; St. Patrick, *Confessio*, in *St. Patrick: His Writings and Muirchu's Life* (Totowa, NJ: Rowman & Littlefield, 1978), 41–54; E. A. Thompson, *Who Was Saint Patrick?* (New York: St. Martin's Press, 1985), 51–78.

12. Bede, *Ecclesiastical History of the English Nation*, trans. John Stevens (New York: E. P. Dutton, 1910), 32–37, bk. 1, chap. 23–26; Peter Hunter Blair, *An Introduction to Anglo-Saxon England* (Cambridge: Cambridge University Press, 1959), 116–20.

13. C. Munier, ed., *Statuta antiqua Ecclesiae*, *CCSL* 148:165–66; Paul F. Bradshaw, *Ordination Rites of the Ancient Churches of East and West* (New York: Pueblo, 1990), 14–15, 222.

14. Gregory of Tours, *The History of the Franks*, trans. Lewis Thorpe (Baltimore: Penguin, 1974), 104–105, bk. 2, chap. 1. See also 129–30, 162–63, 200–1, 229–30, bk. 2, chaps. 13, 21; bk. 3, chap.1; bk. 4, chaps. 6–7; bk. 4, chaps. 35–36.

15. See the *Statuta antiqua Ecclesiae* (n. 13 above) compiled around 475; the Second Council of Arles (453–473); the Council of Clermont (535); the Second, Third, and Fifth Councils of Orleans (533, 538, 549); the Third, Fourth, and Fifth Councils of Paris (556–573, 561–562, 614); and the Council of Chalons-sur-Saône (647–653). C. Munier, ed., *Concilia Galliae A. 314–A. 506*, *CCSL* 148 (Turnhout: Brepols, 1963), and Charles de Clercq, ed., *Concilia Galliae A. 511–A. 695*, *CCSL* 148A (Turnhout: Brepols, 1963).

16. *Formulae Marculfi*, bk. 1, nos. 5–7, *MGH Formulae Merowingici et Karolini Aevi*, 45–47; Rosmini, *Five Wounds*, chap. 4, pt. 1, art. 79, n. 19.

17. José Vives, *Concilios Visigóticos e Hispano-Romanos* (Barcelona–Madrid: CSIC 1963), 86–87.

18. Vives, *Concilios*, 198–200, 202–203. Also see VIII Toledo (c. 3), and XI Toledo (c. 9); Vives, *Concilios*, 277, 362; Jocelyn Hillgarth, "Popular Religion in Visigothic Spain," in *Visigothic Spain: New Approaches*, ed. Edward James (Oxford: Clarendon Press, 1980), 8, 45–46.

19. Isidore of Seville, *De Officiis ecclesiasticis*, bk. 2, chap. 5, *CCSL* 113:56–63.

20. Willibald, *Life of St. Boniface*, trans. G. W. Robinson (Cambridge, MA: Harvard University Press, 1916), 57–64; *The Letters of Saint Boniface*, trans. Ephraim Emerton, Records of Civilization 31 (New York: Columbia University Press, 1940), 136–41; *MGH Concilia Aevi Karolini*, 1:1–4; Pierre Riché, *The Carolingians: A Family Who Forged Europe*, trans. Michael Idomir Allen (Philadelphia: University of Pennsylvania Press, 1993), 54–58.

21. Tierney, *Crisis*, 20–23; McBrien, *Lives*, 121–23, 129–31.

22. Heinrich Fichtenau, *The Carolingian Empire*, trans. Peter Munz (Oxford: Basil Blackwell, 1957), 129–30.

23. *MGH Concilia Aevi Karolini*, 1:110–71; *MGH Capitularia Regum Francorum*, 1:78, no. 28; H. R. Loyn and John Percival, *The Reign of Charlemagne: Documents on Carolingian Government and Administration* (New York: St. Martin's Press, 1975), 47–49, 56–63; Patrick Geary, *Readings in Medieval History* (Peterborough, ON.: Broadview Press, 1989), 313.

24. *MGH Capitularia Regum Francorum*, 2:399; *MGH Epistolae Karolini Aevi*, 6:73, no. 81; Walter Ullmann, "The Election of the Bishops and the Kings of France in the Ninth and Tenth Centuries," in *Election and Consensus in the Church, Concilium* 77, ed. Giuseppe Alberigo and Anton Weiler (New York: Herder and Herder, 1972), 79–86.

25. Joannes Dominicus Mansi, *Sacrorum Conciliorum nova et amplissima collectio*, new ed., 53 vols. in 60 (Paris: H. Welter, 1901–1927), 15:7, chap. 7; Ullmann, "Election," 82–83.

26. Nicholas I, *Epistolae*, 41, *PL* 119:841–42; Hincmar, *Epistolae*, 9, 12, *PL* 126:258, 260, 268–69; Rosmini, *Five Wounds*, chap. 4 pt. 1, art. 79–80, nn. 30, 37; Raymond Davis, trans., *The Lives of the Ninth-Century Popes (Liber Pontificalis): The Ancient Biographies of Ten Popes from A.D. 817–891*, (Liverpool: Liverpool University Press, 1995), 194–96, 234–38, chaps. 58–63; McBrien, *Lives*, 138–40.

27. See Theodor Klauser, *A Short History of the Western Liturgy: An Account and Some Reflections* (Oxford: Oxford University Press, 1979), 54–59, on the compilation of the liturgical books.

28. Michel Andrieu, *Les Ordines Romani du haut moyen âge*, 4 vols. (Louvain: Spicilegium Sacrum Lovaniense, 1931–1957), 3:535–41, 603–13; Sharon L. McMillan, *Episcopal Ordination and Ecclesial Consensus* (Collegeville, MN: Liturgical Press, 2005), 20–32; Bradshaw, *Ordination Rites*, 14, 32, 101, 218–24.

29. Leo Cunibert Mohlberg, OSB, ed., *Missale Francorum* (Rome: Herder, 1957), 10–14, chap. 9; McMillan, *Episcopal Ordination*, 51–59; Bradshaw, *Ordination Rites*, 223–30.

30. Cyrille Vogel and Reinhard Elze, *Le Pontifical romano-germanique du dixième siècle*, 3 vols. (Vatican City: Biblioteca Apostolica Vaticana, 1963–1972), 1:194–240, chaps. 56–67; McMillan, *Episcopal Ordination*, 71–135 (*PRG* texts in English, 77–78, 82–83, 89, 93–94; in Latin, 87–88, 98–99).

31. *MGH Concilia Aevi Karolini*, 2:86; *The Lives of the Ninth-Century Popes (Liber Pontificalis)*, 215; McBrien, *Lives*, 124–25.

32. *MGH Epistolae Karolini Aevi,* 2:136; Sidney Z. Ehler and John B. Morrall, *Church and State through the Centuries* (Westminster, MD: Newman Press, 1954), 13–15; McBrien, *Lives*, 133–34.

33. McBrien, *Lives*, 144–51.

34. John X, *Epistolae*, 7–8, *PL* 132:803–8; Wilhelm Kölmel, "Episcopal Elections and Political Manipulation," in Alberigo and Weiler, *Election and Consensus*, 69–70.

35. Uta-Renate Blumenthal, *The Investiture Controversy: Church and Monarchy from the Ninth to the Twelfth Century* (Philadelphia: University of Pennsylvania Press, 1988), 28–63; McBrien, *Lives*, 157–60.

36. Fulbert of Chartres, *Epistolae*, 8, *PL* 141:219; Jean Gaudemet, "Bishops: From Election to Nomination," in *Electing Our Own Bishops, Concilium* 137, ed. Peter Huizing and Knut Walf (New York: Seabury Press, 1980), 11; Blumenthal, *Investiture Controversy*, 89–90.

37. Tierney, *Crisis*, 33–42; Blumenthal, *Investiture Controversy*, 75–76, 89–92.

38. Tierney, *Crisis*, 31–32; Gaudemet, "Bishops," 11; Blumenthal, *Investiture Controversy*, 56–58, 70–79; McBrien, *Lives*, 170–75.

39. Tierney, *Crisis*, 42–44; Ehler and Morrall, *Church and State*, 25–28.

40. McBrien, *Lives*, 177–80.

41. Ephraim Emerton, ed., *The Correspondence of Pope Gregory VII* (New York: W. W. Norton, 1969), 1–4; Tierney, *Crisis*, 45–52.

42. Tierney, *Crisis*, 51–52; Blumenthal, *Investiture Controversy*, 106–27.

43. Colman Barry, *Readings in Church History*, rev. ed., 3 vols. in 1 (Westminster, MD: Christian Classics, 1985), 238–52; Tierney, *Crisis*, 53–73; McBrien, *Lives*, 180–88.

44. Tierney, *Crisis*, 45–46.

45. McBrien, *Lives*, 190–92.

46. Suger, *The Deeds of Louis the Fat*, trans. Richard Cusimano and John Moorhead (Washington, DC: Catholic University of America Press, 1992), 49–50.

47. Tierney, *Crisis*, 89–90; McBrien, *Lives*, 192–93.

48. Tierney, *Crisis*, 91–92; Ehler and Morrall, *Church and State*, 48–49; Blumenthal, *Investiture Controversy*, 135–42, 167–73; McBrien, *Lives*, 195–96.

49. Tanner, *Decrees*, 1:190–91.

50. Florence of Worcester, *Chronicle*, trans. T. Forester (London: H. G. Bohn, 1854), 211–18; Norman F. Cantor, *Church, Kingship and Lay Investiture in England 1089–1135* (Princeton, NJ: Princeton University Press, 1958); Blumenthal, *Investiture Controversy*, 142–58.

51. Hugh of Fleury, *Tractatus de regia potestate, MGH Libelli de lite*, 2:472; Tierney, *Crisis*, 83–84; Blumenthal, *Investiture Controversy*, 159–66.

To the Eve of the Protestant Reformation **4**

T HE TWELFTH CENTURY USHERED in a notable period in the history of western Europe, marked by the revival of trade, the development of towns and the rise of the middle class, the emergence of universities founded on the formal study of theology and canon law, and the growth of national monarchies. Clashes between the papacy and empire, each contending for preeminence in Christendom, continued into the following century. After the collapse of the empire, papal claims to supremacy in both the spiritual and temporal realms seemed unchallenged. Yet the king of France, exemplifying new ideas about royal sovereignty, dared to dispute the papal position and humiliated the papacy. During the fourteenth century when the popes abandoned Rome, their episcopal see, and settled in Avignon in southern France, French dominance of the papacy seemed evident to all. After an exile of seventy years the papacy was returned to Rome, but a disputed papal election resulted in the Great Western Schism that divided Christian Europe for nearly forty years. Efforts to resolve that tragic episode gave rise to the doctrine of conciliarism, which emphasized that ultimate authority in the Church rested in a general council representing the whole body of the faithful. Although the papacy recovered, the spread of heresy foreshadowed the more serious doctrinal divisions resulting in the Protestant Reformation.

The Canons of the Cathedral Chapter as Electors

During the four hundred years following the resolution of the quarrel of investitures, the principle of free episcopal elections was further eroded as the body of electors was steadily reduced. Perhaps with the model of the College of Cardinals as the papal electoral body in mind, the canons of cathedral chapters, to the total exclusion of the ordinary clergy and laity, reserved the right of election to themselves. The canons, the bishop's counselors and collaborators in the administration of the diocese, were usually drawn from the elite classes whose interest and mentality they represented. Ambitious canons often sought the office of bishop and at times disputes arose between factions. As in the past, secular rulers continued to intervene in the process by nominating candidates, whom the electors seldom dared to reject. The French king Philip Augustus, for example, in 1190 required the canons, before proceeding to an election, to obtain royal permission and then to elect "a priest who is pleasing to God and useful to the realm." Many bishops, especially those serving in the more important sees, were members of the royal family or the nobility.[1] The role of the nonordained was restricted to a formal consent during the bishop's ordination.

The Second Lateran Council (the second ecumenical council held in the West) summoned by Pope Innocent II (1130–1143) in 1139 acknowledged the electoral responsibility of the canons, but in a conditional manner. An election had to be held within three months of the bishop's death, but the canons were forbidden to "exclude religious men from the election. . . . But let a virtuous and suitable person be elected as bishop with their advice" (c. 28). The intent of this canon was to affirm the right of monks living in the diocese to take part in the election, but by implication they seem already to have been excluded. However that may be, the canon was never enforced.[2]

The emphasis placed by the reformers on returning to the principles of the early Church encouraged the collection of ancient canons, many concerning episcopal elections. Canon law, founded on these collections, became a formal subject of study in the schools, and a class of professionally trained canon lawyers, who subsequently wielded exceptional influence in the Church, emerged. Prominent among them was the monk Gratian (d. 1160), whose *Concordance of Discordant Canons*, more commonly known as the *Decretum*, reaffirmed the tradition that no one should be counted as a bishop who was not elected by the clergy, requested by the people, and consecrated by the metropolitan and provincial bishops. Although Gratian cited many texts in support of that proposition, he made very clear the different roles of the clergy and people: "Election belongs to clerics; consent to the people." He intended not only to eliminate royal intrusion as in the era of lay investitures, but also to prevent the direct participation of the people. The process, as he envisioned it, involved a vote by the clergy and the consent of the people given by acclamation. Following that the bishop-elect had to be confirmed by the metropolitan (*Distinctio* 62–64). Later canonists reiterated the idea that the people should have no real role in the election.[3]

Henceforth there was no question that the cathedral canons were the proper electors. The introduction into the electoral process of the phrase, "the greater or wiser part (*maior vel sanior pars*)," suggested to some that the wisdom of the wiser part, even though it might be a minority, was preferable; thus the will of the majority could be set aside. Disagreements resulting from the interpretation of these words often meant that a bishop could not be elected for months or even years.[4]

Pope Alexander III (1159–1181) introduced a certain degree of clarity into papal elections. Chosen by the majority of the cardinals in 1159, he nevertheless had to contend with a minority candidate enjoying imperial support. After the emperor yielded, the pope convoked the Third Lateran Council in 1179; this council established that the opinion of the greater *and* wiser part of the electors (*maior et sanior pars*) was determinative. In papal elections a two-thirds majority was necessary (c. 1). That regulation remained in effect until 1945, when it was set at two-thirds plus one, but John Paul II reinstated the earlier rule. Recapitulating earlier decrees, the council required that a prospective bishop had to be at least thirty years of age, of legitimate birth, literate, and "shown to be worthy by his life and learning" (c. 2).[5]

In the next generation the German emperors, Otto IV and Frederick II, seeking to win the support of Pope Innocent III (1198–1216), swore in their coronation charters of 1209 and 1213 to uphold the right of cathedral chapters to freely elect their bishops. In the Golden Bull of Eger in 1213, for example, Frederick II, expressing his desire to abolish abuses by certain of his predecessors, guaranteed that henceforth "the one placed over a widowed church would be the one whom the whole chapter or the *maior et sanior pars* elected." He also promised not to seize the property of vacant bishoprics. In time, however, he found reason to ignore these pledges.[6]

Royal and Papal Intervention in Episcopal Elections

Two English controversies illustrate the role of the cathedral chapter and the king's determination to have his way in episcopal elections. On the death of the archbishop of Canterbury in 1161, King Henry II informed the monks of Christ Church, Canterbury, who traditionally had the right of election, that he granted them "full freedom of election . . . provided that you elect a man worthy of the office and equal to the burdens." That man was the royal chancellor, Thomas à Becket, through whom the king hoped to control the Church; despite some grumbling, Becket was chosen.[7]

Three years later, King Henry presented to the English bishops the Constitutions of Clarendon, which repeated restrictions imposed on the Church by William the Conqueror and the Concordat of London. When a bishop died, custody of the diocese and all its revenues would pass into the king's hands. In the meantime he would summon the chief persons of the church, that is, the cathedral canons, to hold an election in the royal chapel, with his consent and the counsel of those persons whom he summoned for that purpose. The bishop-elect had to pledge homage and swear fealty to the king prior to consecration (art. 12). Becket's refusal to accept the constitutions incited a long and bitter quarrel that ended with his murder in 1170. Although the king had to make some concessions, the constitutions regulating the election of bishops and the royal right to the revenues of vacant bishoprics remained in effect.[8]

The second contentious episode occurred following the death of another archbishop of Canterbury in 1205. Without first seeking the king's consent, the monks of Christ Church, anxious to choose one of their own number, free of interference by the provincial bishops, elected their subprior and sent him to Rome to be consecrated by the pope. When King John learned of this he ordered the monks to elect his candidate, who was also sent to Rome. Setting aside both elections, Innocent III required the monks to choose an English cardinal-priest, Stephen Langton. The king refused to accept him because his own right of patronage had been violated. In response the pope imposed an interdict on England in 1208 and excommunicated the king the next year. As John demanded that pastoral ministry continue, the interdict was a failure. However, the threat of deposition and a possible French invasion induced the king to submit in 1213. He agreed to accept Langton, to restore church property, and to become a papal vassal, promising payment of an annual tribute. Defeated in his subsequent struggle with his barons, King John recognized limitations on his authority in the Magna Carta, which was issued in 1215. In the first article he confirmed the liberty of the Church and the right of free elections as essential to it.[9]

Although King John bowed to the pope and accepted an archbishop whom he did not want, royal control over the appointment of bishops remained the norm. The twelfth-century Pontifical of Magdalen College, for example, reserved the election to the king "with the consent of the clergy and the people." The medieval custom whereby the king authorized the cathedral canons to hold an election, but forbade them to choose anyone other than the person he named, continued in use after the Reformation.[10]

The Fourth Lateran Council and the Electoral Process

The Fourth Lateran Council of 1215, the capstone of Innocent III's pontificate, summarized the electoral procedure as it had developed by the beginning of the thirteenth century. In subsequent years this procedure was incorporated into the law of the Church. Recognizing the canons of the cathedral chapter as the sole electors, the council ignored the clergy and laity entirely. If the electors failed to provide a bishop within three months of a vacancy, they would lose their right of election, which would devolve upon the immediate superior, who, with the counsel of his chapter and other prudent men, was obliged to provide a suitable pastor for the widowed church within three months. The new bishop should be chosen from that church, but if a suitable person could not be found, someone from another diocese might be chosen (c. 23). Aside from recognizing the necessity of filling episcopal sees within a reasonable time, the council's reference to the widowed church acknowledged the traditional notion that the bishop was wedded to his see, now bereaved by his death. The requirement that the bishop should be chosen from the local church also affirmed the older tradition, but the exception allowing someone to be chosen from another see ultimately opened the way to the abandonment of that custom.

In order to establish uniformity, the council acknowledged that there were three valid electoral procedures, namely, scrutiny, compromise, and inspiration. When all the electors were present three trustworthy persons would be chosen to gather privately and individually the votes of each elector. Once the votes were tabulated and the result announced, no further appeal was permitted; the person agreed upon by all or by "the greater or wiser part of the chapter" would be elected. A compromise occurred when the electors entrusted the right of choosing the new bishop to certain worthy persons whose decision would be accepted by all. When absolute unanimity existed among the electors, "as if by divine inspiration," it was believed that the Holy Spirit made manifest the one to be elected. Should anyone be lawfully prevented from attending, he might designate a proxy to act for him. Secret elections were forbidden. As soon as the election took place, the result would be made public (c. 24). Most elections were decided by scrutiny, but factionalism among the cathedral canons sometimes led to the procedure by compromise. An election carried out under secular auspices was invalid and the person elected was declared ineligible to hold any office without dispensation (c. 25).

Once the election was complete, the one responsible for confirming it had to review the process and investigate the bishop-elect to ascertain that he was indeed worthy. A person of insufficient knowledge or "dishonest life" or illegitimate birth was deemed unworthy. Ordinarily the archbishop would confirm the newly elected bishop, but prelates directly subject to the pope had to receive confirmation in person, or send a record of the election to Rome for that purpose (c. 16).[11]

The reference to the "greater or wiser part of the chapter"—"*maior vel sanior pars capituli*"—spurred new attempts by popes and canonists to interpret the phrase's meaning. Suggestions that the zeal and dignity of the electors, as well as the zeal and merit of the candidates, ought to be taken into account served only to sow further confusion. So long as a minority could claim to be the *sanior pars*, an appeal could always be directed to Rome. By the second half of the thirteenth century, however, a consensus acknowledging the identity of the greater and wiser parts was reached. In other words, the decision of the majority was accepted as best.[12]

In spite of the council's exclusion of secular rulers from the election, the rulers continued to nominate the candidates. While incorporating the decrees of the Fourth Lateran Council into his great legal compilation, the *Siete Partidas* (1, 5, 17–25), Alfonso X of Castile insisted that no election could take place without royal authorization and that the cathedral chapter should elect the person whom he nominated. Kings enjoyed these rights, he said, because they had conquered the land from the Moors, transforming mosques into churches, founding new churches and endowing others. Not only did the king authorize the bishop-elect to take possession of episcopal lands, but also, on the death of the bishop, he occupied the temporalities of the see until a new bishop was elected.[13]

Papal elections exhibited many of the same problems as episcopal elections. Although some popes were elected within a day or so of the death of their predecessor, vacancies of eighteen months and four months preceded the elections of Innocent IV in 1243 and Clement IV in 1265 respectively. Nearly three years, however, elapsed before the politically divided cardinals elected Gregory X (1272–1276). The vacancy might have been prolonged, save for the fact that the people of Viterbo, where the cardinals had gathered, locked the cardinals in and removed the roof of the building, thus exposing them to the weather, and threatened them with starvation if they failed to elect a pope. Rather than await that fate, they elected Gregory X.[14]

The Second Council of Lyon summoned by Gregory X in 1274 laid down detailed regulations for future papal elections. The election had to be held within ten days of the death of the preceding pope in the city where he died. The assembled cardinals would be locked in—hence the word *conclave*—and faced with the possibility of being put on a diet of bread, wine, and water if they were unable to come to agreement within a certain time.

No bargain or promise made in exchange for a vote was binding (c. 2). Concerned about "long and dangerous vacancies," the council required the one elected to consent within a month or else lose his right. If he accepted, within three months he had to seek confirmation by the metropolitan. In disputed elections, appeals could be addressed to the papacy in proper form, but they could not be frivolous. If the majority agreed on a candidate, the minority could not base an appeal on the lack of zeal, merit, or authority on the part of the majority or their candidate (cc. 3–10).[15]

Liturgical Texts for the Ordination of a Bishop

The steady growth of papal influence is reflected in the dissemination of Roman liturgical texts for the ordination (now commonly called *consecration*) of a bishop. In many respects the elements already described continued in use but there were some significant changes. The consent of the clergy and people of the diocese as well as that of the metropolitan and provincial bishops was downplayed. Only the diocesan clergy were mentioned as being present at the ceremony, and the bishop-elect's reference to his confreres who elected him reveals the minimal role of the laity. The decree of election was not read nor was there any reference to letters recommending the elect and asking that he be consecrated. In case of a suffragan of the Roman see, the ceremony began with the kissing of the pope's foot, a privilege derived from Gregory VII's claim in the *Dictatus Papae* (art. 9). During the rite there was no proclamation of consensus. After the examination a new statement was added: "It is for the bishop to judge, interpret, consecrate, consummate, ordain, offer, and baptize." In addition to conferring the staff and ring, the pope gave him the Gospel book with the instruction, "go, preach to the people committed to you." At the conclusion of the liturgy he received the miter. The offering of the gifts of bread and wine by the bishop-elect, his promise of fidelity, and reception of the staff and ring from the hands of the consecrating bishop seem to emphasize, as McMillan notes, a new personal bond between the elect and the consecrator, rather than the ecclesial one between the bishop and the faithful of his diocese; the consecrator's consent replaced theirs.[16]

In the late thirteenth century, Guillaume Durand, bishop of Mende in southern France (d. 1296), composed a pontifical of great significance. The metropolitan, attended by two provincial bishops, examined the elect on a Saturday. The archpriest, archdeacon, and two canons of the diocese—laypeople were not mentioned—appeared before the metropolitan, who questioned the archdeacon in the traditional form and asked that the decree of election be read. Whereas earlier versions of the decree mentioned the clergy and people, Durand's text emphasized that the cathedral canons were the electors. Next the elect entered the church in a candlelight procession accompanied by the canons, archpriest, and archdeacon. In response to the metropolitan's question he said: "My fellow brothers elected me, although unworthy, to preside over them as pastor." After the examination, the metropolitan repeated the ancient formula "because the desires of all have agreed upon you" and set the consecration for the next day, Sunday.

Two bishops presented the elect, vested in amice, alb, cincture, stole, and cope, to the metropolitan, saying: "Reverend father, holy mother Catholic church asks that you elevate this presbyter to the burden of the episcopacy." The consecrator asked: "Do you know him to be worthy?" They replied: "As far as human frailty allows [us] to know, we know and believe him to be worthy." After examining the elect, the consecrator asked him to promise fidelity to Blessed Peter the Apostle, to his vicars, the popes, and to the metropolitan. In a gesture of submission the elect then kissed the hand of the consecrator. In presenting the elect, the two bishops, who may or may not have been provincial bishops, did so, not in the name of the clergy and people of the diocese, but in the name of the whole Church. Nor were the clergy and people of the diocese called on to attest to his worthiness; the two bishops did that. By drawing on Roman models, Durand required the elect not only to promise obedience to his metropolitan, but also to the pope as the vicar of St. Peter. The mass followed in the usual form, with the laying on of hands and anointing, and the presentation of the Gospel book, the staff, ring, and miter, "the helmet of protection and salvation." Although liturgists believe that Durand burdened the ceremony with excessive details that distract from the core, his pontifical gained widespread use and served as a model for the papal revisions of the late fifteenth and sixteenth centuries.[17]

Prior to the conversion of Constantine the dress of bishops and priests scarcely differed from that of their secular contemporaries, but thereafter, distinctive liturgical garments came into vogue. By the twelfth century the symbols of the episcopal office included the bishop's staff, ring, miter, chair, pectoral cross, and pallium. Innocent III described the ring, first mentioned in the seventh century, as a *fidei sacramentum*, a contract of love and faith between the bishop and his church. The pope echoed the prayer said by the metropolitan as he gave the ring to the bishop: "Receive the ring, the sign of faith, so that, adorned with undefiled faith, you may protect without harm your bride, namely, the holy church of God."[18] By analogy with Christ as the Bridegroom of the Church, the bishop was said to be wedded to his see and the ring was the visible sign of that nuptial bond. The analogy was carried further as, at least from the time of the Council of Chalcedon (c. 25), the diocese whose bishop had died was described as the "widowed church." Thus, the transfer of a bishop from one see to another, as Innocent III noted, constituted a form of spiritual adultery. The bishop's ring was often made of silver or gold and set with precious stones. Shaped like a shepherd's crook, the staff or crosier, also mentioned in the seventh century, was the sign of the bishop's responsibility to lead and protect the sheep entrusted to his care. Often elaborately worked in silver and encrusted with jewels, the crosier bore little resemblance to a shepherd's simple, wooden staff. The right to wear the miter, originally the papal headdress, was granted to other bishops from the eleventh century onward. A sort of folded conical cap with two strips of cloth called *lappets* hanging down in back, the miter might be one of several types used on different occasions. In addition to the plain white miter, there were two others varying only in their rich ornamentation. The pectoral cross and the skullcap were both mentioned in the thirteenth century. The bishop's chair (*cathedra*), the sign of his teaching authority, was originally placed in the apse behind the altar so that, facing the people, he could instruct them. The chair developed into an ornate raised throne, often covered with gilt and red damask, with a tasseled canopy above. Under the influence of late medieval chivalric custom, bishops also began to use coats of arms as a sign of their nobility. From the fourteenth century a bishop, when not vested for mass, often wore a flat, green, wide-brimmed hat with a low crown and six tassels hanging down behind. When he died his hat was raised to the roof of the cathedral, where it remained until it disintegrated. The pallium, a strip of white wool worn around the neck and a sign of the archbishop's authority, was conferred on him by the pope.[19]

Papal Reservation of Episcopal Appointments

From the late thirteenth century onward, papal intervention in episcopal elections tended to increase, chiefly because of the failure of the cathedral canons to carry out their electoral responsibility appropriately. The canons, for example, sometimes attempted to control the direction of the diocese through electoral capitulations setting limitations on a future bishop. Once consecrated, however, a bishop was likely to ignore such restraints. When controversies arose, appeals were frequently directed to Rome, allowing the pope to set an election aside and to impose his own candidate. Boniface VIII (1295–1303), for example, asserted that the pope could quash an irregular election or the election of someone lacking the appropriate qualifications. By virtue of their claim to confirm both archbishops and their suffragans, the popes also were in a position to nullify elections.[20]

During the fourteenth century the popes resident at Avignon in southern France developed a highly centralized and lucrative administration
and greatly expanded their claim to name bishops. Alleging responsibility
to care for all the churches, they reserved to themselves appointment to
bishoprics vacated by the death of the incumbent at the curia, as well as in
the case of disputed elections, suspensions, transfers, resignations, or depositions. In this way they were able to provide for members of the curia, their
own relatives, and the sons and brothers of kings and nobles whose alliance
they wished to cultivate. Claims to the property of a deceased bishop and
the obligation of a newly appointed bishop to pay annates, the first year's
revenue of his see, as well as other fees, supplied the papacy with significant
sources of income.[21]

As bishops were not required to reside in their sees, but often spent
their time at either the papal or royal court, the problem of absenteeism
was widespread. An absentee prelate, while collecting the revenues of his
distant diocese, usually appointed a vicar to handle day-to-day administration. Plurality of benefices also became a serious concern as bishops often
held more than one ecclesiastical office, sometimes even more than one
bishopric. A Portuguese cardinal in the fifteenth century, for example, held
not only the archbishoprics of Braga and Lisbon, but five other sees, as well
as the abbacies of twelve monasteries, and a number of lesser positions, all
furnishing him with a substantial income. The gap between bishops and the
clergy and people grew ever wider, as bishops were no longer chosen from
the diocesan clergy, and were frequently transferred, rather than serving one
diocese for life. The ambitious careerism decried by Cardinal Bernard Gantin in the twentieth century was much in evidence from the late Middle
Ages onward. Thus were laid the foundations of the present papal claim to
appoint all the bishops.[22]

As might be expected, papal nomination of bishops and other ecclesiastics and increasing papal taxation evoked strenuous protest throughout
Europe. The deepening hostility toward the papacy was reflected not only
in the literature of the age, but also in the law. Marsiglio of Padua, in his
provocative treatise, *The Defender of the Peace* (*Defensor Pacis*), written in
1324, turned the hierarchical pyramid upside down, as he insisted that all
authority in the Church derives from the whole body of the faithful (*uni-
versitas fidelium*). While dismissing papal claims to primacy as a historical
construct, he stated that the bishop should be elected by the community:
"The immediate efficient cause of the assignment or appointment of a
prelate . . . is or ought to be the entire multitude of believers of that place
through their election or expressed will." He added: "Since, therefore, a

better election can be made by the whole body of the faithful than by a single man, even a bishop, or by a single group, it is clear that such election or appointment of an overseer ought to pertain to the whole body of the faithful rather than to a single official or group." Thus he insisted on the right of parishioners to elect their pastor, the people of the diocese to elect their bishop, and a general council representative of the whole body of the faithful to elect the pope. In addition, the electoral bodies would have the authority to remove a bishop who failed in his duties.[23]

Upholding the royal right of patronage, the Statutes of Provisors enacted by the English parliament in 1351 and 1390 reiterated that "the free elections of archbishops and bishops, and [of] all other dignities and benefices that are elective in England, shall continue to be held." Foreigners were excluded from English benefices and the papal claim to appointment was denied. Despite this language, kings worked hand in glove with the papacy to share in the naming of bishops. Nevertheless, the statutes provided the monarchy with legal weapons that could be used to justify royal domination of the Church.[24]

Avignon and the Great Western Schism

By residing in the comparative tranquility of Avignon for the greater part of the fourteenth century, the bishops of Rome exemplified the problem of nonresidence that was so troubling to the late medieval Church. The seven popes of that era were French, leading to the charge that the papacy was in thrall to the political ambitions of the French king. In 1352 the cardinals, now inured to a lavish lifestyle worthy of princes of the Church, attempted by means of a preelectoral capitulation to enhance their position by proposing the sharing of revenues between pope and cardinals. Once chosen, nevertheless, Innocent VI (1352–1362) repudiated the capitulation. The Avignon Papacy came to an end in 1377 when Gregory XI (1371–1378), responding to the entreaties of St. Catherine of Siena, returned to Rome. His death the following year, however, touched off the Great Western Schism.[25]

For the first time in more than seventy years, a papal election took place in Rome. The demand by the populace that a Roman pope—or at least an Italian—be elected reflected the general European hostility to foreign bishops and represented an appeal to the ancient tradition of electing bishops from the diocesan clergy. Although the cardinals heeded the popular wish by electing Urban VI (1378–1389), an Italian, they soon turned against him and elected a rival, Clement VII, a Frenchman, who returned to Avignon. All of Europe was now divided in its allegiance. A practical consequence of the schism was that in some dioceses there were two bishops, one adhering to Rome and the other to Avignon. Over the years various proposals were made to resolve the crisis, such as mutual resignation, but to no avail. Eventually the cardinals on both sides, disgusted by the intransigence of their respective pontiffs, convoked the Council of Pisa in 1409. The council deposed the popes of Rome and Avignon and elected a new pope, but the expectation that this would end the schism was thwarted and a threefold division of Europe ensued. Finally, in 1414 at the urging of the emperor, John XXIII, the Pisan pope, summoned the Council of Constance, which accepted the resignation of the Roman pontiff and deposed the other two claimants. The election of Martin V (1417–1431) by twenty-three cardinals and six representatives from each of five nations present at the council brought this disastrous era in the history of the Church to a conclusion.[26]

The Council of Constance also attempted to correct abuses. In addition to condemning papal reservations, papal claims to the property of deceased bishops, and simony, the fathers prohibited anyone to hold a bishopric without being consecrated. Commenting that "when prelates are translated, there is commonly both spiritual and temporal loss and damage of a grave nature for the churches from which they are transferred," the council determined that bishops could not be transferred without their consent unless there was "a grave and reasonable cause."[27]

The Age of Conciliarism

The termination of the schism by the action of the bishops gathered in council ushered in the age of conciliarism. Reacting against the extreme centralization of papal power, the Council of Constance enacted two fundamental ecclesiological decrees. Claiming to represent the whole body of the faithful, the council declared in *Haec Sancta* that all members of the Church, including the pope, were subject to its authority. The second decree, *Frequens*, envisioned the regular convocation of general councils every ten years.[28] This assertion of the supremacy of a general council was an attempt to return to an earlier time when bishops meeting in council resolved fundamental issues of doctrine and discipline. Nevertheless, the battle between Pope Eugene IV (1431–1447) and the Council of Basel, summoned in 1431 in accord with the decree *Frequens*, ultimately weakened the conciliarist movement. Emboldened by that fact, in 1460 Pius II (1458–1464) condemned anyone who would presume to appeal to the authority of a council against that of the pope.[29] Despite that papal pronouncement, conciliarist ideas persisted, as Francis Oakley has shown, and found expression in succeeding centuries. As a consequence of conciliar-ism, "the democratic idea," according to Anton Weiler, "broke through in the Church."[30]

Other than quarreling with the pope, the prelates assembled at Basel enacted legislation concerning episcopal elections. Stressing that bishops "must firmly uphold the church by the strength of their doctrine and merits," and that "great care should be taken in their election, for they are appointed for the government of souls," the council condemned papal res-ervations. As earlier councils had "established that each church and college or convent should elect a prelate for itself," Basel reminded the electors of their obligation to choose a worthy person "in the presence of God and of the people." On the day of the election, the electors would gather in church to hear the mass of the Holy Spirit and to be inspired "to elect a worthy pastor." They were admonished to confess their sins and to receive the Eucharist. Before proceeding to the election they would swear in the hands of the chapter president to elect the most suitable person and not to vote for anyone offering gifts or bribes, the sin of simony. An elector could designate a proxy to act in his name. The person elected had to be "of lawful age, of serious character and adequate education, already in sacred orders and suitable in other respects in accordance with canonical regula-tions." The council also exhorted kings, princes, and others not to intrude into the process by written recommendations, threats, or pressure of any sort. The results of the election would be publicly announced. The bishop-elect would be confirmed by the one having that responsibility, usually the metropolitan, who would do so after careful inquiry into the qualifications of the candidates and the canonicity of the proceedings. Three years later the council reiterated its condemnation of papal reservations.[31] The thrust of this article was to affirm the right of the cathedral chapter to conduct an election in the presence of the people, without external interference, but it is clear that the ordinary clergy and people did not participate.

In his major work, *The Catholic Concordance* (*De Concordantia catholica*), written around 1433, Nicholas of Cusa (initially a conciliarist though later put off by the more extreme actions of the Council of Basel), stressed that the unity of the Church could best be preserved if the members chose their leaders. Bishops appointed by the pope, but unknown to the clergy and people of the diocese, often failed to establish harmonious relations with them. Recalling the statements of Celestine I and Leo I, he updated Celestine's principle by stating, "The pope may not give a bishop to the unwilling"—"*Papa enim invitis episcopum dare non potest.*" Effective reform required a restoration of the threefold custom of episcopal election by the clergy, the consent of the people, and the judgment of the archbishop. A bishop elected by the community already enjoyed its confidence and so could act forthrightly, knowing that his actions would be effective and have validity because the clergy and people were with him. Outsiders, on the contrary, had to win that trust over time; as many did not, they were often transferred, to the detriment of the Church. Nicholas also proposed that bishops, with the consent of the clergy, should elect archbishops; archbishops, with the consent of the bishops, should elect the cardinals; and the cardinals, with the consent of the archbishops, should elect the pope.[32]

The Response of the Secular Princes

While Eugene IV wrangled with the fathers gathered at Basel, kings, emperors, and princes were settling on their response to the crisis. A synod of French bishops summoned by King Charles VII at Bourges in 1438 enacted twenty-three decrees that upheld the conciliarist decrees (*Haec Sancta, Frequens*) of the Council of Constance and approved the reforms of Basel. The king's edict, known as the Pragmatic Sanction of Bourges, gave legal force to these reform proposals, abolishing papal reservations, expectatives (appointment to a church office should it become vacant), annates, and denying the right to appeal to Rome (arts. 4–7). Papal authority to nominate bishops was also curtailed. "Election is reestablished for ecclesiastical offices, but the king, or the princes of the kingdom, without violating the canonical rules, may make recommendations when elections are to occur in the chapters or the monasteries" (art. 3). In effect the electoral right of the cathedral chapter was confirmed, but, contrary to the Council of Basel, the royal right of nomination was reasserted. Although Louis XI, at the urging of Pope Pius II, revoked the Pragmatic Sanction in 1461, receiving the title of "Most Christian King" as his reward, he soon enacted new laws that restored liberties traditionally viewed as pertaining to the French, or Gallican, Church.[33]

The stance taken by the Holy Roman Empire was ultimately much more favorable to the papacy. The Concordat of Vienna concluded in 1448 between Emperor Frederick III and Pope Nicholas V (1447–1455) provided that episcopal elections should be free, but the pope retained the right of confirmation. Moreover, if he and the cardinals believed that the worthiest candidate had not been chosen, they could set the election aside and the pope would make a new appointment. Similarly, if the election was not in conformity with the canons or if the papacy was not notified within a fixed time, the pope could appoint the bishop (art. 2). The tradition reserving to the pope appointment to all offices, including bishoprics, vacated at the papal curia, was reaffirmed (art. 1). While the concordat dissolved the tension between the papacy and Germany and effectively undercut the Council of Basel, it did not bring about serious reform of the Church. Issues allowed to fester helped to bring on the Lutheran Reformation. The Concordat of Vienna remained in place until the secularization of 1803.[34]

In Spain, King Ferdinand and Queen Isabella, seeking to restore royal authority following a period of instability and civil war, determined to subordinate the Church. Distressed by papal appointment of foreigners and absentees, they approached Pope Sixtus IV (1471–1484), who initially rejected their proposals. However, in 1482 he reluctantly allowed them to nominate the bishops subject to papal approval. Four years later Innocent VIII (1484–1492) granted them the right of appointment (*patronato*) of suitable persons to all the principal benefices in the kingdom of Granada then being conquered. Subsequent concessions by Alexander VI (1491–1503) in 1493 and Julius II (1503–1513) in 1508 extended that right to all ecclesiastical offices in the New World. By granting the kings of Spain this authority, the papacy averted the possibility of a violent confrontation such as occurred elsewhere during the Protestant Reformation.[35]

Meantime, papal discontent with the Pragmatic Sanction of Bourges and the implied autonomy of the French Church prompted Julius II, the warrior pope, to condemn it during the Fifth Lateran Council in 1512. In 1516 when Pope Leo X (1513–1521) and King Francis I concluded the Concordat of Bologna, abolishing the Pragmatic Sanction, tension between the papacy and the French crown was eased. Nevertheless, the pope, while acknowledging the freedom of cathedral chapters to elect their bishops, conceded to the king the right of nomination within six months of a vacancy. The nominee had to be a master or licentiate in theology or a doctor in both laws or in civil or canon law and at least twenty-seven years of age. The appointment was subject to papal confirmation. If the pope rejected an unqualified person, the king had to submit another nomination within three months. If he failed to do so in due time, the pope was free to name whomever he wished. One notable exception to royal nomination was the right of the pope to appoint to churches made vacant by the death of the incumbent while visiting the papal curia. Moreover, if two irregular appointments were made, the pope could make the appointment himself. The Concordat of 1516 remained in effect until 1790.[36]

Convened in 1512 and dissolved in 1517, the Fifth Lateran Council did little to achieve its stated purpose, the reform of the Church. Although the council condemned simony in papal elections, it failed in every other respect as a reforming body.[37] The irony of this is that in the very year that

Leo X closed the council, thinking he had reformed the Church in head and members, Martin Luther nailed his ninety-five theses to the door of Wittenberg cathedral.

The Roman Pontifical of 1485

Meantime, in 1485 Pope Innocent VIII ordered the preparation of a new pontifical for the consecration of bishops, one that drew heavily on Durand's work of two centuries before. McMillan remarks: "For the first time in history the rite for the ordination of a bishop is given a title referring to only half of its constitutive elements, 'consecration.'" Any reference to the process of election was eliminated and the rite was transformed from a two-stage process of election and ordination to one of consecration. As the theologians did not recognize the ordination of a bishop as part of the sacrament of holy orders, the rite became a rite of consecration. As in Durand's pontifical, two bishops presented the elect, asking, in the name of holy mother Church, that the consecrator raise him to the episcopacy. Entirely omitted is the metropolitan's question, "Do you know him to be worthy?" and the response affirming his worthiness. Instead the consecrator asked: "Do you have the apostolic mandate?" Now, instead of the decree recording the election and the consent of the clergy and people, only the papal mandate was required. After the mandate was read, the consecrator briefly examined the elect and asked him to promise fidelity to Blessed Peter and to his vicars, the popes. Then the elect kissed the consecrator's hand.

The Pontifical of 1485, used henceforth not only in Rome but throughout the Church, helped to weaken the ties hitherto linking the bishop to the clergy and people of his diocese, to his fellow bishops, and to his metropolitan. Indeed, the consecrating prelate may not have been his metropolitan. Instead of being presented by the clergy and people, he was now presented in the name of the whole Church; instead of promising fidelity to the metropolitan, he now pledged allegiance to the pope. The introduction to the text explained that as the apostolic see had the right to provide for or to confirm elections to "churches widowed of a pastor," the examination of the elect and testimony to his worthiness by the clergy and people, the provincial bishops, and the metropolitan was unnecessary. The papal mandate sufficed for all that.[38]

Recapitulation

On the eve of the Reformation, "the unreformed Church," in Robert McNally's phrase, suffered from numerous abuses.[39] Juridicism was now ingrained in the life of the Church so that spiritual and religious questions

were viewed through the lens of canon law. The Church groaned under
the burden of papal taxation to support the curia; the sale of curial offices
was rife while papal appointments to ecclesiastical benefices and plurality
of benefices greatly increased. The free election of bishops by the clergy
and people of the diocese was now a dim memory, as the effective power
of naming bishops, with papal connivance, was vested outright with kings
and emperors. The royal right to authorize the election and to designate the
candidate was justified because kings restored and endowed old bishoprics
or founded new ones. The function of the cathedral canons was ever more
a mere formality of approving the monarch's choice rather than independently electing their own man. The appointment of young nobles still in
their early teens as canons diluted the wisdom that one would expect of the
body charged with the weighty responsibility of electing a bishop.

The Fourth Lateran Council of 1215 described the three customary
modes of election, namely, scrutiny, compromise, and inspiration. Whether
the election should be determined by the "wiser or greater part" of the
electors was debated for many years and sometimes resulted in long delays
in filling a see. By the late thirteenth century the decision of the majority was acknowledged as preferable. The pontifical of Guillaume Durand
acknowledged the electoral role of the cathedral canons, but the required
promise of obedience to the pope, as well as to the metropolitan, enhanced
papal influence over the whole Church. During the High Middle Ages
episcopal dress and the other accoutrements of the office assumed the form
generally known today.

The episcopal office became a sinecure for royal princes and the younger
sons of noblemen who were thus provided with a source of income. Not
having been consecrated because of their youth, once they reached adult-
hood some gave up the episcopacy to pursue secular careers. As the office
of bishop was a position of power and influence, most bishops preferred to
live at court where they could have the ruler's ear. Frequently foreigners
and absentees, the main concern of many was to accumulate bishoprics
and other benefices so as to increase their income. The pastoral care of the
people, every bishop's fundamental charge, suffered grave neglect by reason
of episcopal absenteeism.

Protests against papal intervention in episcopal elections became more
frequent during the Avignon era, and the Great Western Schism further
dimmed papal prestige. Adding to papal difficulties was the Council of
Constance's proclamation that a general council, representative of the
whole body of the faithful, had final authority in the Church. Once that
test was overcome, the papacy conceded the right of naming bishops to

secular rulers subject to papal confirmation. The Pontifical of 1485 tacitly acknowledged the growing irrelevance of the electoral stage by eliminating any reference to it. By stressing obedience to the pope the pontifical further weakened the link between the bishop, his people, and his metropolitan. This era came to a close and the sixteenth century opened with the Fifth Lateran Council, notable for its failure to effect any meaningful reform.

Notes

1. Wilhelm Kölmel, "Episcopal Elections and Political Manipulation," in *Election and Consensus in the Church, Concilium* 77, ed. Giuseppe Alberigo and Anton Weiler (New York: Herder and Herder, 1972), 72; Bernhard Schimmelpfennig, "The Principle of the *Sanior Pars* in the Election of Bishops during the Middle Ages," in *Electing Our Own Bishops, Concilium* 137, ed. Peter Huizing and Knut Walf (New York: Seabury Press, 1980), 19–23; John W. Baldwin, *The Government of Philip Augustus* (Berkeley: University of California Press, 1986), 64–70.

2. Norman Tanner, *Decrees of the Ecumenical Councils*, 2 vols. (London: Sheed & Ward; Washington, DC: Georgetown University Press, 1990), 1:203; Jean Gaudemet, "Bishops: From Election to Nomination," in Huizing and Walf, *Electing Our Own Bishops*, 12; Richard McBrien, *Lives of the Popes: The Pontiffs from St. Peter to John Paul II* (San Francisco: HarperSanFrancisco, 1997), 197–99.

3. Gratian, *Decretum*, in *Corpus Iuris Canonici*, ed. Emil Friedberg, 2 vols. (Leipzig: B. Tauchnitz, 1881); Robert L. Benson, *The Bishop-Elect: A Study in Medieval Ecclesiastical Office* (Princeton, NJ: Princeton University Press, 1968), 23–55; Gaudemet, "Bishops," 10–12; Michael Buckley, SJ, "Resources for Reform from the First Millenium," in *Common Calling: The Laity and Governance of the Catholic Church*, ed. Stephen J. Pope (Washington, DC: Georgetown University Press, 2004), 73.

4. Schimmelpfennig, "*Sanior Pars*," 16–23; Gaudemet, "Bishops," 12–13.

5. Tanner, *Decrees*, 1:211; Brian Tierney, *The Crisis of Church and State* (Englewood Cliffs, NJ: Prentice Hall, 1964), 113–14; Sidney Z. Ehler and John B. Morrall, *Church and State through the Centuries* (Westminster, MD: Newman Press, 1954), 63–64; McBrien, *Lives*, 203–5.

6. *MGH Constitutiones et Acta Publica Imperatorum et Regum*, 2:58–59; Schimmelpfennig, "*Sanior Pars*," 16–17.

7. Richard Winston, *Thomas Becket* (New York: Knopf, 1967), 105–24, esp. 115.

8. David C. Douglas and George C. Greenaway, eds., *English Historical Documents, 1042–1189* (London: Eyre & Spottiswood, 1953), 718–22.

9. Harry Rothwell, ed., *English Historical Documents, 1189–1327* (London: Eyre & Spottiswood, 1975), 3; Sidney Painter, *The Reign of King John* (Baltimore: Johns Hopkins University Press, 1966), 164–202.

10. H. A. Wilson, *The Pontifical of Magdalen College, with an Appendix of Extracts from Other English MSS of the Twelfth Century* (London: Henry Bradshaw Society, 1910), cited by Joseph Lécuyer, "The Bishop and the People in the Rite of Episcopal Consecration," in Huizing and Walf, *Electing Our Own Bishops*, 45; Owen

Chadwick, "The Anglican Practice in the Election of Bishops," in Alberigo and Weiler, *Election and Consensus*, 140–46.

11. Tanner, *Decrees*, 1:246–48; McBrien, *Lives*, 209–11.

12. Schimmelpfennig, "*Sanior Pars*" 16–21. The First Council of Lyon in 1245 regulated appeals in elections and declared that only unconditional votes were valid (cc. 4–5); Tanner, *Decrees*, 1:284–85. Geoffrey Barraclough, "The Making of a Bishop in the Middle Ages," *The Catholic Historical Review* 19 (1934): 275–319, esp. 275–78.

13. *Las Siete Partidas*, trans. Samuel P. Scott, ed. Robert I. Burns, SJ, 3 vols. (Philadelphia: University of Pennsylvania Press, 2001), 56–57; Joseph F. O'Callaghan, *The Learned King: The Reign of Alfonso X of Castile* (Philadelphia: University of Pennsylvania Press, 1993), 49–52.

14. McBrien, *Lives*, 215–18.

15. Tanner, *Decrees*, 1:314–21; McBrien, *Lives*, 219–20.

16. Michel Andrieu, *Le Pontifical romain au moyen âge*, 4 vols. (Vatican City: Bibliotheca Apostolica Vaticana, 1938–1941), vol. 1 (*Le Pontifical romain du XIIe siècle*), and vol. 2 (*Le Pontifical de la Curie romaine au XIIIe siècle*); Sharon L. McMillan, *Episcopal Ordination and Ecclesial Consensus* (Collegeville, MN: Liturgical Press, 2005), 136–71 (Latin texts, 156–58, 169–71).

17. Andrieu, *Pontifical romain*, vol. 3 (*Pontificale Guillelmi Durandi*); McMillan, *Episcopal Ordination*, 171–202 (Latin text, 192–96).

18. *Ordo 35B.35* in Andrieu, *Ordines Romani*, 4:108, and *Le Pontifical romain du XIIe siècle* in Andrieu, *Pontifical romain*, 1:149; Benson, *Bishop-Elect*, 122–23, 145.

19. Benson, *Bishop-Elect*, 168–88; Theodor Klauser, *A Short History of the Western Liturgy: An Account and Some Reflections* (Oxford: Oxford University Press, 1979), 61; Herbert Norris, *Church Vestments: Their Origin and Development* (Mineola, NY: Dover, 2002).

20. Friedberg, *Corpus Iuris Canonici*, 6, 1, 6, c. 18; Barraclough, "Making of a Bishop," 284–319; McBrien, *Lives*, 229–32.

21. Michel Mollat, *The Popes at Avignon, 1305–1378* (New York: Harper Torchbooks, 1965), esp. bk. 3.

22. Gaudemet, "Bishops," 13–14; John E. Lynch, "The History of Centralization: Papal Reservations," in *The Once and Future Church: A Communion of Freedom*, ed. James A. Coriden (Staten Island, NY: Alba House, 1971), 57–110.

23. Marsilius of Padua, *The Defender of Peace: The Defensor Pacis*, trans. Alan Gewirth (New York: Harper Torchbooks, 1967), 254–66, esp. 258, disc. 2, chap. 17.

24. Carl Stephenson and Frederick Marcham, *Sources of English Constitutional History: A Selection of Documents from A.D. 600 to the Present* (New York: Harper & Row, 1937), 226.

25. Mollat, *Popes*, 44–63; Walter Ullmann, *The Origins of the Great Schism: A Study in Fourteenth Century Ecclesiastical History* (Hamden, CT: Archon, 1967); McBrien, *Lives*, 242–47.

26. Tanner, *Decrees*, 1:403–51; August Franzen, "The Council of Constance: Present State of the Problem," in *Historical Problems of Church Renewal*, Concilium 7, ed. Roger Aubert and Anton G. Weiler (Glen Rock, NJ: Paulist Press, 1965), 29–68; McBrien, *Lives*, 247–55.

27. Tanner, *Decrees*, 1:443 (sess. 39, October 9, 1417), 448 (sess. 43, March 21, 1418); Colman Barry, *Readings in Church History*, rev. ed., 3 vols. in 1 (Westminster, MD: Christian Classics, 1985), 1:494–500; Christopher Bellitto, *The General Councils: A History of the Twenty-One Church Councils from Nicaea to Vatican II* (Mahwah, NJ: Paulist Press, 2002), 81–89.

28. Tanner, *Decrees*, 1:408–9 (sess. 4, March 30, 1415), 438–39 (sess. 39, October 9, 1417); Brian Tierney, *Foundations of the Conciliar Theory: The Contribution of the Medieval Canonists from Gratian to the Great Schism* (Cambridge: Cambridge University Press, 1955), 20–59.

29. Tanner, *Decrees*, 1:453–591; Ehler and Morrall, *Church and State*, 132–33; Barry, *Readings*, 1:502–3; McBrien, *Lives*, 255–58; Bellitto, *Councils*, 89–95.

30. Francis Oakley, "Constitutionalism in the Church?" in *Governance, Accountability, and the Future of the Catholic Church*, ed. Francis Oakley and Bruce Russett (New York: Continuum, 2004), 76–87, and *The Conciliarist Tradition: Constitutionalism in the Catholic Church, 1300–1870* (Oxford: Oxford University Press, 2003); Anton G. Weiler, "Church Authority and Government in the Middle Ages," in Aubert and Weiler, *Historical Problems*, 123–36, esp. 125.

31. Tanner, *Decrees*, 1:469–72 (sess. 12, July 13, 1433), 504–5 (sess. 23, March 16, 1436).

32. Nicholas of Cusa, *The Catholic Concordance*, trans. Paul E. Sigmund (Cambridge: Cambridge University Press, 1991), 178–87, bk. 2, chap. 32; Anton G. Weiler, "Nicholas of Cusa on the Reform of the Church," in Alberigo and Weiler, *Election and Consensus*, 94–103.

33. Ehler and Morrall, *Church and State*, 114–21; Oakley, *Conciliarist Tradition*, 50, 56–57.

34. Ehler and Morrall, *Church and State*, 125–31; Francis Xavier Funk, *A Manual of Church History*, trans. P. Perciballi and W. H. Kent, 2 vols. (London: Burns, Oates and Washbourne, 1938), 2:45–46; Kölmel, "Episcopal Elections," 73; McBrien, *Lives*, 258–60.

35. Enrique Dussel, "The Appointment of Bishops in the First Century of 'Patronage' in Latin America (1504–1620)," in Alberigo and Weiler, *Election and Consensus*, 113–21; Joseph F. O'Callaghan, *A History of Medieval Spain* (Ithaca, NY: Cornell University Press, 1975), 665; Jocelyn Hillgarth, *The Spanish Kingdoms, 1250–1516*, 2 vols. (Oxford: Clarendon Press, 1978), 2:396–99.

36. Tanner, *Decrees*, 1:598–600 (sess. 4, December 10, 1512); Ehler and Morrall, *Church and State*, 136–44.

37. Tanner, *Decrees*, 1:600–3 (sess. 5, February 16, 1513); Nicholas H. Minnich, *The Fifth Lateran Council (1512–1517): Studies on Its Membership, Diplomacy, and Proposals for Reform* (Brookfield, VT: Ashgate, 1993); Bellitto, *Councils*, 96–99.

38. *Pontificalis ordinis liber incipit in quo ea tantum ordinata sunt que ad officium pontificum pertinent* (Rome: Stephan Planck, 1485); McMillan, *Episcopal Ordination*, 203–19 (Latin text, 220–24).

39. Robert McNally, *The Unreformed Church* (New York: Sheed and Ward, 1965).

From the Protestant Reformation to Vatican II

5

THE FAILURE OF THE CHURCH to reform itself in head and members as so many had demanded had the consequence of ushering in the Protestant Reformation in the sixteenth century. The resulting religious divisions spread throughout the whole world and persist until the present. Unable to destroy the other or to impose religious uniformity, by the middle of the seventeenth century both sides settled into an uneasy truce. Intellectuals of the eighteenth-century Enlightenment, spurred by an abhorrence of violence in the name of religion and the development of natural science, concluded that many religious teachings were irrational. The French Revolution dealt a deathblow to the old regime of privilege and, trumpeting the slogan "liberty, equality, and fraternity," gave impetus to the growth of nationalism and democracy. Perceiving these new movements as hostile in the extreme, the papacy clung to outmoded ideas of the union of church and state and continued to demand that Catholicism be the only officially recognized religion. The proclamation of papal infallibility by the First Vatican Council was seen as a means of restraining unorthodox and dangerous ideas such as liberty of conscience. Wearied by internal oppression, two world wars, and the struggle against fascism, Nazism, and communism, the Church welcomed the Second Vatican Council called by John XXIII (1958–1963), who declared that it was time to open the windows and let some fresh air blow through musty corridors. In the forty years since then the promise of Vatican II remains unfulfilled as John Paul II's (1978–2005) restoration of papal absolutism has polarized the Church.

From Luther to Trent

Aside from challenging Catholic theological positions, Protestant leaders disputed the papal right to appoint bishops, and some even questioned the very concept of *bishop*. Rejecting as "pure invention" the Romanist distinction between clergy and laity, Martin Luther affirmed that through baptism Christians are consecrated into the priesthood of all believers. As the early Christians "chose from their number bishops and priests, who were afterwards confirmed by other bishops, without all the show which now obtains," so too, he argued, the community today has the right to choose its own bishops and priests. Yet he cautioned that no one should assume such an office "without our consent and election. For what is common to all, no one dare take upon himself without the will and the command of the community." He rejected the idea of apostolic succession and reduced the ordination ceremony to a sort of inauguration. John Calvin, basing himself on the ambiguous use of the terms *bishop* and *presbyter* in the New Testament, concluded that there was no need for a bishop as the leader of the Christian community when a presbyter would do as well. Recalling Cyprian, he urged that the minister, whether bishop or presbyter, should be "elected on the consent and approbation of the people." The Presbyterian and other Reformed Churches adhere to his interpretation. Proclaiming himself supreme head of the Church of England, Henry VIII reserved the nomination of bishops to himself. As a consequence of later alterations in the ordinal for the consecration of bishops, Pope Leo XIII (1878–1903) in 1896 declared Anglican orders invalid. In Catholic Europe kings also insisted on the right to name the bishops, and the papacy, fearful of losing the allegiance of more subjects, bowed to their demands.[1]

A residual fear of conciliarism deterred successive popes from responding to the demand that a general council be convened to deal with the issues raised by the Protestants. Eventually, however, Pope Paul III (1534–1549) summoned the Council of Trent in 1545; it met intermittently until 1563. Responding to the conciliarist challenge, the council affirmed papal authority over the whole Church and, as a means of revitalizing the life of each diocese, reasserted the bishop's responsibility as the spiritual leader of his people. The council also addressed several abuses concerning the episcopal office (even debating whether a bishop was obligated by divine law to reside in his diocese) and regulated the process of making bishops.[2]

The focus of the conciliar debate in 1563 was a draft document concerning the examination of potential bishops. When a vacancy occurred, the cathedral chapter, on the instruction of the archbishop, would announce the candidate's name and invite anyone who wished to lodge an objection to do so within a period of two weeks. On an appointed day the archbishop, at least two provincial bishops, the chapter, and representatives of the secular and regular clergy would examine the bishop-designate. In addition to declaring his suitability and willingness for the task, the bishop-designate would proffer written recommendations and witnesses on his own behalf. After discussing his qualifications, the archbishop and his associates would forward to Rome their assessment of the candidate's worthiness and the official record of the proceeding. On the recommendation of the cardinals the pope would then make the appointment.

In the ensuing discussion strong opinions were expressed, chiefly by French bishops, in favor of restoring the ancient custom of election by clergy and people. Citing St. Cyprian, who stated that the people's choice is inspired and willed by God, and Leo the Great, who emphasized that the metropolitan should consecrate only a bishop chosen by the clergy and people, Nicholas Pseaume, bishop of Verdun, was the chief advocate of popular election. Charles de Guise, the Cardinal of Lorraine, also lamented the abandonment of the ancient tradition, though his personal career exemplified some of the problems associated with the contemporary episcopate: named archbishop of Rheims at age thirteen on his uncle's resignation, he was consecrated at twenty. The council contested whether the laity actually had a right of election or only of consenting to the choice made by the bishops and clergy.

Some bishops, recalling ancient conciliar enactments, called on kings to surrender their right of appointment. The notion that boys seated on the throne, or what was worse, women, who were obliged to keep silence in church, should be able to name bishops was quite abhorrent. Nevertheless, royal and imperial ambassadors made it clear that their sovereigns did not intend to yield and many bishops, especially the Spaniards, expressed strong support for them. As the cathedral canons, often mere boys, the sons of the nobility, were generally considered corrupt and susceptible to bribery, no one defended their electoral claims. Although one prelate urged the pope to give up his right of appointment, others argued for the abolition of royal and capitular claims in favor of the papacy.

Determined to uphold papal rights, the Italian bishops gave a hostile reception to the idea of popular election, alleging that it would lead to evils and scandals. One declared that "the people are hopelessly superficial and . . . are moved more by rhetoric, kindness, favours, serious requests and sometimes by bribes than by a straightforward sense of responsibility." A Spaniard wondered whether "the *vox populi* is not the *vox* of the devil himself." Rejecting the ancient tradition as out-of-date and no longer applicable, the Jesuit General and papal theologian, Diego Laínez, contended that the devil was behind the proposal. In the hierarchy of human beings, he argued, as the clergy are superior to the laity, an election made by the clergy is worthier than one made by the laity. The worthiest election was one carried out by the pope, followed in descending order by elections by the archbishop and bishops, and then by the cathedral chapter. When the debate concluded, the argument favoring popular election was set aside in favor of the status quo.[3]

In the decree On the Sacrament of Order, Trent confirmed the papal right to name bishops and anathematized anyone who denied that a papal appointee was a legitimate bishop. Once a see fell vacant the chapter was instructed to order public and private prayers calling on God to "grant clergy and people a good pastor," but nothing further was said of the chapter's role in making that choice. The ultimate decision would be made in Rome by the pope after the cardinals reviewed the candidate's qualifications. Some specific regulations concerning bishops were laid down. The requirement that no one could be made a bishop if he had not served as an ordained priest for at least six months can hardly be considered a reform, if one considers that such a person was not likely to have any real pastoral experience. Insistence that newly elected bishops had to be consecrated within three months of election did address a long-standing problem that allowed the younger sons of kings and nobles to receive the revenues of bishoprics until they were prepared to receive orders or to pursue other career options. The appointment of coadjutor bishops with the right of succession was abolished. Nepotism, plurality of benefices, expectatives, and absenteeism were condemned. It seems unbelievable that a church council had to enact decrees obliging bishops to reside in their sees (Rome was the habitual residence of a hundred or more); to preach every Sunday and holy day; to visit each church in their diocese once a year; and to personally ordain the priests of their diocese. This simply emphasizes how far the idea of the bishop as shepherd of a flock had departed from reality. To ensure fraternal cooperation and correction, the council required that bishops summon diocesan synods each year and that archbishops convene provincial synods every three years. Bishops were admonished to adopt a frugal lifestyle and to refrain from participation in political and financial intrigues. They were also cautioned to be mindful of their role as fathers and pastors and not to display unworthy servility to the king's ministers or the nobility. Frugality, political and financial intrigue, and toadying to the king and his ministers, remained so many dead letters.[4]

Given that the bishops and other ecclesiastical leaders were usually drawn from the nobility, one ought not to be surprised by their elitist positions and disdain for the majority of the people who made up the Body of Christ. In an age of absolute monarchy the restoration of the popular election of bishops would have been incongruous. While dismissive of the cathedral chapters, the council seemed content to continue to allow kings and emperors, with papal confirmation, to control episcopal appointments. Bokenkotter summed up the council's structural reform: "Under the papal autocrat they placed episcopal autocrats by giving the bishop absolute control over his diocese. And they left no room for participation by the laity in the administration of the Church. In sum, they bequeathed to modern Catholics a highly authoritarian, centralized structure that was still basically medieval."[5]

The Pontifical of 1595 and Episcopal Consecration

The Tridentine view of the bishop and his relationship to the pope was set forth in the Pontifical of 1595 issued at the direction of Pope Clement VIII (1592–1605). Repeating the Pontifical of 1485 with only minor changes, the new text was intended to replace all others and remained in use with little change until 1968. Before the ceremony could begin, the consecrator had to have before him the papal mandate or, if he were a cardinal, to have received the pope's direct oral command. If the consecration was held outside the Roman curia, it should be done in the bishop-elect's cathedral or at least within the province. Although the text referred to him as the elect, in fact he was not elected by the clergy or people of the diocese, but rather appointed by the pope. As in 1485, two bishops asked, in the name of holy mother Church, that the bishop-elect be elevated to the episcopacy. After the papal mandate was presented and read, the bishop was examined and asked to promise fidelity in all things to Blessed Peter and to his vicar, the present pope, and his successors. The Pontifical of 1595 differed from that of 1485 in specifying "in all things" and in citing the name of the present pope. McMillan points out that the bishop's selection by the pope and pledge of obedience stressed that the bishop's most important relationship was with the pope rather than with the clergy and people of his diocese, his fellow bishops, and his metropolitan. She sums up the character of the Pontifical of 1595: "The consecration is celebrated in no particular church for no particular church by no particular church."[6]

Challenges to the Tridentine Ecclesiological Model

The bitter division of Christianity after the Council of Trent ushered in a period of religious wars that tore Europe apart. Under the circumstances, the reception of the Tridentine decrees was difficult, especially as Catholic rulers, while continuing to profess belief in essential dogmas, were reluctant to give up their right of patronage and to fully comply with the new regulations concerning bishops. Like their Protestant colleagues, they hoped to exercise direct control over the Church in their respective countries. Emperor Maximilian II and the Catholic estates of the Holy Roman Empire assembled in the Diet of Augsburg in 1566 accepted Trent, but the territorial princes recognized that the decrees concerning the episcopate were contrary to their interests. Philip II of Spain published the decrees but with the proviso that they not prejudice his right to appoint bishops and abbots. Through the Council of the Indies he controlled the appointment of bishops and other ecclesiastics throughout the Spanish overseas empire.[7]

Nowhere was this quarrel more difficult than in France. During the council, the French bishops strongly upheld the liberties of the French Church embodied in the term *Gallicanism*, and the French kings never officially accepted the Tridentine reforms, although an ecclesiastical assembly in 1615 did so. The desire of the French Church to be independent of external control by the papacy gained new strength under King Louis XIV. Rejecting any subordination to the papacy in temporal matters, he took up the defense of Gallican liberties in the expectation of subjecting the Church to royal rule. Reasserting the right claimed by his predecessors since the twelfth century, he insisted that he could occupy episcopal lands until a new bishop was appointed. When Pope Innocent XI (1676–1689) rejected his claim, the king summoned an assembly of the clergy who recognized the *jus regale* and published the Declaration of the Gallican Church, or Four Articles, in March 1682. The articles affirmed that kings are not subject in temporal matters to the pope; that a general council is superior to the pope; that the pope cannot decide anything contrary to the inviolable ancient rules, customs, and institutions of the Gallican Church; and the decisions of the pope in matters of faith are not unalterable unless they receive the consent of the Church.[8]

As a consequence of the pope's repudiation of the Four Articles and his refusal to confirm the election of bishops who accepted them, thirty-five bishoprics were allowed to remain vacant for six years. Although Pope Alexander VIII (1689–1691) also condemned the Declaration in 1690 and refused to confirm royal appointments to bishoprics, both sides soon realized the need for a rapprochement. In 1690 the king, while retaining the right to name the bishops, announced that he would not require the Four Articles to be taught in seminaries. The new Pope Innocent XII (1691–1700) yielded on the issue of the *jus regale* and agreed to give canonical institution to the bishops appointed since 1682 who had not subscribed to the declaration; when those who had subscribed withdrew their signatures, the pope invested them as well. Despite the settlement, Gallican ideas continued to pervade the French Church.[9]

Meantime, the relationship between the papacy and bishops of different countries continued to be debated. Reflecting the influence of conciliarism and Gallicanism, Johan Nikolaus von Hontheim, auxiliary bishop of Trier (d. 1790), writing under the pseudonym Justin Febronius, in 1763 published a book, *On the State of the Church and the Legitimate Power of the Roman Pontiff*, in which he challenged papal primacy and jurisdiction. Drawing on extensive research in Church history, he argues that as the power of the keys was given to the whole Church, final authority rests with a general council. Refuting claims put forth by Gregory VII in the eleventh century, he holds that only the bishops had the right to confirm episcopal elections, to translate or depose bishops, to name coadjutor bishops, to establish new sees, and to erect metropolitan or primatial sees. Translated into various languages, his book had wide circulation, but as it stressed the power of national bishops and minimized papal authority, the popes condemned it and placed it on the Index of Prohibited Books. In 1778 Febronius issued a retraction, though it was not convincing. Meantime, the German archbishops of Mainz, Trier, and Cologne, and the prince-bishop of Salzburg, meeting at Ems in 1786 restated Febronius's principles in a document called *The Punctation of Ems*. The majority of German bishops, however, were reluctant to follow that lead. Interest in pressing episcopal claims against the papacy waned after the secularization of church property in 1803 and the loss of civil jurisdiction by the German prince–bishops.[10]

Nevertheless, Febronius's ideas gained acceptance by the Holy Roman Emperor Joseph II, whose ecclesiastical policy came to be known as *Josephism* or *Josephinism*. Intending to curtail papal influence in Germany and especially in Austria, the center of Habsburg power, he maintained his right to name the bishops and forbade them to communicate with Rome without his permission. Papal letters could be published only with his acquiescence. In addition to suppressing monasteries and confiscating Church property, he reordered the structure of parishes. When he appointed a new archbishop of Milan, Pius VI (1775–1799) protested, but in a concordat of 1784, Pius ceded the right of nominating the bishops in the duchies of Milan and Mantua to the emperor. With the backing of the emperor's brother Leopold II, Grand Duke of Tuscany, the Synod of Pistoia of 1786 convoked by Bishop Scipio Ricci accepted the Gallican Articles and Febronianism as a means of restoring episcopal authority and curbing the intrusion of the papacy in diocesan affairs. The Tuscan bishops assembled at Florence in the following year, however, refused to agree to the Pistoian decrees and in 1794 Pius VI condemned the Synod.[11]

As other rulers imitated Joseph II's policies, the eighteenth-century popes, in a series of concordats, acknowledged the right of the kings of

Sardinia-Piedmont, the Two Sicilies, Spain, Portugal, and Poland, to nominate to ecclesiastical offices, including bishoprics.

The French Revolution and Napoleon

The French Revolution, however, presented an even more formidable challenge to the Church. The Civil Constitution of the Clergy enacted by the French National Assembly in 1790 effected a sweeping reform of the ecclesiastical structure. The number of French sees was reduced from 139 to 83 (with ten metropolitan sees) corresponding to the departments, or new civil provinces, into which the country was divided. Departmental electors who chose civil officials would also elect the bishops by a written ballot; an absolute majority was necessary for election. Only a priest who had served in ecclesiastical ministry in the diocese for at least fifteen years was eligible for election. Within a month the bishop-elect had to present himself, together with the written record of his election, to the metropolitan (the title of archbishop was abolished), who, in the presence of his council, would examine the bishop-elect concerning his doctrine and morals. If the bishop-elect were qualified the metropolitan would confirm the election and require him to take an oath professing the Roman Catholic religion. If the bishop-elect were chosen for the metropolitan see he had to seek confirmation from the oldest bishop in the department. No bishop could ask the pope to confirm his election, but he could write to him as the visible head of the universal Church. If the metropolitan and his council determined that the candidate was unworthy and so refused confirmation, they had to issue a written statement of explanation, but the electors were entitled to an appeal. Before consecration the bishop-elect had to take a solemn oath "to watch with care over the faithful of the diocese entrusted to him, to be faithful to the nation, to the law, and to the king, and to maintain with all his power the Constitution decreed by the National Assembly and accepted by the king." All bishops (and other ministers of religion) were obligated to reside in their dioceses and to carry out their responsibilities in person. As the tithe, a principal source of their income, was abolished, the government would pay their salaries and provide them with suitable dwelling places. Bishops and priests also had to perform their duties without charge to the faithful.[12]

Although the constitution affirmed the electoral principle, it said nothing of the right of the clergy and people to elect, nor of the participation of the provincial bishops. Rather, the electors were a secular body, representative of neither the clergy or nor the people, and might indeed be non-Catholics. In that sense the bishop was treated as simply another state official. The requirement that the metropolitan confirm the bishop-elect was traditional, but the possibility that the departmental electors might appeal his rejection of a candidate was not. By prohibiting the bishop from seeking papal confirmation, while at the same time allowing him to recognize the pope as the visible head of the Church, the constitution reflected the Gallican tradition.

Most bishops and clergy ignored the constitution until the assembly required them to take an oath supporting it. Only seven bishops, including Talleyrand of Autun, who was to have a great future as a politician and statesman, and about half the ordinary clergy did so. Bishops were soon elected to replace the nonjurors and Talleyrand helped to consecrate them.

As might be expected, Pius VI declared the constitution unacceptable and suspended all prelates who took the required oath. His denunciation of the election of bishops by "laymen, heretics, infidels, and Jews" is a curious reflection of the papal mentality as it consigns the laity to the company of heretics and non-Christians. He also condemned new consecrations, suspending the consecrators, and prohibiting the newly consecrated bishops to exercise jurisdiction. His condemnation of the constitution and excommunication of the juring clergy confirmed the division in the Church.[13]

The ecclesiastical situation remained turbulent for several years until Napoleon came to power as first consul. Together with Pius VII (1800–1823) he concluded the Concordat of 1801, which remained in effect until 1905. The concordat accepted previous actions of the revolutionary government, such as the confiscation of church property, the suppression of the monasteries, and the abolition of the tithe. However, the papacy and the government jointly would make a new division of dioceses. The pope would request the resignation of all current bishops so that Napoleon, within three months, could appoint new ones. Should a bishopric become vacant in the future, the first consul would nominate a successor. Canonical institution of all the bishops, that is, effective possession of the office, was reserved to the pope. Newly appointed bishops had to take an oath of loyalty to the first consul, the same oath in use prior to the change of government. All non-alienated churches would be restored to the bishops. The government also agreed to continue payment of salaries to bishops and priests. Should any of Napoleon's successors not be Catholic, a new convention would be drafted to regulate the appointment of bishops. Although the papacy complained about the Concordat of 1801, Roberts remarked that it "gave the Pope a right of entry into France which he had never enjoyed before and gained for him a secure position from which he could dominate the French clergy and, to an extent, even influence other aspects of French affairs."[14]

In accordance with the concordat, all the constitutional bishops—that is, those who had signed the Civil Constitution—resigned, but forty-five of the ninety-seven nonjurors did not. Nevertheless, Napoleon nominated sixty bishops, one for each of the newly created dioceses. Twelve were jurors, sixteen were not, and thirty-two were priests. The concession of the right to name bishops was regarded as a continuation of the practice dating back to the sixteenth-century Concordat of Bologna. Napoleon extended further control over the Church through the Organic Articles published in 1802. Reaffirming the Gallican Declaration of 1682, he prohibited the publication of papal documents or the convocation of synods without governmental authorization. As the pope denied canonical institution, many bishoprics remained vacant. Consequently, a national council convened at Paris in 1811 by Napoleon, emperor since 1804, declared that, if the pope failed to do so within six months, the metropolitan could confirm the nomination of a candidate presented by the emperor. This formed part of the Concordat of Fontainebleau, which was concluded in 1813 by the emperor and the pope, then a captive in France (art. 4). Napoleon's overthrow soon after, however, made this new concordat a dead letter.[15]

The Restoration

Following the overthrow of Napoleon, the Congress of Vienna in 1815 attempted to return to the order that had prevailed prior to the French Revolution although that was clearly impossible. Restored to the French throne, Louis XVIII proposed the abolition of the Concordat of 1801 and the Organic Articles, the reestablishment of suppressed bishoprics, and the reinstatement of the Concordat of 1516. Pius VII, however, was unwilling to accept this plan because he realized that the Concordat of 1801 gave him greater influence over the French Church.[16]

Elsewhere the popes signed concordats with various European states, permitting the head of state to nominate bishops. The Concordat of 1817 with Bavaria typically allowed the king and his Catholic successors "to name to vacant archiepiscopal and episcopal churches in the Kingdom of Bavaria worthy and suitable ecclesiastics, endowed with those qualities that the sacred canons require." The pope would grant canonical institution (art. 9). That right of appointment was also given to the Catholic kings of the Two Sicilies, Spain, and Portugal. The Concordat of 1855 with Austria-Hungary, for example, while acknowledging the imperial right of patronage confirmed by past papal privileges, stipulated that the emperor would take counsel with the provincial bishops before presenting a nominee to the pope for canonical institution (art. 19).[17]

Just as the pope was unwilling to allow Protestant rulers to nominate bishops, so too were the Protestant rulers averse to allowing him to do so. Thus different arrangements had to be developed. Seeking an accommodation with England, the papacy was prepared to concede to the English monarch the right to veto unacceptable candidates for Irish bishoprics. Irish opposition was so intense, however, that the plan was jettisoned.

The so-called Irish veto was offered to five Protestant states of the Upper Rhineland, Prussia, and Hanover, where circumstances were somewhat different. In 1818 the Upper Rhineland states proposed that the cathedral chapters and rural deans present three candidates to the ruler, who would select one. After examination by the archbishop, the candidate's name would be forwarded to the pope for confirmation within six months. In fear of creeping democracy in the Church, Pius VII objected, however, to the inclusion of the rural deans in the electoral process. More importantly, he refused to admit that a non-Catholic ruler could designate a bishop, but he was disposed to concede the Irish veto permitting the ruler to reject a candidate as unacceptable. An agreement with Prussia in 1821 provided that within three months of a vacancy, the cathedral chapters, after first ascertaining the king's opinion concerning the acceptability of possible candidates, would elect the bishops in accordance with canon law. If the archbishop determined that the bishop-elect was worthy, the pope would confirm the election. In 1824 a similar arrangement authorized the king of Hanover to declare unacceptable one or more candidates from the proposed list, provided that there remained a sufficient number to enable a real choice. Three years later an agreement with the states of the Upper Rhineland allowed cathedral chapters to exercise their traditional right of election, but the pope reminded them to elect candidates acceptable to the ruler.[18]

Whereas the role of the cathedral chapters (who were hardly representative of the majority of priests) in episcopal elections continued to be acknowledged, the freedom of the electors was gravely compromised by allowing secular rulers, whether Catholic or Protestant, to intrude into the process either by directly nominating candidates or by objecting to others. Emperors, kings, and princes claimed the right of patronage based on the principle that they or their predecessors had founded the churches and thus ought to have the right of appointment. Ironically, the possibility that a Protestant monarch or his Protestant ministers might determine who would be bishop underscores the incongruity of allowing non-Catholics a voice in the election that was denied to the majority of the Catholic people. The papacy seems to have preferred this arrangement as it effectively sidelined the cathedral canons, kept democracy in check, and allowed the popes to negotiate appointments with secular rulers.

The situation in Ireland and England was somewhat different as over-sight of the Church in both countries rested with the Congregation for the Propagation of the Faith, or, simply, the Propaganda. Despite the Penal Laws, the Irish bishops continued to function. Bishops and clergy usually chose candidates for vacant bishoprics and forwarded the names of one or more to Rome for confirmation. In 1825 the Propaganda refused to accept the nomination of a candidate and a recommendation including the word "elected" because that implied that the curia had to accept a fait accompli and would have no real part in the appointment. Given the confusion hith-erto prevailing, in 1829 the Propaganda determined that when a see became vacant, the vicar general should summon the canons and parish priests; each of them would secretly write the name of the candidate he considered most appropriate. The names of the three candidates receiving the most votes were submitted to the provincial bishops, who would forward them to Rome with their own comments; but they could not introduce other names. This was the first time that the *terna*, or list of three, was used. The new system gave parish priests a greater voice than before, inasmuch as they drew up the original list of three. Still, laypeople were entirely excluded.[19]

Since the seventeenth century, vicars apostolic appointed by the pope were responsible for the Church in England, so that neither the clergy nor the people had any say in episcopal appointments. After Catholic Emanci-pation in 1829 restored civil and religious liberties to Catholics, the idea of reestablishing the English hierarchy and restoring the traditional electoral process was broached. In 1850 Pius IX restored the Catholic hierarchy in England, appointing Nicholas Wiseman, rector of the English College in Rome, as archbishop of Westminster, with twelve suffragan sees. The pope also created cathedral chapters that had responsibility for the nomination of bishops. When a see fell vacant, the chapter, convened by the archbishop, would prepare an alphabetical list of three names (*terna*) to be sent to Rome with the comments of the provincial bishops. Trisco comments that whereas someone chosen by a cathedral chapter had "a presumptive right" to the vacant see, no one in the *terna* could have any such expectation. The pope was free to set the list aside and nominate whomever he wished.[20]

The Condemnation of Liberalism and Reassertion of Papal Authority

The tendency of the papacy to negotiate the appointment of bishops with the secular authority and to downplay the electoral role of the cathedral chapters contributed to the increasing centralization of power that resulted in the imperial papacy of the late nineteenth and twentieth centuries. The popes viewed with suspicion, indeed with hostility, any democratic tendency that might lead to a liberalization of Church government. Pope Gregory XVI's bull *Mirari vos*, issued in 1832, reflected the papal attitude, as he condemned indifferentism in religion; liberty of conscience; freedom of publication (he noted that "the Church has always taken action to destroy the plague of bad books"); the growing lack of "trust and submission due to princes," and movements "devoted to impairing and destroying all rights of dominion while bringing servitude to the people under the slogan of liberty"; and the separation of church and state.[21]

In the very same year, however, Antonio Rosmini, a distinguished philosopher, theologian, and staunch Romanist, perhaps echoing those denounced by Gregory XVI, argued that the Church was indeed in need of "restoration and regeneration." In his book, *The Five Wounds of the Church*, Rosmini identifies five grave problems: (1) the division between people and clergy caused by the inability of the people to understand the Latin liturgy, (2) the poor education of the clergy, (3) disunion among bishops arising from their dispersal throughout the world, (4) the nomination of bishops by the secular power, and (5) the wealth of the Church. In objecting to the right of civil rulers to nominate the bishops subject only to confirmation from Rome, he assails the principles of Josephism and the appointment of bishops by the Austrian emperor in northern Italy. As a free society, the Church, he asserts, has the right to choose its own leaders, a right that it cannot surrender to any government without destroying itself. He concludes that any "absolute concession of this kind is invalid, a contract without foundation, a pact without substance, and like every other agreement to evil, null and void." In effect he condemns concordats and other arrangements that allowed secular rulers to name the bishops. Rather than permit episcopal appointments to be decided in the secrecy of cabinet meetings, he proposes a return to the ancient tradition of election by the clergy and people of the diocese. By divine right, he argues, they should participate in the choice of their bishop and not be compelled to accept someone whom they did not know or in whom they had no confidence. As Jesus said, the sheep know their shepherd as he knows them. He urges greater unity and collaboration among the bishops, pointing out that in ancient times they knew one another personally, were in constant correspondence with one another, often visited together, and gathered in provincial councils under the authority of the metropolitan. The pope, of course, had authority over them all. The Holy Office of the Inquisition condemned Rosmini's book in 1849 and placed it on the Index of Forbidden Books. However, in 1854 all his works were said to be above suspicion.[22]

Meanwhile, Pope Pius IX (1846–1878), faced with the failed attempt to establish a Roman republic in 1848, continued to oppose any significant change in the Church and became a staunch opponent of liberalism and nationalism. His *Syllabus of Errors*, published in 1864, denounced many of the same ideas as Gregory XVI's *Mirari vos*, namely, freedom of religion and the separation of church and state. The proclamation of papal primacy and infallibility in 1870 by the First Vatican Council was a major step toward giving the pope absolute authority over the Church. In the minds of many, the pope for all practical purposes was the only Catholic whose opinion counted. At the very time when absolute monarchy was in decline, papal jurisdiction over the whole Church became more centralized than ever before.[23]

Church and State Adjustments

The revolutions of 1830 and 1848, the intensification of national feeling, the occupation of Rome and the Papal States, the proclamation of the kingdom of Italy, the Franco-Prussian War of 1870, and the proclamation of the German Empire resulted in increasingly tendentious relationships between church and state. In the effort to reach some adjustment, the right of secular governments to have a say in the appointment of bishops came to the fore once again.

Challenging the Church's autonomy, the Protestant government of Prussia, for example, in the 1870s required all churchmen to be German citizens and graduates of German universities and refused to permit bishops or priests to function without governmental authorization. Although several bishops were deposed, exiled, or imprisoned for refusal to abide by these rules, the severity of the laws was gradually mitigated. The papal claim to freely appoint all bishops set forth in the new Code of Canon Law in 1917 (c. 329) became a source of contention two years later. When the cathedral canons of Cologne announced their intention to elect a new archbishop, the papal nuncio ordered them to await further instruction from Rome. The Prussian government, however, insisted that the agreement of 1821 allowing the chapter to elect, once the king gave his consent to the candidate, was still in force. In acquiescence, Rome acknowledged the right of the canons to elect in that instance, but gave no assurance for the future.[24]

After the downfall of the Second Empire of Napoleon III, whose troops had long protected the papacy, the Third French Republic adopted a decidedly secularist and anticlerical position. The government provoked a controversy over the language used when a nominee for an episcopal see was presented to Rome. Seeking to be accommodating, Leo XIII agreed that the president of the republic should use the phrase "we name him and present him to your holiness." When the pope refused canonical institution to one of three persons nominated by the government, the French prime minister insisted on "all or none." An impasse was reached and the three dioceses were left vacant. As tensions continued to mount during the pontificate of Pius X (1903–1914), the French government in 1905 abrogated the Concordat of 1801 that had regulated church-state affairs since Napoleon. Henceforth the papacy was free to appoint the French bishops without the participation of the government.[25]

Relations between the newly proclaimed kingdom of Italy and the papacy were also strained. While the government adopted measures to limit Church influence, Pius IX declared himself a prisoner in the Vatican and his successors forbade Catholics to participate in public life or to vote. Nevertheless, the Lateran Treaty concluded in 1929 by Benito Mussolini, the fascist dictator, and Pius XI (1922–1939) brought this difficult period to a close. The Italian government recognized not only the State of Vatican City but also that "the choice of the archbishops and bishops belongs to the Holy See." However, before any bishop (or coadjutor with right of succession) could be nominated, the Holy See would inform the government to determine whether it had any objection of a political character. This was to be done with the greatest care and secrecy so that the candidate's name would not be revealed until nomination (art. 19). Italy also renounced any right of royal patronage over benefices as well as any right to the income of bishoprics during vacancies (arts. 24–25).[26]

A few years after coming to terms with Mussolini, Pius XI in 1933 entered a similar concordat with Adolf Hitler, the German chancellor and Nazi dictator. While acknowledging the Church's right to name its own officials without governmental participation, the government stipulated that nominations should first be submitted for review lest there be objections of a political character (art. 14.2). A supplementary protocol stipulated that if no objection were made within twenty days, the papacy could make the nomination. Until that announcement, the strictest secrecy was to be maintained. This arrangement was not to be construed as giving a right of veto to the state, but in practical terms it did act as a restraint. Bishops had to be German citizens; alumni of German universities or ecclesiastical colleges, or of a papal college in Rome (art. 14.1); and had to take an oath of loyalty to the German state (art. 16).[27]

In 1941 Pius XII (1939–1958), who, as papal secretary of state, had negotiated the concordat with Hitler, also reached an agreement concerning the appointment of bishops with the fascist regime in Spain headed by Generalissimo Francisco Franco. As soon as a see became vacant or the papacy determined to name a coadjutor bishop with right of succession, the apostolic nuncio would inform the government. Having obtained the government's agreement, the nuncio would send a list of at least six suitable persons to Rome. The pope would select three names, but if he was unable to find three acceptable candidates on the original list, he was permitted to choose three others and to forward their names to Spain. Even when there were three acceptable candidates, he was free to add other names. Within thirty days the government had to make known its objections. If there were none, Franco, as chief of state, within thirty days would present one of the candidates for appointment by the pope. This arrangement was confirmed in the Concordat of 1953 (art. 7).[28]

Thomas Reese emphasized that from the end of the nineteenth century one of the primary goals of papal diplomacy was to secure a free hand in the appointment of bishops. To that end papal diplomats negotiated directly with secular governments. Church leaders in different countries were not actively involved in negotiations resulting in concordats. As a consequence, whereas 80 percent of the bishops were appointed locally and confirmed by the papacy at the opening of the nineteenth century, today the pope appoints 80 percent.[29]

The Church in the United States

When the United States achieved independence late in the eighteenth century, the Church was removed from the jurisdiction of the vicar apostolic in London and steps were taken to name a bishop.[30] American Catholics led by John Carroll were insistent that the bishop should be an American, not an Englishman or a Frenchman. At the time it was estimated that there were about 25,000 Catholics in the United States served by thirty-four priests, chiefly Anglo-Americans and former Jesuits (Pope Clement XIV had suppressed the society in 1773). In 1784 the papal nuncio in France approached Benjamin Franklin, then the American ambassador, about the appointment of an American bishop. Although the Continental Congress, in response to Franklin's query, asserted that it had no jurisdiction over the matter, Franklin apparently recommended John Carroll.[31]

Robert Trisco, who has traced the subsequent history of attempts to secure the election of bishops in the fledgling United States, may serve as our guide through this period.[32] In 1788 the American clergy petitioned

Pius VI to allow them to elect a bishop, "at least for the first time." They expressed the hope that the pope "after hearing the petitions of our priests of approved life and experience, and considering the character of our government, will adopt some course by which future elections may be permanently conducted." In justification they argued that it was important that the appointment of the bishop be "rendered as free as possible from suspicion and odium" on the part of their fellow Americans, especially the Protestants. The Propaganda, which had jurisdiction over the American Church until 1908, acceded "on this first occasion at least." With papal consent, "as a special favor and for this time," the General Chapter of the American clergy, meeting at Whitemarsh, Maryland, elected John Carroll as bishop of Baltimore in 1789. Twenty-four of the twenty-six priests attending elected him. Confirmed by the pope, he was consecrated in England. The priests at Whitemarsh meantime proposed that the clergy have the right to elect bishops in the future, but nothing further was heard of this idea. Indeed, the papal brief erecting the diocese of Baltimore emphasized that the right of election had been conceded for the first time, but henceforth the pope would appoint the bishop.[33]

When Carroll proposed that the diocese be divided and that the clergy elect the new bishop, the Propaganda instead preferred to give him a coadjutor bishop. Carroll was asked to consult with the "older and more prudent priests," and the pope would appoint the person they recommended. Thus two of his coadjutor bishops, elected by the General Chapter, were appointed by Rome. When four additional dioceses (Boston, New York, Philadelphia, and Bardstown, Kentucky) were established in 1808 (with Baltimore as the metropolitan see), however, the pope, without consulting the American bishops, appointed the new bishops. Thus the participation of the clergy in the naming of bishops was terminated. During the course of the nineteenth century, ethnic tensions involving the original core of Anglo-American clergy and the immigrant French, Irish, and Germans became acute. The bishops, several of whom were French, were disinclined to allow the clergy, many of whom were Irish, a voice in choosing their bishops. Bishop John England of Charleston in 1833 indicated that the best persons were not always appointed and that it would be erroneous "to say that either the clergy or the great body of the laity is content with nominations procured privately" (arts. 7–9). He urged that some system for making recommendations to the Holy See be established.[34]

Meantime there was much debate over the possibility of creating cathedral chapters, like those that existed in Europe, with the right to elect bishops and also to check the apparently unlimited authority of the bishops. Given the dispersal of the diocesan clergy over large areas, however, some bishops argued that cathedral chapters were not yet feasible. As an alternative, in 1855 the Eighth Provincial Council of Baltimore proposed the establishment of a body of ten or twelve priest consultors who, on the death of the bishop, would recommend to the archbishop (or, in case of his death, the senior bishop), a suitable successor.[35]

In the year following the death of Bishop Bernard O'Reilly of Hartford, who was known for bitter disputes with his clergy, an anonymous author cited the manner of appointing bishops as one reason for animosity between bishops and priests. A man otherwise unsuitable for the office was likely to be appointed if he had an influential patron. The selection of young, inexperienced bishops set them at loggerheads with older priests who neither respected nor obeyed them. The consequent scandal was harmful to the Church. Three Hartford pastors echoed these sentiments when they complained that the favorites of powerful prelates, by reason of personal friendship or wealth, were appointed despite their limited accomplishments and middling piety. When priests believed themselves to be as pious, learned, and zealous as their bishop, strained relations resulted. Commenting that the gap between bishops and their priests ran contrary to the country's republican spirit, Samuel Mazzuchelli, an Italian Dominican with many years of missionary service in the United States, suggested that a greater degree of republicanism in the Church would yield a better clergy.[36]

Louis Leitner, a German pastor in the Diocese of Philadelphia and former professor of sacred scripture, described the unfortunate consequences of the system of selecting bishops. Neighboring bishops set out to choose a new bishop for a vacant diocese without knowing its needs or the abilities of its priests. When the new man enacted new rules and regulations, nullifying those of his predecessor whom he deemed less zealous for the faith, the clergy responded with disobedience and disrespect, even satirizing him in the press. The Propaganda and the Holy See, because of their responsibility for the appointment, also came under attack. Leitner argued that one could not reproach the priests, many of whom were more experienced and talented than the incompetent stranger imposed upon them. He concluded that, if examined in Rome, a third of the American bishops would not even have been ordained. The fact of being male was their only qualification for the episcopal office.[37]

While Leitner believed that the time was not propitious to entrust priests with the election of their bishops, he argued that those nominated should be examined either in Rome or in the United States by examiners chosen by the Propaganda. He also suggested that pastors, at least, ought to have a limited privilege of accepting a nominee. In order to avert the appointment of unqualified men, the bishop-electors should publish their nominations so that any unfavorable information could be forwarded to the Propaganda. Acknowledging defects in the system, the prefect of the Propaganda in 1859 asked the American archbishops for suggestions for improvement, but they failed to advocate giving a voice to the priests.[38]

The Second Plenary Council of Baltimore in 1866 rejected a proposal to establish cathedral chapters, whose members would be responsible for nominating candidates for the office of bishop. In the discussion preparatory to the council, Archbishop Peter Kenrick of St. Louis noted that if the chapter made the choice, the role of the provincial bishops would be restricted, if not eliminated entirely. A draft text proposed that consultors be permitted to propose names or to comment on the merits of candidates put forward by the bishops and that the names be made public. However, a committee of theologians urged that the procedure be secret and advised against publication of the names either to the clergy or to the people, a proposal with which the Propaganda concurred. While noting that various methods for making bishops had been used in the past, the council decreed that the choice now rested with the Supreme Pontiff "for the wisest of reasons." The council repeated various decrees issued by the Propaganda summed up in 1861. Every third year all the bishops should forward to their archbishop and to the Propaganda the names of priests deemed worthy to govern a diocese. This was to be done in the greatest secrecy lest ambitions be stirred. When a see fell vacant all the bishops should be gathered in a synod under the presidency of the archbishop (or if he was deceased, the senior bishop) to discuss potential candidates. The public discussion should touch on each priest's name, age, nationality, diocese, education, health, pastoral experience, languages known, offices held, administrative capability, reputation for prudence, firmness, honesty, moral integrity, observance of the rubrics, and gravitas. Voting would be secret, as each bishop placed his ballot in an urn. The archbishop or senior bishop would take a report of the acts of the assembly to the Propaganda.[39]

As the century wore on, relations between bishops and priests scarcely improved. As the United States was still treated as a missionary territory without canonically erected parishes, priests objected that they were subject to removal or transfer at the whim of the bishop and that they had no say in the choice of their bishop. In 1868 William Wheeler, a priest of St. Louis, argued that the time had come to give the priests authority to choose their bishops. "The *valet de chambre* manner in which priests are nominated . . . is to me, truly, disgusting. . . . The rule always was, and is, that the obsequious wirepuller with influential ladies at his back, was and is sure to succeed rather than the hard-working zealous retiring priest."[40]

A decade later, George Conroy, bishop of Ardagh in Ireland, sent by Rome to inquire into conditions in the United States, emphasized the importance of episcopal patronage in choosing bishops. A candidate who enjoyed the favor and protection of a bishop, usually because of services performed, would likely be appointed, as no serious effort was made to discover the best candidates or to assess the character and habits of those proposed. Moreover, the secrecy of the proceedings precluded the presentation of any negative information about a candidate. Conroy's commentary on the quality of the current crop of American bishops was devastating. Most were men of mediocre ability with scarcely any knowledge of theology and therefore did not command the respect of the clergy. He concluded that the bishops, prior to presenting their nominations to Rome, should consult pastors more widely, but he did not favor giving them a deliberative voice.[41]

In 1883 Patrick Corrigan, a priest of Hoboken, New Jersey, complaining about financial mismanagement and the lack of accountability on the part of some bishops, argued that it would be in the best interests of the Church to allow qualified priests a role in episcopal nominations. If that occurred, it would reduce tensions between bishops and priests and result in the appointment of experienced persons. A bishop's personal holiness and theological wisdom were secondary in importance to a detailed knowledge of the diocese and its priests. In light of ethnic tensions, especially between Germans and Irish, he held that a bishop ought to be a native American or one reared in and attuned to the spirit of the United States. The veto power of the provincial bishops would eliminate unsuitable candidates proposed by diocesan priests. No doubt expressing the views of many of his confreres, he commented that bishops, clergy, and laity often received the first authentic notice of episcopal appointments from "a pious lady convert at Rome." The lady in question, Ella B. Edes, "a New England spinster . . . possessed of a biting tongue and a talent for gossip and conspiracy," was the Roman correspondent for the *Catholic News* of New York.[42]

Decrying the harmful potential of Patrick Corrigan's work, issued without an imprimatur, his bishop, Winand Wigger of Newark, demanded its suppression and witnessed the destruction of the plates by the publisher. Undaunted, however, Corrigan returned to the fray, urging priests to petition Rome for a say in episcopal elections. After adducing evidence from earlier centuries showing that priests had participated in episcopal elections, he stressed the validity of applying to Church affairs the principle of self-government, on which the country had been founded; he denied that to do so would be revolutionary or result in the Americanization of the Church.[43]

The issue of priestly participation in the selection of bishops was presented in the Third Plenary Council of Baltimore in 1884. In preparation for the council, the Propaganda proposed that when a vacancy occurred, the diocesan administrator should gather the irremovable rectors to draw up a list of three suitable candidates to be sent to the provincial bishops. After reviewing it and possibly rejecting some names (and providing reasons for doing so), the bishops would send the final list to Rome. When this proposal was discussed at the council, Bishop John Lancaster Spalding of Peoria worried ominously: "If priests are given the right of electing [their bishop] the people will also covet it." Despite that, the council, under pressure from Rome, agreed to the appointment of consultors, rather than a chapter of canons. The consultors, assembled together with irremovable rectors under the presidency of the archbishop, would recommend those whom they believed most worthy. The presiding bishop would send their recommendations to the provincial bishops and to the Propaganda. The assembly of provincial bishops would draw up a *terna* of three candidates to be sent to Rome. If the bishops rejected any of the names presented by the clergy they had to explain their reasons for doing so. Thus some priests had an opportunity to voice their opinions, but the bishops were not obliged to follow them.[44]

As the nineteenth century drew to a close, ethnic rivalries—principally between German- and Irish-Americans—often prompted demands that a new bishop be chosen from one or another national group. Nevertheless, the prefect of the Propaganda argued that this was not in the best interests of the Church. At the same time Edward McGlynn, an outspoken priest of the New York archdiocese, attacked as inadequate the role of consultors in the nomination of bishops. The consultors were too few and as appointees of the bishop they were not really representative of the majority of priests. Furthermore, the lists they prepared were often revised or ignored by the bishops. In his judgment Rome needed an outside source of information concerning prospective candidates and suggested that this could be one of the tasks of the apostolic delegate first appointed in 1893.[45]

In contrast to McGlynn, George Peries, a Frenchman and a canonist at the Catholic University of America, defended the existing system. Arguing that it accorded with ancient custom, modified by the elimination of abuses that had crept in, he insisted that the consultors and irremovable pastors represented the best of the clergy and were attuned to the desires of the people. Furthermore, the provincial bishops, with their experience and knowledge of the people, were well placed to act for the good of the Church, and the Propaganda, where the final determination would be made, was free of any national or regional bias. He concluded: "We ask any unprejudiced man, is there aught more grand, more wise, more regardful of all interests than this manner of selecting the pastors of the faithful?" One may suspect that many contemporaries, thought to be reasonably lacking in prejudice, would have answered with a resounding "Yes!"[46]

The nomination process underwent important changes early in the twentieth century. Complaints were made that when the names of candidates were publicized, they were often unjustly attacked and reputations were grievously damaged, sometimes beyond hope of repair. As a consequence many qualified men did not wish to be considered for the episcopal office. In addition, public discussion thwarted Rome's right to choose freely and without prejudice. Thus in 1910 the Sacred Consistorial Congregation required consultors and irremovable pastors to take an oath of secrecy, on penalty of removal from office, not to reveal the names of any persons they might discuss. Bishops and the members of the apostolic delegation and all those persons whose recommendations were requested were also obliged to preserve secrecy.[47]

A few years later, in 1916, the Consistorial Congregation modified the process again. Given prolonged delays in filling a see once it became vacant, the congregation decided that it would be helpful to receive nominations in anticipation of a vacancy. Thus bishops were asked every other year to nominate to their metropolitan one or two priests judged worthy of being bishops. The diocesan consultors and irremovable pastors, individually, and not as a group, would be asked to do the same. The bishops might also consult prudent men, including members of the regular clergy. None of the archbishops or bishops were bound to follow the advice given by anyone, but were admonished only to remember their responsibility to account for their actions to God. The nominations being made were not for a specific diocese; rather, they provided Rome with a roster of names of men considered suitable for the episcopal office, but not necessarily in the dioceses from which they came. All of this strengthened Rome's hand in the process and the influence of the apostolic delegate, while undercutting the significance of priestly participation. This was the situation when the Code of Canon Law was promulgated in 1917.[48]

Throughout the period under review emphasis was placed on securing a voice for the priests in the selection of their bishops. Patrick Corrigan's arguments, denounced by his bishop, seem mild today as even he was not prepared to argue that all the clergy should have a say in the matter. Whereas some urged the establishment of cathedral chapters similar to those in Europe, with the right of nomination restricted to a small number of canons, the American bishops generally opposed that idea. The privilege of recommending candidates ultimately was accorded to a select few: the diocesan consultors and irremovable pastors. After 1916, however, even their input was drastically curtailed. No one spoke up in favor of allowing the laity to have a say; indeed, Bishop Spalding warned against it.

The Code of Canon Law of 1917

The Code of Canon Law, promulgated by Pope Benedict XV (1914–1922) in 1917, summarized the canons regulating the office of bishop. Bishops were declared to be the successors of the apostles presiding by divine institution over particular churches and ruling them with ordinary power under papal authority. "The Roman Pontiff freely nominates them" (c. 329). Legrand commented that "this is the first time in history that such a statement appeared in a legislative text, at least in such categorical and general terms. Hence the untrammeled right of the pope to appoint any bishop is not traditional. In the course of two thousand years of history, even if the letter of the law was often twisted, the norm professed by the Church was that of election."[49]

However, if the right of electing the bishop had been granted to any college (that is, a cathedral chapter or similar body), the prescription of Canon 321 requiring an absolute majority of votes had to be observed. The worthiness of a candidate should be established according to a process determined by the Apostolic See, which alone may judge his suitability. He had to be of legitimate birth, at least thirty years of age, ordained at least five years, distinguished by good morals, piety, zeal for souls, prudence, and other gifts suitable for governing a diocese. He should also have a doctorate or a licentiate in sacred theology or canon law granted by an institute approved by the Holy See, or be solidly grounded in those disciplines. Whether elected or nominated by the civil authority, in accordance with a concordat, he had to receive canonical investiture from the pope after making a profession of faith and taking an oath of fidelity to the Holy See. Within three months of receiving papal investiture he had to be consecrated and take up residence in his see within four months (cc. 329–333). The code acknowledged the right of colleges such as cathedral chapters to elect but required that they do so within three months of a vacancy. Should they not act, the one who had the right of confirming the election might then freely appoint someone of his own choice (c. 161). In effect, that meant that the pope would do so.

During the nineteenth and twentieth centuries the electoral role of cathedral chapters was steadily eclipsed, as the papacy and secular governments worked together to name the bishops. By reserving the right of canonical institution the pope could exercise a veto over a royal nomination. The later concordats gave the pope greater influence because he could refuse to accept any of the names presented to him. In negotiating these accords the papacy sought to protect the Church against oppression by the state. In recompense for the confiscation of Church property during the French Revolution the papacy agreed to arrangements whereby the bishops and clergy, as though they were civil employees, received salaries from the state. Unable to accept the principle of separation of church and state and fearful of democracy, successive popes were unwilling to grant the rank and file of the clergy or laity any voice in the selection of bishops. The irony is that secular monarchs (or their ministers) who were often non-Catholic or anticlerical, or, in the twentieth century, irreligious dictators hostile to Catholicism, had a greater voice in choosing bishops than faithful Catholics.

Vatican II and the Ordination of a Bishop

The Second Vatican Council meeting from 1962 to 1965 altered the prevailing concept of the Church by emphasizing the People of God, the whole body of the faithful, including pope, bishops, priests, and laity. Nevertheless, chapter 3 of *Lumen Gentium* on "The Hierarchical Structure of the Church" reinforced the top-down model of church government hitherto in vogue. This is also evident in *Christus Dominus, The Decree on the Pastoral Office of Bishops*, which affirms that the "apostolic office of bishops was instituted by Christ the Lord" and that the pope "has the proper, special, and, as of right, exclusive power to appoint and install bishops." Nevertheless, the concordats cited above had conceded to secular governments some participation in the process. On that account the council expressed the desire that in the future "no rights or privileges [should] be conceded to the civil authorities in regard to the election, nomination, or presentation to bishoprics. The civil authorities . . . are respectfully asked to initiate discussions with the Holy See with the object of freely waiving the aforesaid rights and privileges which they at present enjoy by agreement or custom" (*CD* 20).[50] In addition, bishops impeded from carrying out their responsibilities by reason of age, illness, or some other "grave cause" would be invited to resign by the pope (*CD* 21).

In his letter implementing *Christus Dominus*, Paul VI (1963–1978) reaffirmed "the right of the Roman Pontiff freely to nominate and institute bishops," but he also authorized episcopal conferences in each country to propose in secret names of candidates suitable for the episcopal office (art. 10). Reiterating the request that a bishop submit his resignation on reaching the age of seventy-five, the pope declared that, after review, he would determine whether to accept it. A bishop who resigned could continue to reside in the diocese, which was obligated to provide him with "a worthy and appropriate living" (art. 11).

In accordance with Vatican II's *Constitution on the Sacred Liturgy* ordering the revision of liturgical books, especially to provide for the participation of the people, a commission was appointed to prepare a new pontifical for the ordination of a bishop (arts. 25, 31). In light of *Lumen Gentium*'s emphasis on the People of God, the Roman Pontifical of 1595 was deemed inadequate. In 1968 Paul VI published the new text, *The Ordination of a Bishop*.[51]

Instead of referring to the consecration of a bishop, the new version opted to return to the ancient term *ordination*. The laying on of hands by the ordaining bishops and the prayer of ordination were cited as essential to the validity of the rite. In order to encourage attendance by large numbers of the faithful, the ordination should take place on a Sunday or holy day in the bishop-elect's cathedral. In addition, so that the faithful might participate more fully, seats for the consecrating bishops, the bishop-elect, and his assisting priests should be placed so that the people have an unobstructed view of the ceremony (art. 9a–b). This emphasis on the importance of the assembly was nearly invisible in the Pontifical of 1595.

Following the gospel, one of the assisting priests addressed the principal consecrator: "Most Reverend Father, the church of N. asks you to ordain this priest, N., for service as bishop" (art. 16). The consecrator then asked for the papal mandate and ordered it to be read. Instead of acclaiming the bishop-elect as worthy, as in earlier times, by saying, "All present say: 'Thanks be to God' or give their assent to the choice in some other way, according to local custom" (art. 17), after discoursing on the duties of a bishop, the consecrator declared that it was the ancient custom of the Fathers to question the bishop-elect in the presence of the people. He then asked whether the bishop-elect was determined to preserve the faith handed down by the apostles, to care for the people of God and lead them toward salvation, to serve the needs of the poor, the homeless, and the suffering. Next he inquired: "Are you resolved to build up the Church as the body of Christ, and to remain united to it within the order of bishops under the authority of the successor of the apostle Peter? Are you resolved to be faithful in your obedience to the successor of the apostle Peter?" (art. 19). The rite continued with the anointing and ordination prayer. The blessing of the ring, pastoral staff, and miter took place before the ordination.

In earlier pontificals the presentation, examination, and consent to the ordination of the newly elected bishop had taken place before the celebration of the liturgy. Now it was incorporated into the liturgy immediately after the Gospel. McMillan remarks that "for the first time since the sixth century episcopal ordination in the Roman Church retains not even a remnant of its traditional two-stage structure" of selection and consecration. As the first stage of selection, presentation had "ceased to be an authentic expression of communal consensus by the thirteenth century (if not earlier)," one might say that the new version "brought the liturgy of episcopal ordination into line with ecclesiastical reality." But she suggests that the editors had missed an opportunity to affirm an earlier Roman tradition.

The request that the bishop be ordained, presented in the name of "the Church of N.," instead of "holy Mother Catholic Church," restored the important role of the vacant see. But no decree of election, nor any testimony concerning the worthiness of the candidate, was offered, as in ancient times, because the clergy and people of the local church had not in fact elected their bishop. The papal mandate was still all that counted. The ceremonial "Thanks be to God" or some other form of assent tried to restore some semblance of acceptance and approval but there was ambiguity as to the identity of those giving assent. Who were they? The assembly gathered for the ordination or the clergy and people of the diocese? The latter had not had any role in electing their bishop, so their assent here was hardly essential. There was no expectation that they might now dissent. The "Thanks be to God" was mere ritual rather than a real expression of consent by the community for which the bishop was being ordained. Kleinheyer points to this anomaly: "The consent of the community to the prayers of those who are appointed to serve at the altar, which is rightly asked in the liturgical celebration, will have all the more weight if the communities are given greater responsibility in the choice of candidates for offices in the Church."[52] The promise of obedience to the pope reaffirmed that the bishop's principal allegiance would always be to the successor of St. Peter. The bishop-elect's relationship to his metropolitan was not mentioned.

A revision published in 1990 clarified the 1968 version by stressing the role of the local church. The two assisting priests, for example, were identified as priests of the diocese and one of them requested the ordination of the bishop in the name of the local church. The two priests might be seen as representing their diocese, but neither they nor the other clergy and people of the diocese had participated in the process of choosing their bishop. The statement that all the faithful have the duty "to pray for the one to be elected their Bishop and for the Bishop once elected" seems to imply that an electoral process will occur, when, in fact, that was not the case. Nevertheless, the clergy and other faithful would be invited to the bishop's ordination because he is "constituted for the sake of the entire local church." Moreover, if the ordination occurred in the diocese, the newly ordained bishop, rather than the ordaining bishop, should preside at the concelebration of the liturgy.[53]

While the versions of 1968 and 1990 attempted to reestablish the connection between the bishop and the diocese for which he was being ordained and to give new prominence to the clergy and people of that church, much remains to be done. These texts are limited by the fact that there is no true election by the community, nor is there any indication that the provincial bishops and the metropolitan have any role in the choice of the bishop. Fundamentally, the pope appoints the bishop and the presentation of the papal mandate justifies the ordination. The bishop's promise of obedience to the pope, without reference to his metropolitan or fellow bishops, stresses the absolute nature of papal authority. A revision that would recognize an actual election by clergy and people, with the consent of the provincial bishops and the metropolitan, is very much in order.

Recapitulation

One of the consequences of the Protestant reformation was that it prompted the Council of Trent to debate the wisdom of returning to the ancient tradition of the election of bishops by the clergy and people of the diocese. Rather than endorse that idea, however, the council, while minimizing the electoral role of cathedral chapters, upheld the papal right to name bishops. Otherwise the council obliged bishops to reside in their dioceses, to preach, and to hold annual diocesan synods and triennial provincial synods. The Pontifical of 1595, reflecting the prevailing understanding of the process of making a bishop, lacked any reference to election and further relaxed the bonds between a bishop and a particular church. Though willing to accept some of Trent's decrees, secular monarchs were not prepared to yield their power to name bishops. Louis XIV's insistence on Gallican liberties directly challenged papal authority in France with the result that many bishoprics were left vacant until a compromise confirming the rights of royal appointment and papal confirmation resolved this long dispute. In the eighteenth century, Febronius, by defending conciliarism and the right of bishops to confirm elections, to transfer and depose bishops, and to establish new sees, launched an additional attack on papal prerogatives.

The Civil Constitution of the Clergy enacted by the National Assembly in 1790 effected a radical change in the French ecclesiastical structure as the election of bishops was assigned to departmental electors who might not even be Catholic. Finding this unacceptable, Pius VI concluded the Concordat of 1801 with Napoleon: a new division of dioceses was made and the right to name bishops was conceded to Napoleon, subject to papal confirmation. When the Third French Republic abrogated the concordat in 1905, the papacy was free to designate the bishops without governmental interference. After Napoleon's downfall, the papacy signed concordats with other European states, recognizing the papal right of instituting bishops named by the head of state. Pius VII was unwilling to yield the right of appointment to Protestant rulers but he did agree that they could reject a candidate as unsuitable. The *terna*, or list of three nominees drawn up by the bishops and clergy and sent to Rome so that the pope could select one, was first used in Ireland. Restoring the English hierarchy in 1850, Pius IX appointed the bishops, but in the future he authorized newly created cathedral chapters to prepare a *terna* from which he or his successors would make the final selection. In arguing against the appointment of bishops by secular rulers, Antonio Rosmini urged a return to popular election, but his position was rejected. Threatened by liberalism, democracy, and nationalism, the papacy tried to strengthen its hold over the Church by the First Vatican Council's proclamation of papal primacy and infallibility.

Meanwhile, John Carroll, the first American bishop, was elected by his priests, but thereafter the pope appointed the bishops. Lamenting the poor quality of the American bishops, witnesses attacked the system of episcopal appointments on the grounds of secrecy, patronage, intrigue, and the failure to consult priests. Although the provincial bishops and some priests were eventually asked to draw up a *terna*, the laity had no role in the choice of their bishops.

The Code of Canon Law in 1917 forthrightly stated the papal right to appoint all the bishops. That right was confirmed in the Lateran Treaty of 1929 between the Vatican and Italy and the concordats with Germany in 1933 and Spain in 1941, provided, however, that the government had no political objection to the candidates. Vatican II reiterated papal authority in this respect but expressed the belief that secular governments should have no say in the matter. Reflecting Vatican II's teaching on the People of God, *The Ordination of a Bishop*, a revised liturgical text issued in 1968, endeavored to foster greater participation by the people of the diocese in the ceremony of episcopal ordination, but made no reference to election or to the relationship between the bishop and his metropolitan. The papal mandate appointing the bishop was essential and the bishop's promise of obedience to the pope transcended all other responsibilities. This was the legacy of the late twentieth-century Church.

Notes

1. Martin Luther, "Open Letter to the Christian Nobility of the German Nation," in Colman Barry, *Readings in Church History*, rev. ed., 3 vols. in 1 (Westminster, MD: Christian Classics, 1985), 2:628–34, 668–69, 682–84; John Calvin, *Institutes of the Christian Religion*, 2 vols., trans. Henry Beveridge (Edinburgh: T. & T. Clark, 1863), 2:321–24, bk. 2, chaps. 8, 15; Thomas Bokenkotter, *A Concise History of the Catholic Church*, rev. ed. (New York: Doubleday Image Books, 1990), 186–200.

2. Hubert Jedin, *A History of the Council of Trent*, 2 vols. (St. Louis: Herder, 1957); Owen Chadwick, *The Reformation* (Baltimore: Penguin, 1964); Philip Hughes, *A Popular History of the Reformation* (Garden City, NY: Image Books, 1960), 206–67; Christopher Bellitto, *The General Councils: A History of the Twenty-One Church Councils from Nicaea to Vatican II* (Mahwah, NJ: Paulist Press, 2002), 96–111.

3. Societas Goerresiana, ed., *Concilium Tridentinum: Diariorum, actorum, epistolarum, tractatuum nova collectio*, 13 vols. in 19 (Freiburg im Breisgau: Herder, 1950–2001), 9:477–589; Jean Bernhard, "The Election of Bishops in the Council of Trent," in *Electing Our Own Bishops, Concilium* 137, ed. Peter Huizing and Knut Walf (New York: Seabury Press, 1980), 24–32; Robert Trisco, "The Debate on the Election of Bishops in the Council of Trent," *The Jurist* 34 (1974): 257–91; Marvin R. O'Connell, *The Counter Reformation, 1560–1610* (New York: Harper & Row, 1974), 98–103; J. H. Elliott, *Europe Divided, 1559–1598* (New York: Harper & Row, 1968), 145–50.

4. Norman Tanner, *Decrees of the Ecumenical Councils*, 2 vols. (London: Sheed & Ward; Washington, DC: Georgetown University Press, 1990), 2:744–53, 759–61, 784–94 (sess. 23, "On the Sacrament of Order," c. 8, and "On Reformation," chaps. 1–2; sess. 24, "On Reformation," chap. 2; sess. 25, "On Reformation," chaps. 1, 17).

5. Bokenkotter, *History*, 217, 222.

6. *Pontificale Romanum Clementis VIII P.M. iussu restituum atque editum* (Rome: Jacob Luna, 1596); Sharon L. McMillan, *Episcopal Ordination and Ecclesial Consensus* (Collegeville, MN: Liturgical Press, 2005), 224–37 (Latin text, 234–37).

7. Elliott, *Europe Divided*, 245–50; Henry Kamen, *Spain, 1469–1714: A Society in Conflict*, 2nd ed. (London and New York: Longman, 1991), 174–84.

8. Barry, *Readings*, 2:821–22; Francis Oakley, *The Conciliarist Tradition: Constitutionalism in the Catholic Church, 1300–1870* (Oxford: Oxford University Press, 2003), 173–78.

9. Richard McBrien, *Lives of the Popes: The Pontiffs from St. Peter to John Paul II* (San Francisco: HarperSanFrancisco, 1997), 310–15; Bokenkotter, *History*, 242–44; Gerald R. Cragg, *The Church and the Age of Reason, 1648–1789* (Harmondsworth: Penguin, 1970), 24–25.

10. Justin Febronius, *De Statu Ecclesiae et de Legitima Potestate Romani Pontificis* (Frankfurt: Bullioni, 1764); Oakley, *Conciliarist Tradition*, 182–93; Henri Daniel-Rops, *The Church in the Eighteenth Century* (New York: Doubleday Image, 1964), 286–91; Bokenkotter, *History*, 244–45; William W. Bassett, "Subsidiarity, Order and Freedom in the Church," in *The Once and Future Church: A Communion of Freedom*, ed. James A. Coriden (Staten Island, NY: Alba House, 1971), 205–65, esp. 240.

11. Funk, *Manual*, 2:177–78; Daniel-Rops, *Church*, 291–99; Cragg, *Church*, 219–26.

12. J. H. Stewart, *A Documentary Survey of the French Revolution* (New York: Macmillan, 1951), 172–81; Sidney Z. Ehler and John B. Morrall, *Church and State through the Centuries* (Westminster, MD: Newman Press, 1954), 169–81; Bernard Plongeron, "The Practice of Democracy in the Constitutional Church of France (1790–1801)," in *Election and Consensus in the Church, Concilium* 77, ed. Giuseppe Alberigo and Anton Weiler (New York: Herder and Herder, 1972), 122–31.

13. Stewart, *Documentary Survey*, 184–89 (*Charitas*, April 13, 1791); McBrien, *Lives*, 328–30.

14. Ermino Lora, ed., *Enchiridion dei Concordati: Due Secoli di Storia dei Rapporti Chiesa-Stato* (Bologna: EDB, 2003), 2–9 (arts. 2–6, 12–14, 17); Angelo Mercati, ed., *Raccolta di Concordati in materie ecclesiastiche tra la Santa Sede e la autorità civili* (Vatican City, 1954), 1:561–65, no. 74; Barry, *Readings*, 3:943–45; William Roberts, "Napoleon, the Concordat of 1801, and Its Consequences," in *Controversial Concordats: The Vatican's Relations with Napoleon, Mussolini, and Hitler*, ed. Frank J. Coppa (Washington, DC: Catholic University of America Press, 1999), 34–80, esp. 53, 91–193 (text of the concordat); Robert Trisco, "The Variety of Procedures in Modern History," in *The Choosing of Bishops*, ed. William W. Bassett (Hartford, CT: Canon Law Society of America, 1971), 33–34.

15. Lora, *Enchiridion*, 16–21 (Concordat of Fontainebleau); Mercati, *Raccolta*, 1:579–85; Bokenkotter, *History*, 248–58; E. E. Y. Hales, *The Church in the Modern World* (Garden City, NY: Doubleday Image, 1960). 34–71.

16. Lora, *Enchiridion*, 42–48 (Concordat of 1817); McBrien, *Lives*, 330–33.

17. Lora, *Enchiridion*, 28–42 (Bavaria), 48–70 (Two Sicilies, February 16, 1818, art. 28), 239 (Austria-Hungary, August 18, 1855); Mercati, *Raccolta*, 1:594, no. 79 (June 5, 1817), 825, no. 102 (August 18, 1855); Trisco, "Variety," 33–34.

18. Andreas Advocatus Barberi, ed., *Bullarii Romani continuatio*, vol. 15 (Mainz, 1855), 406–7, no. 985 (July 16, 1821), 16:32–37, no. 23 (March 26, 1824), 17:54–56, no. 206 (April 11, 1827); Mercati, *Raccolta*, 1:653–54, 665–66, 689–96, 700–3, nos. 84, 87, 89; Trisco, "Variety," 37–38; Wilhelm Kölmel, "Episcopal Elections and Political Manipulation," in *Election and Consensus in the Church, Concilium* 77, ed. Giuseppe Alberigo and Anton Weiler (New York: Herder and Herder, 1972), 76–77.

19. John H. Whyte, "The Appointment of Catholic Bishops in Nineteenth-Century Ireland," *Catholic Historical Review* 48 (1962): 12–32.

20. Trisco, "Variety," 38–42; Hales, *Church*, 107–10.

21. Barry, *Readings*, 3:959–66; Hales, *Church*, 90–95; McBrien, *Lives*, 336–39.

22. Antonio Rosmini, *The Five Wounds of the Church*, trans. Denis Cleary (Leominster, MA: Fowler Wright Books, 1987), esp. chap. 4. See the text at www. rosmini-in-english.org/fivewounds. Gregory Baum, "Ratzinger Explains How Condemnation Was Right Then, but Wrong Now," *National Catholic Reporter*, January 25, 2002.

23. Tanner, *Decrees*, 2:815–16 (sess. 4, chap. 4); Barry, *Readings*, 3:992–1001; Bokenkotter, *History*, 261–94; Hales, *Church*, 100–47; Bellitto, *Councils*, 117–25; McBrien, *Lives*, 343–47.

24. Ehler and Morrall, *Church and State*, 295–96; Hales, *Church*, 212–27; John Cornwell, *Hitler's Pope: The Secret History of Pius XII* (New York: Viking, 1999), 87–90.

25. Ehler and Morrall, *Church and State*, 358–71; Barry, *Readings*, 3:971–81; Roberts, "Napoleon," 71–72; Hales, *Church*, 233–40; McBrien, *Lives*, 347–55.

26. Frank J. Coppa, "Mussolini and the Concordat of 1929," in Coppa, *Concordats*, 81–119, 193–205 (text of the concordat); Lora, *Enchiridion*, 728–48; Barry, *Readings*, 3:1196–1202; Hales, *Church*, 228–30, 268–70; McBrien, *Lives*, 358–61.

27. Joseph A. Biesinger, "The Reich Concordat of 1933: The Church Struggle against Nazi Germany," in Coppa, *Concordats*, 120–81, 205–14 (text of the concordat); Lora, *Enchiridion*, 864–85; Ehler and Morrall, *Church and State*, 487–96; Barry, *Readings*, 3:1203–11; McBrien, *Lives*, 358–63.

28. Lora, *Enchiridion*, 996–1000 (1941), 1099–1128 (1953); McBrien, *Lives*, 363–66.

29. Thomas J. Reese, SJ, *Inside the Vatican: The Politics and Organization of the Catholic Church* (Cambridge, MA: Harvard University Press, 1996), 234; James L. Heft, "Accountability and Governance in the Church: Theological Considerations," in Oakley and Russett, *Governance*, 130, citing Garrett Sweeney, "The 'Wound in the Right Foot': Unhealed?" in *Bishops and Writers*, ed. Adrian Hastings (Wheathampstead, UK: Anthony Clarke, 1977), 207.

30. James Hennesey, SJ, *American Catholics: A History of the Roman Catholic Community in the United States* (New York: Oxford University Press, 1981), 69–100, and "'To Chuse a Bishop': An American Way," *America*, September 2, 1972, 115–18; Jay P. Dolan, *The American Catholic Experience: A History from Colonial Times to the Present* (Notre Dame, IN: University of Notre Dame Press, 1992), 100–24; Robert Trisco, "Democratic Influence on the Election of Bishops and Pastors and on the Administration of Dioceses and Parishes in the U.S.A.," in Alberigo and Weiler, *Election and Consensus*, 132–38; John Tracy Ellis, "On Selecting American Bishops," *Commonweal*, March 10, 1967, 643–49, and "On Selecting Catholic Bishops for the United States," *The Critic* 26 (1969): 42–48, and "The Selection of Bishops," *American Benedictine Review* 35:2 (June 1984): 111–27.

31. James Hennesey, SJ, "The Tradition of American Catholicism," in *Catholicism in America*, ed. Philip Gleason (New York: Harper & Row, 1970), 34–37; Ellis, "Selection of Bishops," 115.

32. Robert Trisco, "Bishops and Their Priests in the United States," in *The Catholic Priest in the United States: Historical Investigations*, ed. John Tracy Ellis (Collegeville, MN: Saint John's University Press, 1971), 111–292.

33. John Tracy Ellis, *Documents of American Catholic History* (Milwaukee: Bruce, 1956), 167–71, no. 53 (November 6, 1789); Trisco, "Bishops," 111–13.

34. "Report on the State of the Church in the U.S.," in "Papers Relating to the Church in America from the Folios of the Irish College at Rome," *Records of the American Catholic Historical Society* 8 (1897): 460–61; Trisco, "Bishops," 123.

35. "Decreta Concilii Baltimorensis Provincialis VIII," no. 6, in *Acta et Decreta Sacrorum Conciliorum Recentiorum. Collectio Lacensis*, 7 vols. (Freiburg im Breisgau: Herder, 1875), 3:161–62; Trisco, "Bishops," 129–30.

36. Trisco, "Bishops," 132–34. Trisco's citations (and translations) in this and the following notes (37, 38) are to documents in the Archives of the Congregation De Propaganda Fidei.

37. Trisco, "Bishops," 136–37.

38. Trisco, "Bishops," 137–38.

39. *Concilii Plenarii Baltimorensis II, in Ecclesia Metropolitana Baltimorensi, a die VII., ad diem XXI. Octobris, A.D. MDCCCLXVI, habiti, et a Sede Apostolica recogniti, Decreta* (Baltimore: John Murphy, 1868), 69–75, title 3, chap. 3; Peter Guilday, *A History of the Councils of Baltimore* (New York: Arno Press and the New York Times, 1969), 205–6; Trisco, "Bishops," 141–49.

40. Trisco, "Bishops," 155–56, citing Wheeler's letter to James McMaster, October 19, 1868, McMaster Papers at the University of Notre Dame.

41. Trisco, "Bishops," 197–200, citing a document from the Archives of the Congregation De Propaganda Fidei.

42. Patrick Corrigan, *Episcopal Nominations: Do the Interests of the Church Require that Priests Should Have the Power of Nominating the Bishops?* (New York: Sullivan & Schaefer, 1883); Charles R. Morris, *American Catholic: The Saints and Sinners Who Built America's Most Powerful Church* (New York: Random House, 1997), 91–92.

43. Patrick Corrigan, *What the Catholic Church Most Needs in the United States, or, The Voice of the Priests in the Election of Their Bishops* (New York: American News, 1884); Trisco, "Bishops," 214–25.

44. *Acta et Decreta Concilii Plenarii Baltimorensis Tertii in Ecclesia Metropolitana Baltimorensi habiti a die IX. Novembris usque ad diem VII. Decembris A.D. MDCCCLXXIV* (Baltimore: John Murphy, 1886), 12–14, title 2, chap. 1, nos. 15–16; Spalding's comment, November 24, 1884, *Acta et Decreta Concilii Plenarii*, lii–liii; Guilday, *Councils of Baltimore*, 231; Trisco, "Bishops," 228, 233, 244–45.

45. Trisco, "Bishops," 259, 264, citing Edward McGlynn, "The Results of Cardinal Satolli's Mission," *The Forum* 22 (1897): 695–705: Hennesey, "American Catholicism," 43–44.

46. George Peries, "Episcopal Elections," *American Catholic Quarterly Review* 21 (1896): 81–105, esp. 105; Trisco, "Bishops," 265–66.

47. Trisco, "Bishops," 266–67, citing *Acta Apostolicae Sedis* 2 (1910): 286–87.

48. Trisco, "Bishops," 267–68, citing *Acta Apostolicae Sedis* 8 (1916): 400–4.

49. *Codex Iuris Canonici* (Westminster, MD: Newman Book Shop, 1946); Legrand, "Theology," 33.

50. Hartmut Zapp, "The Nomination of Bishops in Accordance with Existing Law and the Draft *Liber II de Populo Dei* of 1977," in Huizing and Walf, *Electing Our Own Bishops*, 57–62; Jean-Louis Harouel, "The Methods of Selecting Bishops Stipulated by Church-State Agreements in Force Today," in Huizing and Walf, *Electing Our Own Bishops*, 63–66; Lamberto de Echeverría, "The Appointment of Bishops in Spain since Vatican II," in Huizing and Walf, *Electing Our Own Bishops*, 77–80; Jean Gaudemet, "The Choice of Bishops: A Tortuous History," in *From Life to Law. Concilium* 1996/5, ed. James Provost and Knut Walf (Maryknoll, NY: Orbis, 1996), 59–65.

51. *De Ordinatione Episcopi, Presbyterorum et Diaconorum*, rev. ed. (Vatican City: Libreria Editrice Vaticana, 1990); *Ordination of a Bishop*, in *Rites of Ordination of a Bishop, of Priests, and of Deacons* (Washington, DC: United States Conference of Catholic Bishops, 2003), 5–63; McMillan, *Episcopal Ordination*, 240–76.

52. Bruno Kleinheyer, "Consensus in the Liturgy," in Alberigo and Weiler, *Election and Consensus*, 27–30; Joseph Lécuyer, "The Bishop and the People in the Rite of Episcopal Consecration," in Huizing and Walf, *Electing Our Own Bishops*, 44–47.

53. McMillan, *Episcopal Ordination*, 266–71.

Contemporary Appointment of Bishops

6

IN THE CHURCH TODAY SCARCELY any vestige remains of the ancient tradition of the election of bishops by the clergy and people of the diocese. Rather, throughout the Latin Church the notion that the pope, without challenge, appoints the bishops as he wishes is generally accepted. Whereas Vatican II, by emphasizing the idea of the Church as the People of God, seemed to set the hierarchical pyramid on end, steps toward greater popular participation in the making of bishops have been sporadic and generally ineffectual. Any possible trend toward democracy in the Church, as the concept of the People of God seemed to imply, has been stifled and efforts to loosen the iron grip of the papacy on the appointment of bishops have been thwarted.

In the pages that follow the current system for appointing bishops is outlined and specific proposals for reform are offered.

Norms for the Selection of Bishops and the Code of Canon Law

In 1972 in response to Pope Paul VI's directive that episcopal conferences should annually and in secret propose candidates for the episcopacy to the papal nuncio, the Vatican's Council for the Public Affairs of the Church issued a series of "Norms for the Selection of Bishops." Through personal inquiry and individual consultation with both clergy and laity, conducted in secret, bishops were urged to draw up lists of candidates whose qualifications would be reviewed by national episcopal conferences. Each bishop, however, had the right to make recommendations directly to Rome (arts. 1–2). Prospective bishops were expected to be good pastors and teachers, prudent, even tempered, stable, versed in dogmatic and moral theology, upholders of the orthodoxy of the faith, "devoted to the Apostolic See, and faithful to the magisterium of the Church." In addition, they were to be men of moral probity and piety, endowed with pastoral zeal, an awareness of the signs of the times, and a capacity for administration. Their "family background, health, age, and inherited characteristics" should also be considered (art. 6). Omitted from this description is any reference to fidelity to the People of God in the local Church entrusted to the bishop's care.[1]

After a written ballot by the provincial bishops in conference, the papal nuncio would send the list of names to Rome. However, the pope was not obliged to adhere to the list and could appoint someone not already nominated (arts. 3–11). Prior to appointment, the nuncio would carry out a thorough inquiry concerning the candidate, consulting bishops, priests, religious people, and "prudent and generally reliable lay people" (art. 12). In the case of a specific diocese the apostolic administrator would prepare a detailed description of the diocese and its needs. The nuncio could consult clerics and laity, "especially through their canonically established representative bodies . . . as well as religious" (art. 13.1). The nuncio's final responsibility was to send to the Congregation for Bishops in Rome a list of three candidates, together with the opinions of the metropolitan and suffragan bishops, and the president of the episcopal conference (art. 13.2-3). Ever concerned about secrecy, the Vatican forbade open consultation concerning specific persons (art. 14). Collective consultation by the nuncio with clergy or laity, or bodies representing them, is a dead letter; moreover, it is not permissible for any group of priests, religious people, or laypeople to initiate the process.

Reaction to the Norms was not enthusiastic. Donald E. Heintschel, president of the Canon Law Society of America, pointed out that "the ecclesiology implied . . . seemed to be pre-conciliar" and that the process of consultation, while broader than before, "was still too restrictive, and did not seem to reflect the awakening consciousness of the responsible People of God." Other canonists were equally negative. Ladislas Orsy commented on the failure to reflect the principles of collegiality and subsidiarity stressed by Vatican II and the minimal consultation of priests and laity. John F. Fahey observed: "Alleged to be an implementation of the insights of Vatican II, the regulations are instead a reassertion of authoritarian practices that run counter to collegiality and subsidiarity. . . . Most American Catholics who recognize the importance of episcopal selections will react with chilled dismay."[2]

The Code of Canon Law of 1983 largely embodies the Norms outlined above. The pope freely appoints bishops or confirms those lawfully elected, that is, those elected by certain cathedral chapters, as, for example, in Germany and Switzerland, and by episcopal synods of the Eastern rites. The bishops in each ecclesiastical province or episcopal conference should draw up "by common accord and in secret" a list (*ternus*) to be sent to Rome of priests suitable to be bishops. Individual bishops could also submit names. The papal legate must seek suggestions from the archbishop and suffragans of each province as well as from the president of the episcopal conference. He should also hear from "some members of the college of consultors" or of the cathedral chapter, and he may seek suggestions "in secret" from other clerics and laypersons "of outstanding wisdom." He then sends his recommendations to the Congregation for Bishops. Reflecting earlier battles, the civil authorities were to be excluded from any role in episcopal elections or appointments (c. 377.1-5).

The person appointed should be outstanding in faith, morals, piety, zeal for souls, wisdom, prudence, and human virtues; be held in good esteem; be at least thirty-five years old and a priest for a minimum of five years; hold a doctorate or a licentiate in scripture, theology, or canon law from an institute of higher studies approved by the Apostolic See, or be well versed in those disciplines. After weighing this information, the Congregation for Bishops makes a final recommendation to the pope. The person chosen must be consecrated within three months and before taking possession of his office he must take an oath of fidelity to the Apostolic See (cc. 378–380). Once again there is no mention of the bishop's faithfulness toward the people of his diocese.

The Appointment of Bishops in Practice

Prior to the enactment of the 1972 Norms or the 1983 Code, petitions were addressed in 1968 to the papal nuncios in France and Germany asking that clergy and laity be consulted before appointments were made to the sees of Paris and Speyer. In the latter instance the request was denied because "a desire for a voice in the choice of episcopal candidates" could not be derived from the teachings of Vatican II. Priests of the diocese of Freiburg, however, pointed out that "the present electoral method contradicts the spirit of collegial co-responsibility" and argued for greater representation of both clergy and people in the body of electors. The cathedral chapters of several dioceses in the Netherlands initiated a similar move toward a more open and democratic process. When the canons of Haarlem decided to solicit popular counsel through the newspapers, the papal nuncio warned that that had "never been the practice and that a nomination based on such a procedure would not make a good impression." In Den Bosch, about 10,000 people responded when asked their expectations of a new bishop and their recommendations of suitable candidates. A bishop ought to be collaborative, able to bring together persons of differing views, and be an effective leader enjoying the confidence of the faithful. Tens of thousands similarly participated in a consultation in the Diocese of Rotterdam. After receiving nominations, the cathedral chapter sent a list of three names to Rome. The new bishop was usually appointed from that list, but under John Paul II the popular wish was often ignored as men of a conservative bent were named. Acknowledging the suffering that his decisions had caused, he stated in 1985 that he had appointed the person he thought most suitable for the office. But he queried: "Must he [the pope] explain his choice? Discretion does not permit him to do so." Honesty and transparency and a desire to enjoy the confidence of the faithful, however, would seem to oblige him to do just that.[3]

Meantime, the Second Synod of Bridgeport held in 1971 under the auspices of Bishop Walter W. Curtis, recognizing that Christians have traditionally participated in the choice of their bishops, proposed "to develop means whereby priests and laity may have a voice in nominations for the Episcopal Office." Like other bishops, Bishop Curtis apparently asked the priests of the diocese every year to suggest names of potential bishops, and he even consulted with some laypersons of "outstanding wisdom."[4] In 1979 the apostolic delegate instructed Leroy T. Mathiesen, then administrator of the diocese of Amarillo, Texas, to provide the names of every diocesan priest, a representative number of deacons and religious women, and of 100 laypeople to be consulted concerning the vacancy. This practice gradually was abandoned, however, prompting Bishop Mathiesen to conclude: "Small wonder that many on the parish level feel alienated and that the divide between them and the hierarchy continues to widen."[5]

Thomas Reese, who studied the selection process as it worked in the American Church of the 1970s and 1980s, can be our guide in the following discussion. Prior to that time certain bishops such as Cardinal Francis Spellman of New York, a close friend of Pius XII, acted as kingmakers, naming many bishops and auxiliary bishops. For many years thereafter no one had that influence, although Cardinal Bernard Law of Boston, before his resignation in disgrace, emerged as the principal kingmaker. In the 1970s in Baltimore, Santa Fe, and St. Louis the Priests' Senate organized the process of consultation in accord with the procedure proposed by the Canon Law Society. In most instances one of the three nominated was appointed as bishop. After Cardinal Spellman's death, some 563 priests of the New York archdiocese offered suggestions for his replacement. Consultation sometimes becomes impossible, however, when the announcement of a bishop's resignation or retirement is followed quickly by the appointment of his successor.[6]

The process usually begins when the bishop, sometimes annually, asks his priests to name three of their colleagues whom they deem worthy of the episcopate. Nevertheless, the response often is small, perhaps a sign that the clergy have little expectation that their suggestions will be attended to. Bishops tend to recommend priests whom they know best, especially chancellors and other diocesan officials, seminary rectors, and bishops' secretaries. The bishop forwards his recommendations to his archbishop and to the other provincial bishops. After the vote the archbishop sends their list to the nuncio with specific recommendations for a diocese, archdiocese, or the position of auxiliary bishop. The names are also given to the standing Committee on the Selection of Bishops of the NCCB (now the USCCB), but the effectiveness of this committee seems to be minimal.[7]

The nuncio plays the most important role as he may ask for more information and carry out more extensive consultation with the president of the NCCB, bishops and archbishops, or individually with the diocesan consultors, or laypersons of "outstanding wisdom." The last are usually active in diocesan affairs and are often listed in the Catholic Directory. Presidents of the NCCB have often indicated that they knew little about the candidates being suggested. In carrying out his investigation the nuncio makes use of a questionnaire drafted by the Congregation for Bishops. Those consulted are asked to evaluate the candidate's personal characteristics and human qualities; his human, Christian, and priestly formation; his behavior, cultural preparation, orthodoxy, and discipline; pastoral fitness and experience, leadership qualities, administrative skills, and public esteem.[8]

Without doubt, the greatest weight is given to questions 6 and 7, which relate to the candidate's orthodoxy and discipline. The questionnaire asks about his "adherence with conviction and loyalty to the doctrine and Magisterium of the Church"; his attitude concerning pronouncements "of the Holy See on the Ministerial Priesthood, on the priestly ordination of women, on the Sacrament of Matrimony, on sexual ethics and on social justice"; his "fidelity to the genuine ecclesial tradition and commitment to the authentic renewal promoted by the Second Vatican Council and by subsequent pontifical teachings" (question 6). Next the questionnaire inquires about the candidate's "loyalty and docility to the Holy Father, the Apostolic See, and the Hierarchy"; his "esteem for and acceptance of priestly celibacy"; and his "respect for and observance of the general and particular norms governing divine worship and clerical attire" (ques. 7).[9]

It seems likely that a candidate favoring a modification of the rule of celibacy or the ordination of women or who is less than adamant in condemning contraception and abortion will not be recommended. The phrase "loyalty and docility" suggests an unquestioning, even abject, obedience to the pope and the pronouncements of the papal curia. Phrases such as the "genuine ecclesial tradition" and "authentic renewal promoted by the Second Vatican Council and by subsequent pontifical teachings" are clearly open to different interpretations; but there is no reason to doubt that the candidate is expected to adhere to the interpretation of that tradition and renewal advanced by the curia. Someone of independent mind would seem to have little hope of being approved. Candidates who have studied in Rome and have imbibed the spirit of *Romanità* are often thought to be preferred, but that is not always the case.

After an investigation usually of two to four months, the nuncio weighs all this information about the candidate and the diocese for which he is being proposed and prepares a report for the Congregation for Bishops. Although some consultation with diocesan consultors and laymen of outstanding wisdom may take place, it is very clear that archbishops, cardinals, and the papal nuncio have a major voice in appointments. Among others, John Tracy Ellis, the eminent historian of the American Catholic Church, observed the incongruity of entrusting to the nuncio, a foreigner with no pastoral office in the United States, the principal role in choosing the bishops.[10]

The Congregation for Bishops consists of curial cardinals living in Rome (the majority) as well as others who are residential bishops. Many of the noncurial cardinals, such as Cardinal Terence Cooke, archbishop of New York in the seventies, did not attend the meetings. Cardinal John O'Connor, Cooke's successor, tried to learn Italian so he could participate, especially when American appointments were under consideration. Given the sporadic attendance of the noncurial cardinals, it is not surprising that their curial confreres should wield the greatest influence. Once deliberations are concluded the prefect or head of the Congregation presents a recommendation to the pope, who usually accepts it though he may ask for further study. After the nominee gives his consent, the appointment is announced. Four to eight months usually elapse from the time a vacancy occurs until the appointment is made public.[11]

A bishop normally serves as an auxiliary for six years before appointment to a diocese of his own. In most instances he will not be promoted to the diocese where he has been an auxiliary. An archdiocese (and sometimes a diocese) may be of such great territorial extent or population size that the archbishop may feel the need for one or more auxiliaries. The person recommended by the archbishop, once the nuncio is convinced of the need, is usually appointed. If a new archbishop is selected, his predecessor's auxiliaries are usually advanced to sees of their own so the new archbishop can name his own men. Ellis comments that archbishops frequently chose auxiliaries willing to remain in the shadows and to be obedient. Often they were men of mediocre capabilities who were eventually given responsibility for sees of their own. Thus, mediocrity sometimes becomes a qualification for leadership.[12]

In addition to diocesan and auxiliary bishops, coadjutor bishops are sometimes appointed. That is often the case when a bishop is old or ill and requires the assistance of someone who can take full responsibility for diocesan administration. The coadjutor is always named with right of succession after the bishop dies or retires (c. 403.3). The liberal policies of Archbishop Raymond Hunthausen of Seattle displeased John Paul II, who in 1987 appointed a coadjutor to assume day-to-day control of the archdiocese.[13]

A potential influence on the selection of bishops is the United States government. The United States does not have a concordat allowing the government to express its opinion for or against a candidate, but it is well known that in 1939 President Franklin Roosevelt tried unsuccessfully to have Bernard Sheil named archbishop of Chicago and later proposed him for the archdiocese of Washington, DC. The issue of governmental interference in the appointment of bishops was raised after the establishment of diplomatic relations with the Vatican in 1983. In a court challenge the National Association of Laity (now defunct) argued that diplomatic ties would allow the government to intrude into the internal affairs of the Church. In response, the Justice Department asserted that if the American ambassador to the Vatican persuaded the pope to appoint a specific person, then the association ought to take that up with the ecclesiastical authorities and not with the government. Reese comments: "Since the court sided with the government, the Justice Department's brief should make Catholics nervous about how the U.S. ambassador to the Holy See might be used."[14]

The Bishops of John Paul II

During the nearly thirty years of his pontificate Pope John Paul II (1978–2005) had the opportunity to appoint nearly all the current bishops of the world. Insisting that this should not be the pope's private choice, several theologians from Germany, Holland, Switzerland, and Luxembourg in 1989 strongly protested that the rights and recommendations of local churches were consistently ignored.[15]

The Canon Law Society of America, in conjunction with CARA, the Center for Applied Research on the Apostolate, developed a demographic profile (age, education, ethnicity, etc.) of the current group of 294 American bishops (87 percent of whom were appointed by John Paul II). Their average age in 2003 was 65 and their average age when appointed was 52. Most (73 percent) were first named as auxiliary bishops and most are white (87 percent).[16]

The men chosen were loyalists who were not likely to challenge the papacy or its teaching on any issue. Richard Gaillardetz suggests that the person most likely to be appointed by John Paul II would be the favorite of a prominent cardinal, a graduate of a Roman university, with service in the curia, or with experience as a seminary professor or rector. Most importantly, he would have "no record of having written or said anything that might be construed as critical of official magisterial pronouncements or Church policies. Notably absent from this list is demonstrated ability as pastoral leader. Presumably, this qualification is currently viewed as ecclesiastical gravy."[17] Contending that "absolute conformists" do not make good leaders, Thomas Gumbleton, the retired auxiliary bishop of Detroit, was passed over for further advancement because he did not fit the mold indicated above, and he declared that the current criteria preclude the advancement of persons "with initiative, courage, [and] imagination" who are "open to new things."[18]

Andrew Greeley describes these papal nominees as "mean-spirited careerists—inept, incompetent, insensitive bureaucrats who are utterly indifferent to their clergy and laity." Deploring the poison of clerical ambition, William Byron, the former president of Catholic University, notes: "If promotion . . . is closed to those who speak up or write on controversial topics—regardless of how powerfully, competently or respectfully they articulate their views—those with no blots on their copybooks and no reprimands in their files will rise to positions of leadership." In Peter Steinfels's judgment the result of Vatican insistence on loyalty to the pope as the principal criterion for appointment "has been paralysis." Reese concludes that it has polarized the Church in different countries and alienated the faithful.[19]

The case of Anthony O'Connell, who was forced to resign as bishop of Palm Beach in 2002, pointed up the inadequacy of the selection procedures. While rector of a seminary in the late seventies, O'Connell sexually abused a teenaged seminarian; the Diocese of Jefferson City reached a financial settlement with the young man in 1996. Meantime, O'Connell had been appointed bishop of Knoxville, Tennessee, in 1988 and transferred to Palm Beach, Florida, ten years later. His predecessor, Keith Symons, was the first American bishop compelled to step down for sexual relations with boys.[20]

The Transfer of Bishops

The transfer of bishops has become increasingly common, so much so that it seems like an embarrassing game of episcopal musical chairs. A few examples will serve to illustrate this point. Justin Rigali, formerly an auxiliary in Los Angeles, after many years' service in Rome, was made archbishop of St. Louis, but was then transferred to Philadelphia on the retirement of Anthony Bevilacqua, who had previously served as bishop of Pittsburgh and before that as auxiliary in Brooklyn. Raymond Burke, bishop of Lacrosse, Wisconsin, was appointed to St. Louis in Rigali's place. John Myers moved from Peoria to the Archdiocese of Newark, vacated by Theodore McCarrick who was made archbishop of Washington, DC. McCarrick had been auxiliary in New York and then bishop of Metuchen, New Jersey. Edward Egan, a native of Chicago, a longtime judge of the Roman Rota, was rewarded in 1985 first by being made auxiliary bishop of New York under Cardinal O'Connor who, according to all reports, did not want him. O'Connor himself, a native of Philadelphia, spent his career as a chaplain in the navy, rising to the rank of admiral, and then was appointed to Scranton to obtain pastoral experience before succeeding Cardinal Cooke in New York. After O'Connor's death, Egan, then serving as bishop of Bridgeport, Connecticut, was advanced to New York.

William Lori, a native of Kentucky and auxiliary bishop of Washington under Cardinal James Hickey, became bishop of Bridgeport after Egan's departure. After serving as auxiliary of Fresno and bishop of Stockton, California, Cardinal Roger Mahony was named to the archdiocese of Los Angeles. Cardinal Francis George of Chicago had previously presided over the see of Yakima, Washington, before being named archbishop of Portland, Oregon. Cardinal Bernard Law was bishop of Springfield-Cape Girardeau in Missouri prior to his appointment as archbishop of Boston in succession to Humberto Medeiros, previously bishop of Brownsville, Texas. After Law was forced out he was replaced by Sean O'Malley, who had formerly served as bishop of Fall River, Massachusetts, and Palm Beach. Several of Law's auxiliary bishops were rewarded for their service by appointments elsewhere. Thus Thomas Dailey became bishop of Brooklyn and Robert Banks became bishop of Green Bay, Wisconsin; William Murphy went to

Rockville Centre on Long Island in succession to James McHugh, formerly bishop of Camden, New Jersey. Alfred Hughes became archbishop of New Orleans and John McCormack, bishop of Manchester, New Hampshire. Wilton Gregory, auxiliary of Chicago, then bishop of Belleville, Illinois, and president of the United States Conference of Catholic Bishops, received his reward for leading the bishops in the development of their Charter for the Protection of Children and Young People by being named archbishop of Atlanta. These examples could be multiplied.

With some exceptions bishops are hardly ever chosen to rule over the diocese where they served as priests and are thus strangers to both the priests and people committed to their care. In 1961, on being transferred to Baltimore, whence he came, Lawrence Shehan, the first bishop of Bridgeport, acknowledged that point: "Almost eight years ago I came to you as a complete stranger."[21] The local community does not have any real knowledge of the new bishop or his policies and behavior in his previous diocese. Furthermore, the recent history of episcopal appointments in the United States makes it clear that smaller dioceses such as Bridgeport, Belleville, Camden, and Stockton are stepping-stones to more important prizes. In the present climate the faithful are entitled to know how a new bishop dealt with cases of priestly sexual abuse in his former see. If he had been an auxiliary bishop, it would be appropriate to ask what advice he gave to his bishop about handling these cases.

Some years ago Cardinal Bernard Gantin of Nigeria, then prefect of the Vatican Congregation for Bishops, complained of "the amazing careerism" among bishops. Many of them, he said, had their eye on the next prize and importuned him for advancement. He concluded that a bishop should not be transferred except under extraordinary circumstances and that canon law should be amended to that effect. Cardinal Jorge Medina Estévez, the prefect of the Congregation for Divine Worship, affirmed that the bishop's "natural place" was one with "pastoral responsibility as the head of one diocese." "The episcopacy," he said, "cannot be the coronation of a career." Cardinal Joseph Ratzinger, then head of the Congregation for the Doctrine of the Faith, agreed that a bishop should usually serve only one diocese and that "there should be no sense of careerism. To be a bishop should not be considered a career with a number of steps, moving from one seat to another, but a very humble service. . . . Even a poor see with only a few faithful is an important service in God's church." He affirmed that "the view of the bishop–diocese relation as matrimony, implying fidelity, is still valid." "Sadly," he added, "I myself have not remained faithful in this regard." When the Code of Canon Law is next revised, Ratzinger said the bishop's commitment of "oneness and fidelity" should be emphasized. On the other hand, Cardinal Camillo Ruini, formerly auxiliary bishop of Reggio Emilia and now the papal vicar for Rome, thought that the *cursus honorum* allowing a bishop to move up the ladder was "quite normal to me, quite logical."[22]

The irony of this discussion among high-ranking prelates in the Vatican is that none of these cardinals was himself faithful to the diocese for which he was first ordained. Gantin was originally bishop of Cotonu in Benin, West Africa, and Medina, bishop of Rancagua and Valparaiso in Chile. Ratzinger served as archbishop of Munich, then in succession as cardinal bishop of Velletri and cardinal bishop of Ostia (two of the suburbican sees of Rome). While acknowledging his lack of fidelity to his previous dioceses, he did not refuse to accept the fisherman's ring as bishop of Rome under the name Benedict XVI.

The transfer of bishops from one see to another, as John Quinn, former archbishop of San Francisco, observes, is inimical to the best interests of the Church. Not only does it foster a spirit of ambition among bishops hoping to rise higher in the hierarchy, but it also reduces the office to an administrative task. In addition to creating a sense of instability, transfers result in frequent and prolonged vacancies. The clergy and people, sensing that their diocese is of little account, and wondering how long their new bishop will be with them, are demoralized.[23]

As his fidelity to his diocese is clearly tempered by his absolute allegiance to the pope, a bishop is likely to put papal interests above those of the people committed to his care. Furthermore, the transfer of bishops is entirely contrary to the ancient tradition of the Church that emphasized that the bishop was chosen by the community from its own members to serve them for life. Ancient texts, as we have seen, spoke of the nuptial bond between the bishop and his see, a union symbolized by the bishop's ring; after the bishop's death, the diocese was described as "the widowed church." Pope Callistus I (217–222) portrayed a bishop who ruptured that bond by reason of transfer as a "spiritual adulterer."[24] When the consecrating bishop places the ring on the new bishop's hand, he says: "Take this ring, the seal of your fidelity. With faith and love protect the bride of God, his holy Church." The modern *Ceremonial of Bishops* affirms that the ring "is the symbol of the bishop's fidelity to and nuptial bond with the Church, his spouse, and he is to wear it always."[25] In this way the ancient idea of the bishop's union with his see has been erased, and he can be moved anywhere without doing violence to the nuptial bond because his loyalty is given not to the local church, but to the universal Church.

Pleas for Reform

As long ago as 1970 the distinguished theologian Bernard Häring, maintaining that "the common good demands the most competent person at a given time," called for "a bold revision" of the process of making bishops. A bishop chosen after a broad investigation would enjoy a greater moral prestige than one selected after a "secret consultation of a few." The American church historian James Hennesey demanded "structured, public participation of the whole People of God in the episcopal selection process." As "the Church is an assembly of believers and not just the hierarchy," Patrick Granfield argued that everyone—bishops, priests, and laypeople—should be involved in choosing bishops. If the bishop's authority derived from the community and was not imposed from above, his position would be reinforced and he would have a sense of accountability to the people he serves, a sense that is necessary to representative government.[26]

Recalling *Lumen Gentium*'s teaching (23) that the bishop is "the visible principle and foundation of unity in his particular church" and "represents his own church," the canonist John Beal concludes that a bishop appointed without significant community participation cannot be "considered a legitimate representative of that church."[27] The Jesuit theologian Michael Buckley warns: "If the present system for the selection of bishops is not addressed, all other attempts at serious reform will founder and ever greater numbers of Catholics will move towards alienation, disinterest and affective schism." Similarly, the ecclesiologist Gerard Mannion observes: "Nowhere is there more need for more genuine consultation than with regard to the appointment of bishops, and yet what little is undertaken is routinely ignored."[28] Andrew Greeley, the sociologist, remarks: "As long as a bishop can be imposed without the consent of priests and people, thus promoting the type of bishops who created the abuse crisis, I do not see how credibility can be restored." In a research study among Catholics in six countries, all familiar with democratic institutions (Spain, Germany, Ireland, Italy, Poland, and the United States), he found that the majority in each country favored the democratic election of bishops.[29]

The Jesuit Thomas Rausch, noting that the Church through a series of concordats allowed secular regimes, "even repressive ones," to object to episcopal appointments on political grounds, argues that local churches should be permitted "to name their own bishops," subject to papal recognition. Citing 1 Timothy's description of the qualities of a bishop, the theologian James Heft suggests that as the people of a parish where a priest had served would best know his abilities, they should be consulted as to his suitability for the episcopal office. The Jesuit William Byron proposes that before the names of candidates are sent to Rome, they should be announced in the parishes, much like the banns of marriage, so that if anyone has an objection it can be voiced.[30] Declaring that the responsibility for choosing its leaders ought to belong to the whole Church, the ecclesiologist Joseph Komonchak asks why the past enactments of popes and church councils should not still retain their force.[31]

Archbishop Quinn maintains that the present system, "with diminished, even inconsequential participation of bishops, and little or no participation of priests and lay people," is a deterrent to the eventual union of the Christian churches. Reiterating Quinn's point, the canonist John Huels and the theologian Richard Gaillardetz suggest that a revision of current procedures would help to alter "perceptions of the Catholic church as a monolithic, quasi-monarchical institution."[32] The theologian Paul Lakeland proposed that future bishops chosen by regional or national episcopal conferences from the community and with community participation would normally serve until they resigned or retired. As the transfer of bishops contravenes ancient tradition and "reinforces an unhealthy careerism . . . destructive of the role of the bishop," it ought to be sharply limited. The National Review Board recommended that "the process for selecting bishops should include meaningful lay consultation."[33] Suffice it to say that there is ample support for a revision of the present system of making bishops.

The previously cited experience of the Netherlands points up the importance of developing a nominating procedure well in advance of the death or resignation of the bishop. Canon law allows the nuncio to consult in secret with diocesan consultors and laypeople of "outstanding wisdom" about possible candidates for the episcopacy, but this leaves the initiative entirely in his hands. Rather than passively awaiting a new papal appointment, local communities can consult the faithful and recommend worthy candidates. After the transfer of Bishop Gregory to Atlanta, the people of Belleville, Illinois, believing they had the support of Cardinal George of Chicago, began an inquiry process; but were greatly distressed when, before they could complete their work, Rome appointed a new bishop, Edward Braxton, previously bishop of Lake Charles, Louisiana. His announcement that he intended to renovate the bishop's residence was not met with favor as it suggested that his first concern was to assure his own comfort.[34] Voice of the Faithful in the Archdiocese of San Francisco held a day of discernment in October 2005 and proposed the names of three diocesan priests whom they considered worthy of filling the vacant see. Needless to say, their suggestions were not heeded, as George Niederauer, bishop of Salt Lake City, was transferred to San Francisco. After studying the history of episcopal elections and the relevant canonical texts, members of Voice of the Faithful in the Diocese of Bridgeport in the fall of 2005 placed an advertisement in several newspapers and distributed flyers soliciting responses to the question, what qualities would you like to see in a prospective bishop? A second advertisement and flyer asked whether the faithful believed that a Diocesan Committee for the Selection of Candidates for the Office of Bishop, as proposed by the Canon Law Society of America, was desirable. These instances reveal the possibilities as well as the difficulties in enabling the people to have a say in the appointment of their bishops.

Proposals of the Canon Law Society of America

The Canon Law Society of America (CLSA) has taken the lead in developing proposals that would allow a broad consultation of the faithful before an episcopal appointment is made. A committee established in 1969 to investigate the question brought together a body of scholars whose contributions were published in 1971 under the title *The Choosing of Bishops*. Among the topics considered were: election or nomination of bishops, the duties of bishops, term limits and the transfer of bishops, the role of minorities in the process, and electioneering. With the Norms mentioned above as a guide, the CLSA in 1971 prepared a *Provisional Plan for Choosing Bishops in the United States*. In introducing this document, Raymond Goedert remarked: "The Church in the United States, immersed as it is in a climate of participative government, has an unprecedented opportunity to lead the way towards the ideal process." The CLSA declared:

> When the manner of selecting church leadership in a country is inconsistent with the social and political experience of its people, anguish results. At present many American Catholics find their exclusion from the process of choosing bishops frustrating and insensitive to their hopes and heritage. Bishops too experience anguish because they often find themselves standing apart from the people they wish to serve rather than in their midst.[35]

The *Provisional Plan* was superseded in 1973 when the CLSA published the more comprehensive *Procedure for the Selection of Bishops in the United States*.[36] The intention, according to Thomas Green, was to create a structure that would facilitate "informed and genuinely representative ecclesial involvement in the selection process."[37] Noting that the papal Norms of 1972 lacked any means of implementation, the *Procedure* recommends the establishment in each diocese of a Committee for the Selection of Candidates for the Office of Bishop. The committee would include eleven persons, one appointed by the bishop, and the others "chosen through either election or appointment by the Diocesan Pastoral Council," namely, two diocesan priests, two nuns, two religious men, two laywomen, and two lay-men. If a Diocesan Pastoral Council did not exist, the Priests' Senate would choose the members, again either by election or appointment. Other than the bishop's nominee, the members of the committee would serve for four years. To assure continuity, half of the members of the original committee would serve for only two years. The Diocesan Pastoral Council should re-view the committee's work from time to time; in the absence of a council, the Priests' Senate should do so (art. 2.1-3).

In its effort to be continually aware of the developing needs of the diocese, the committee ought to enlist the assistance of all the faithful and should ask three questions: (1) In your opinion what are the three most important needs of the diocese today? (2) In light of the needs you have listed, what do you feel are the desirable qualifications of the next bishop of this diocese? (3) Please list three persons you feel would be good choices for the next bishop and explain why (appendix 2).

Every three years the committee should consult the whole People of God concerning the qualifications desired in a bishop and invite them to propose names of persons who meet the criteria. This triennial exercise is intended to guarantee that the information gathered and its assessment are current. Further input would be obtained from the Diocesan Pastoral Council, the Priests' Senate, parish councils, and various religious and lay organizations. Individuals wishing to propose candidates would be free to do so. Nominees could be suggested from either the diocesan clergy or elsewhere. By majority vote the committee would determine those persons who ought to be given "serious consideration." After soliciting information and interviewing the candidates and their acquaintances, the committee would forward to the Priests' Senate a report ranking the candidates according to their qualifications and the needs of the diocese; the dossiers for each candidate would also be included. The report would be made available to the candidates and to all those who took part in the process. In case of a vacancy the procedure would be initiated anew (arts. 2.4–8, and 7.2a–c).

After reviewing the committee's report, the Priests' Senate could add further information on the state of the diocese and the qualities desired in a bishop. The senate would also reduce the list of candidates to no more than ten names and rank them. Next the senate would send the list to the diocesan bishop, the Diocesan Committee, and the Committee on the Nomination of Bishops of the National Conference of Catholic Bishops (NCCB, now USCCB). In case of a vacancy this information would be sent to the administrator of the diocese as well as the Diocesan Committee (arts. 2.9–11, and 7.3–4).

Exercising his responsibility to discover persons worthy of the episcopal office, the bishop (or the administrator, if the see was vacant) should make inquiries "on an individual basis" concerning the candidates proposed by the Priests' Senate and inform the senate of the procedures employed. He may choose only from the list provided by the senate the names of those he wishes to propose to the Regional Meeting of the Bishops (arts. 3 and 7.5). There are thirteen USCCB regions grouping dioceses together.

At the regional meetings held in the spring, a bishop may submit names from the diocesan list with information about the candidate's personal background, education, pastoral and specialized experience, character, qualities appropriate for the office of bishop, and the type of office for which he would be most suited. In order to facilitate intelligent discussion this information should be provided well in advance of the meeting. After a vote on each candidate, the chairman of the region should forward the names and a complete report of the process to the NCCB Committee on the Nomination of Bishops (art. 4).

The NCCB committee, consisting of one bishop from each region, elected by the bishops of that region, following a review of all the documentation and, if necessary, additional consultation with the Diocesan Committee, Diocesan Pastoral Council, and the Priests' Senate, should prepare a list of three to five names with its own recommendations concerning each one. The NCCB Committee should also inform the Diocesan Committee of its actions. The president of the NCCB, who presides over the national committee, should personally present its report to the Vatican and also provide a copy to the apostolic delegate (now the papal nuncio). The final choice should be made from the list drawn up by the NCCB Committee (arts. 5 and 7.6–8). Throughout the process confidentiality concerning the names and personal affairs of candidates should be observed (art. 8).

Although the *Procedure* aims at greater community involvement, there are problems. One is that diocesan pastoral councils do not exist in every diocese. When they do, the bishop often appoints the members, so that they are hardly representative of either the clergy or the people. It is quite possible that they would choose as members of the Diocesan Committee persons not expected to disturb the status quo. In addition, even though the laity constitutes the vast majority of the faithful in any diocese, the *Procedure* fails to acknowledge that fact. Four laypeople is a decided minority in the committee of eleven. Although nuns and religious brothers may be laypeople in canon law, in the popular mind they are associated with the clergy. Nevertheless, the attempt to create a more inclusive process has to be recognized. The Priests' Senate plays a more important role in the *Procedure* because it can eliminate names and determine the ranking of the names sent to the bishop. Further winnowing can take place as the list makes its way through the regional meetings of bishops and the pertinent NCCB Committee. Lay input seems to be limited to the initial work of the Diocesan Committee. Once its list goes forward, the process is entirely in clerical hands. What is most striking about the *Procedure* is that it removes any participation by the apostolic delegate or papal nuncio. In that sense the *Procedure* attempts to guarantee that the list represents at least in some measure the thinking of the American Church rather than the pope's man in Washington.

In 1977 the CLSA drafted a document entitled "A Four-Phase Process for Diocesan Participation in the Process of Selecting Bishops for United States Latin Dioceses." The development of a vision of the diocese, or diocesan mission statement, was the first phase; second was the identification of the specific tasks required of the bishop as opposed to those he can delegate to others; the gathering of names of potential candidates for the episcopacy was the third step; and the fourth occurred when a new bishop personally appropriated the vision of the diocese. James Provost comments, however, that "the response to the CLSA proposal has frankly not been enthusiastic." One reason is that the American bishops are reluctant to act on it because it encourages a bishop to consult collectively, something the Vatican strongly opposes as contrary to the Norms.[38] The CLSA has continued to refine its proposals.[39]

Seconding CLSA's intent to give local bishops and local churches greater influence over the process, Thomas Reese suggests that the priests' council and the provincial and regional bishops "should be allowed to comment on the nuncio's terna. This could be a first step toward the day when these bodies would actually draw up the terna. If Rome cannot trust the priests' council of a diocese or the bishops of a province, then the state of the church is in serious trouble." Reese's proposal, however, is quite limited and does not include the participation of the faithful as a whole.[40]

The Church in America Leadership Roundtable, a conference of bishops and business leaders, proposed that human resource professionals might be enlisted to improve the selection process. "Improvements should include a clear definition of qualifications (including managerial capabilities), face-to-face interviews and well-informed nominations and recommendations from clergy and laity."[41] While the roundtable recognized that current church management is in need of great improvement, this recommendation seems to perpetuate the concept of the bishop as corporate leader or chief operating officer. The roundtable calls for broadening input into the process of choosing bishops, but it limits that to an elite group of human resource professionals, to the exclusion of the vast majority of the People of God whom the bishops are called upon to serve.

The Proposals of Huels and Gaillardetz

In 1999 John Huels and Richard Gaillardetz cited several traditional values that should be kept in mind when speaking of the choice of bishops. Briefly, they are (1) the theological/ecclesial integrity of the local church expressed both in the eucharistic celebration and in the community assembled as the Body of Christ; (2) the bishop's fundamental relationship to the local church comparable to the union between husband and wife and manifested in his pastoral leadership and liturgical presidency; (3) participation by representatives of the whole local church in the selection of the bishop, as a reflection of the *sensus fidelium*; (4) the application of the principle of subsidiarity in preserving a diversity of methods of episcopal selection, which would allow local churches to determine how they would choose their bishops; (5) the elimination of the control or undue influence of powerful rulers over the process; (6) the selection of suitable candidates for the episcopacy; (7) participation by the bishops of the province and the bishop of Rome; and (8) expeditious provision of a vacant episcopal office.[42]

With these considerations in mind the authors proposed several revisions in the current process for selecting bishops and put them in the form of canons that might be incorporated into a new edition of the Code of Canon Law. Upon the vacancy of a see or a bishop's imminent retirement at age seventy-five, the metropolitan should name a visitor who would consult representatives of the diocesan clergy, religious communities, and laity. He would then prepare a confidential report on the needs of the diocese and the most suitable kind of leadership (c. A). Two months after the vacancy his report should be sent to Rome and, where applicable, to the episcopal electors. Everyone receiving the report would be required to maintain secrecy (c. B). The several ways of choosing bishops include: (1) free appointment by the pope or appointment from a *terna* or list prepared by the provincial bishops, Priests' Council, or cathedral chapter; (2) election by the provincial bishops; (3) by the Priests' Council or cathedral chapter meeting under the presidency of a visitor named by the metropolitan; or (4) by another method adopted by the conference of bishops or plenary council and approved by Rome. Whatever that method may be, it would have to be applied throughout the country (c. C). Only priests of the diocese or province would be eligible for election or selection for the *terna* (c. D). If a suitable candidate could not be found, the metropolitan should inform the pope, who may name the bishop (c. E). Should the electors fail to elect a bishop within three months of the vacancy or if the *terna* were not presented to Rome within that period, the pope could freely appoint the bishop (c. F). The metropolitan must confirm the election of a suffragan bishop while the pope must confirm the election of the metropolitan (c. G). If the metropolitan see is vacant, the senior suffragan bishop should act in the metropolitan's place (c. H).[43]

These proposals have much merit but are also deficient in some ways. While it is desirable that a report on the needs of the diocese be prepared together with a description of the sort of person best able to meet those needs, the task is entrusted to one person. Even though the visitor may consult widely, the proposal does not guarantee collective consultation and ultimately leaves the final draft of the report entirely in his hands. Moreover, the contents of the report are revealed only to a limited group of persons and the rule of secrecy is upheld. In this era transparency has to trump secrecy. As Coriden and Ritty affirm: "Secrecy shrouds abuses and favoritism at the same time that it protects reputations and personal feelings; greater transparency is needed and would breed confidence and enhance trust."[44] The recognition of a diversity of methods of electing bishops accords with historical development but it falls short of guaranteeing the full participation of the People of God in the process. Papal appointment, election by provincial bishops, presbyterial councils, or cathedral canons are no substitute for the Church's most ancient tradition of election by the clergy and the people. Lay participation, in particular, appears to be limited entirely to the visitor's initial consultation. The requirement that the bishop be chosen from the diocesan clergy or at least from those of the province is a good one; it seems unlikely that a papal appointment would have to be made for want of a suitable candidate. The possibility of papal appointment, and the consequent loss of the right of election should the electors fail to do their duty, ought to be an incentive for the electors to proceed promptly. Confirmation of the election by the metropolitan and that of the metropolitan by the pope are ancient traditions that demonstrate the unity of the church.

The Proposal of Ghislain Lafont

The responsibility of the Christian community to choose its leaders, according to the French Benedictine Ghislain Lafont, is primarily a spiritual task, as it involves an attempt to discern that person whom God designates as best equipped for the office. The procedures employed are merely the means of discerning "the charism of the Spirit." Focusing initially on the papal office, Lafont comments that the College of Cardinals elects the Supreme Pastor of the Church and only indirectly the bishop of Rome. However, as the bishop of Rome ought to have "real local pastoral care," the clergy and people of the city, "in substantial enough numbers," should fully and rightfully participate in the electoral college. As the College of Cardinals is not truly representative of the church of Rome, the composition of the electoral college ought to be reformed to include elected representatives of the local church, Italian bishops, and presidents of episcopal conferences. Although the proposal to broaden the membership of the electoral college to include the clergy and people of Rome is praiseworthy, it does not envision the participation of representatives of the clergy and people of the universal Church.

Inasmuch as Paul VI in 1975 declared that the church of Rome should elect its pastor, Lafont asks why every other church should not also do so. The right to name bishops, he argues, is not ordinarily part of the "pastoral universal function of the Bishop of Rome." He points out that as a model for local episcopal elections, the long tradition of electing superiors in religious communities, such as the Benedictines and Dominicans, has functioned well and demonstrates that election is "both possible and beneficial." Thus, when a see falls vacant, one or two bishops (perhaps the archbishop, a regional president, or a bishop acting on behalf of an episcopal conference), together with one or two priests or laypersons from other sees, would visit the diocese. Summoning the people to prayer in the cathedral and in the parishes, the visitors would then invite nominations of candidates and a description of qualifications deemed essential for the office. At a later date, the visitors would summon an electoral college, comprised of the Priests' Council, the Diocesan Pastoral Council, and some others. The college would begin its work with a three-day retreat asking the Holy Spirit's guidance in the process of discernment. Following general discussion, one or two candidates nominated perhaps by the presiding bishop would be asked to come to the meeting. The election, taking place after prayer, would require the vote of a two-thirds majority for validity. Provided that the election was held in accord with the canons and in a spiritual manner, the presiding bishop would confirm it and ordain the bishop-elect. The new bishop, expressing his communion, would write to the bishop of Rome as head of the college of bishops, to the bishops of the national episcopal conference, and other bishops. In turn they would send their "greetings of peace."[45]

Imitating in some respects the example of Pope Gregory the Great, this proposal emphasizes the right of the local community to choose its bishop. However, it does not sufficiently highlight the role of the metropolitan of the ecclesiastical province as visitor and presider. Indeed that function could be entrusted to an outsider. Moreover, the suggested composition of the electoral college is vague and not particularly representative of the majority of the clergy or people of the diocese. In addition, while Priests' Councils may exist, many dioceses do not have Diocesan Pastoral Councils. Furthermore, it is not clear that the members of the electoral college may nominate candidates or whether that right is reserved to the presiding bishop. Nevertheless, the proposal eliminates papal appointment and recommends that if the bishop is legitimately elected, his responsibility is not to ask for confirmation from Rome but rather to inform the pope of his election and to declare his communion with him and with all the other bishops, especially those of his ecclesiastical province and country.

Two Proposals: I. The Selection of a Bishop

A return to the ancient custom of local episcopal elections based on full participation by and consent of the clergy and people of the diocese is in order. Two proposals to bring that about may be put forward. The difference between them is signaled by two words: selection and election. The former reflects the top-down model of Church government and does not challenge the assertion of comparatively recent origin that the "pope freely appoints bishops." The use of the word *selection* acknowledges that the pope, on recommendations received from below, will make the ultimate choice. On the other hand, *election*, the word used in the earliest texts, implies something much more radical, namely, a return to the original custom of the Church.[46] Sanctioned by centuries of tradition, *election* reflects the idea that ultimate authority rests with the whole body of the faithful, who confer the right to govern on those elected by the community. One proposal may be regarded as a temporary measure, the other as more permanent; the first may be achievable here and now, but the second will require much patience before it can be implemented.

Amplifying the CLSA's suggested *Procedure for the Selection of Bishops in the United States*, the first proposal offered here encourages the clergy and people to participate in the process of nomination in accordance with current canon law. If the faithful are to have a permanent voice in the matter, then, following the CLSA's *Procedure*, a Committee for the Selection of Candidates for the Office of Bishop should be established in each diocese. A committee elected by and representative of the priests, deacons, religious, and laymen and laywomen of the diocese, however, is preferable to one appointed by the bishop, or appointed or elected by the Diocesan Pastoral Council or the Priests' Council, as it is more likely to reflect the views of the faithful. The number of representatives ought to be in proportion to the size of each group, with the majority being drawn from the laity.

As an example that might be adapted to any diocese, Voice of the Faithful in the Diocese of Bridgeport proposes a committee of nineteen persons, namely, five laymen and five laywomen elected by the parishioners of the five diocesan vicariates; five priests, one from each vicariate, elected by their fellow priests; one deacon, one woman religious, and one man religious, all elected by their respective groups; and another member chosen by the bishop from either the clergy or the laity. The CLSA *Procedure* does not refer to deacons and the declining number of both men and women religious suggests that their participation in the future may be even less. Members should serve for a term of four years; one-half of the original number should serve for only two years in order to assure continuity; at the end of two years new members should be elected to replace them. At its initial meeting the committee should elect its own officers and adopt any necessary procedural rules. So that the members may become familiar with one another and work effectively, the committee should meet at least four times yearly. The diocese should provide a reasonable budget to facilitate the committee's work.[47]

Two situations determine the work of the committee. In the first instance, at its ordinary meetings the committee should assess the current needs of the diocese and the qualities desired in a prospective bishop, and identify diocesan priests who could best serve as bishop. The committee should issue a report of its activities at its final meeting in the spring of each year. The second circumstance would arise when a bishop is approaching his seventy-fifth birthday and is about to offer his resignation to the pope, or when a bishop dies. Within two weeks of the announcement of a vacancy, the committee, meeting in extraordinary session, should review its assessment of diocesan needs and prepare a list of three diocesan priests qualified to fill the office of bishop.

In carrying out its responsibilities, the committee should consult the faithful as widely as possible, utilizing all the means of communication available: announcements in the diocesan newspaper and parish bulletins; postings on diocesan and parish websites; direct mail to all parishioners; advertisements in secular newspapers; and television and radio stories and announcements. The committee should also consult the Priests' Council, the Diocesan Pastoral Council—if there is a viable one—and the parishioners and parish councils where each nominee has served, and any other organization or person likely to have pertinent information. Working groups could be set up in each parish or vicariate to consider the three questions proposed by the CLSA.

The personnel files of candidates who have agreed to be considered should be given to the committee so that it may accurately appraise each one. Candidates may be asked to fill out a questionnaire concerning their own assessment of diocesan needs and their ideas for providing effective spiritual leadership. The committee should adopt appropriate guidelines for confidentiality concerning the use of the information gathered. After completing the process of consultation, the committee should evaluate the candidates, determining first that they meet the requirements of canon 378 and second whether they would be capable of addressing the expressed needs of the diocese. In case of a vacancy, the committee should draw up a list of three candidates, ranked according to their suitability for the office of bishop. In order to accomplish this task in a responsible manner, the committee should endeavor to complete its work of consultation and evaluation within a month. If the diocese is vacant, it is all the more important to act expeditiously so that there will not be a prolonged vacancy.

In keeping with the principle of transparency, the committee should make its report simultaneously available to the people of the diocese (namely, each parish, the Priests' Council, the Diocesan Pastoral Council, and other diocesan organizations as seems appropriate); the diocesan bishop (or, in case of a vacancy, the administrator); the metropolitan and other provincial bishops; and the president of the USCCB. Most importantly, the report containing the committee's assessment of the needs of the diocese, the qualities desired in a bishop, and the list of three candidates, ranked in order of preference, should be forwarded directly to the Congregation for Bishops in Rome. The reason for this is to ensure that the committee's recommendations are transmitted to the congregation without possible watering down by the Priests' Council, the bishops, or the papal nuncio.

This proposal seeks to entrust the primary responsibility for the selection of the bishop to the people who know him best, the people of the diocese. The Diocesan Committee thus has a grave obligation to be sure that its consultation is broad and thorough and that any potential difficulties in the nomination of a particular candidate are discovered and addressed. If the committee is truly representative of the people of the diocese, its members, after conducting a thorough investigation as outlined above, should be the best qualified to identify the needs of the diocese and the priests most suited to serve the faithful. This ought to curb the practice of favoritism decried by so many of the witnesses mentioned above.

Two Proposals: II. The Election of a Bishop

A second proposal that would represent a true return to the ancient tradition of election by the clergy and people of the diocese is described below.

The archbishop, as head of the ecclesiastical province, in a letter to all pastors and parish councils to be read at all the Sunday masses, should announce the vacancy and convoke a diocesan synod to meet on a Saturday in the cathedral, the bishop's traditional seat, for the purpose of electing a bishop. In the month prior to the synod, representatives of pastors, associate pastors, deacons, religious communities working in the diocese, and the people in all the parishes should be elected. The number of representatives should be in proportion to the size of each body. An effort should be made to assure the election of an equal number of laymen and laywomen. Persons registered in parishes and over the age of eighteen who have received the sacraments of initiation should be eligible to vote. If the archiepiscopal see is vacant, the senior provincial bishop should assume this responsibility.

Meantime, a diocesan committee for the election of a bishop, composed of elected representatives of priests, deacons, religious, and laity (comparable to the committee described above), should direct the preparatory steps of the process. Utilizing the diocesan newspaper and website and other means of communication as previously mentioned, the committee should invite all the faithful to respond to the three questions proposed by the CLSA. Candidates should be members of the diocesan clergy who are known both to their fellow priests and the people of the diocese. Church tradition has always emphasized that the faithful of the diocese can testify to the character of a prospective bishop if he has served among them and is not a stranger from another diocese. In addition to the responses of the faithful, the committee should receive for review the complete personnel files of the candidates. After interviewing each candidate, the committee should prepare a written assessment of his strengths and weaknesses. This information should be presented to all those persons who will take part in the synod, so that through a process of discernment, they may seek the guidance of the Holy Spirit as they evaluate the candidates.

When the synod gathers on the appointed day under the presidency of the archbishop, the other provincial bishops should be in attendance. The committee for the election of a bishop should validate the credentials of the representatives elected as members of the synod. Under the archbishop's direction, the synod should elect officers from each of its constituent elements to guide its activities. The committee for the election of a bishop should present the names and evaluations of the candidates to the synod. The candidates, if they wish, should be permitted to address the assembly. Sufficient time should be allowed for plenary discussion of the merits of each candidate. Voting should be by secret, written ballot. A majority of two-thirds should be required for a valid election. The officers of the synod should jointly count the ballots and inform the archbishop of the result. The archbishop should announce the results of the election, ask for the consent of the one elected, and present him for acclamation by the synod. Testifying to the catholicity of the Church, the archbishop should confirm the election. Meantime, a report of the election should be prepared and signed by the officers of the synod as well as the archbishop and the provincial bishops. The archbishop should send this report to the USCCB, to the Congregation for Bishops, and to the pope. After dissolution of the synod, arrangements should be made for the ordination of the bishop-elect in his cathedral by the archbishop and the provincial bishops. The new bishop should also affirm his acceptance of the Catholic faith in letters of communion to the pope and to his fellow bishops.[48]

The implementation of this proposal will not be accomplished easily given that there are several obstacles to overcome. The election of bishops is an international issue transcending every diocese and country. Consequently, the consent of the bishops throughout the world as well as of the Vatican will be required. A major change in the mind-set of the hierarchy is necessary. Suffering from inertia and timidity, the bishops, who may see this proposal as a threat to their power, are not likely to act without their fellow bishops and without obtaining approval from Rome. As episcopal elections will lead to a decentralization of power and a loosening of the ties that keep the bishops dependent on Rome, the curia assuredly will be reluctant to yield its authority and thus will oppose this proposal. As Steinfels remarks: "The idea of electing bishops renders most conservatives and virtually all the hierarchy and Vatican officialdom apoplectic."[49] Nevertheless, many bishops believe that the curia is excessively intrusive and does not acknowledge the importance of the principle of subsidiarity. Moreover, as noted above, there is a consistent body of opinion among churchmen of all ranks that a return to the election of bishops is desirable.

There is also a need to change the mind-set of the laity who have been excluded from any significant decision-making role in the Church and have been persuaded to believe that their function is to "pray, pay, and obey." Long inured to treatment as children, the nonordained, both men and women, must stand up as adults and claim their rightful place in the Church by virtue of their baptism. Priests, too, must exhibit similar backbone.

Declaring that there is no place for politics in the Church, some will object that an election has the potential to create factions among the clergy and/or the people. Many years ago Granfield indicated that election of bishops by the clergy and people could entail the worst features of a political campaign, including the expenditure of large sums of money. At a time when the Church is sharply divided, he argues, the formation of political parties and partisan politics is not desirable. Factionalism of this sort was one reason for the decline in popular elections in the early centuries. Given its size and complexity, the modern diocese lacks a sense of community and thus he suggests that a return to popular election does not seem feasible.[50]

With the CLSA *Procedure* in mind, Cardinal Avery Dulles objects that the election of a diocesan committee would encourage factionalism and power politics. Restriction of the choice to diocesan priests would risk inbreeding and the possibility that a diocese "with an eccentric tradition would perpetuate its own eccentricity." The difficulty of preserving confidentiality would oblige Rome to choose one of those proposed or to explain its failure to choose that candidate, with potential harm to an individual's reputation. Despite some mistakes, the current procedure allowing consideration of a broad spectrum of candidates "has given us a generally excellent body of bishops."[51] That statement was written two years before the scandal of priestly sexual abuse and episcopal cover-up erupted in Boston. Responding to his fellow Jesuit, Ladislas Orsy contended that while the Church need not imitate secular models, the Catholic tradition offers richer alternatives to the present procedure.[52]

The arguments against election by the clergy and people can be summarized as follows: (1) the Church is divine and therefore the democratic procedures of the secular world should not and cannot be applied to it, (2) political campaigning, electioneering, political parties, factionalism, and power struggles are not desirable, (3) limitation of the choice to diocesan clergy will lead to inbreeding, and (4) an open process will result in a loss of confidentiality possibly detrimental to the reputation of losing candidates.

While agreeing that Christ's Body, the Church, is divine, it must also be said that the people who compose it are not. By their very nature, human beings act in political ways. Politics is the means that enables them to organize as communities, to provide for leadership, law and order, and the like. To suggest that politics is not inherent in the life of the Church betrays an ignorance of Church history. As James Provost points out, since the election of the Apostle Matthias, politics has always had a place in determining leadership in the Church. However, "the politics are now carefully limited to what some term a 'power elite' who are not accountable to the people whose very ecclesial lives are intimately bound up with what the power elite are doing in their politics." Over the centuries the Church has borrowed the institutional practices of various political regimes, for example, Roman law, yet its leaders have refused to acknowledge the value of democratic procedures and representative government.[53]

The recent election of Pope Benedict XVI, while carried out in secrecy, was not free of political campaigning, power struggles, and factionalism. Authors such as John Allen, Andrew Greeley, and Robert Blair Kaiser all assessed the chances of various cardinals.[54] The cardinals conversed, albeit in private, about the qualifications of the candidates. Cardinals ambitious of higher rank have been known to travel the world attending conferences, giving speeches, and writing books and essays, fully aware that these are opportunities to make themselves familiar and therefore *papabili*. It is true that the Church is polarized, perhaps more today than it was thirty years ago, but there has seldom been absolute unanimity in the Church. There have always been and always will be diverse opinions and parties. All of this may seem undesirable, but it is the fact that confronts us today.

The election of bishops by the clergy and people of the diocese will guarantee everyone a voice, something denied to most members of the Church today. In times past the lack or inadequacy of formal procedures for the participation of both priests and people in the electoral process contributed to their ultimate exclusion. Stable structures for the transmission of power from one leader to another exist in modern democratic states and can provide a model for the Church. It seems reasonable to believe that modern Catholic Christians, familiar with democratic and parliamentary procedures, are sufficiently wise to devise orderly electoral means that would curb electioneering without abandoning the concept of popular election.

The lack of any real sense of community in today's megadioceses, as Granfield notes, can be an obstacle to effective participation by the clergy and people in the election of their bishop. That difficulty could be overcome and a sense of community restored by creating much smaller dioceses in which the faithful would know who is worthy to be a bishop.

The establishment of a limited term of office would encourage more frequent elections that would ease the removal of an incompetent bishop and also make possible the reelection of an excellent bishop. The idea that the bishop should serve for life can be traced to the First Letter of Clement, which chastises the Corinthians for removing presbyters who have grown old. However, the Church soon recognized that there were circumstances in which a bishop might resign or might be compelled to do so. Even Pope Celestine V (1294), realizing his unsuitability for the task, resigned the papacy after a few months. If a bishop's health failed and he could no longer carry out his duties, he could step down; but he could also be removed by the archbishop and provincial bishops, usually in a provincial council, if he was charged with immorality, simony, heresy, or the loss of the people's confidence (*malitia*, or *odium plebis*). Here the example of Cardinal Bernard Law comes to mind. Since the time of Paul VI bishops on reaching the age of seventy-five have been asked to submit their resignation (c. 401.1). From time to time John Paul II allowed some bishops to remain in office beyond that age. If a bishop can be required to step down at seventy-five, there is no reason why he cannot be limited to a fixed term of office. In 1970 the theological faculty at the University of Tübingen, whose most distinguished members were Hans Küng and Joseph Ratzinger, proposed a term of eight years. At the end of his term, if it were mutually agreeable, the retiring bishop could act as a consultant to his successor.[55]

The argument will be made that the quality of the candidate pool will be lessened if the bishop must be chosen from the local clergy. Experience has shown, however, that able and competent priests, thoroughly familiar with the spiritual and pastoral needs of their people, are to be found in every diocese. One of the greatest bishops, St. Augustine, presided over the see of Hippo in North Africa, not one of the most important cities of the Roman Empire, and yet he exercised an extraordinary influence over the Church for centuries thereafter. The election of a bishop who is known to his people and clergy should provide effective leadership for the diocese. The archbishop's right to confirm and consecrate the bishop-elect should act as a restraint on the election of an unsuitable person. The intrusion of outsiders has contributed to the present malaise affecting the Church, as it is commonly believed that a bishop in a small see will likely be pro-moted—if, as Byron remarks, he has no blots on his copybook—to a larger and wealthier diocese offering the opportunity for greater prestige, power, and influence, and a more luxurious lifestyle.

Confidentiality, or secrecy, we are told, is necessary to prevent unseemly political campaigning and to save potential nominees from embarrassment should they be passed over. In refusing to explain his appointments to the people of the Netherlands in 1985, John Paul II invoked the principle of discretion. Secrecy is the hallmark of the procedure for the appointment of bishops outlined by the 1972 Norms and the 1983 Code of Canon Law. The fundamental reason for secrecy, however, is to preserve for the papacy the untrammeled right to appoint bishops without fear of opposition or contradiction. The public discussion of the qualifications of different can-didates can be a positive thing in focusing attention on the needs of the diocese and in determining the person best able to lead it. Some egos might be bruised in the process, but as William Byron points out, whether a priest is relieved or humbled by not being chosen could, in either case, enhance his growth in holiness. Underlining the importance of relying on "good Christian sense and humility," Ghislain Lafont remarks that "one can be an excellent priest . . . without necessarily being the one deemed the best candidate" for the episcopal office.[56]

As superiors of religious communities, elected through a process of prayer and discernment, usually "give their best," Lafont queries, "why should it not be the same in the churches?" One ought not to "fear an election conducted in a spirit at once prayerful, liturgical, and reflective." Failures are sometimes inevitable, but they will be few "if we have confidence in the Spirit." He concludes: "Are there not also failures in the centralized system of nominations?" Although some persons may be disappointed in the result of an election, he counsels against contesting it without substantial reasons and cautions that higher authorities, for example, the Roman curia, should be reluctant to intervene.[57] The active participation of the archbishop and provincial bishops ought to safeguard the integrity of the election and preclude the possibility of a challenge.

Recapitulation

The response to the publication of the "Norms for the Selection of Bishops" in 1972 (later incorporated into the Code of Canon Law of 1983) was less than positive, as the "Norms" did not resonate with the ecclesiology enunciated by the Second Vatican Council. In actuality, as Thomas Reese emphasizes, the papal nuncio has the principal role in gathering information about a candidate's orthodoxy and loyalty to the pope, and his stand on celibacy, the ordination of women, and sexual morality. After weighing the nuncio's report, the Congregation for Bishops makes a final recommendation to the pope. Not surprisingly, the bishops appointed by John Paul II were characterized principally by their fidelity to the papacy. Cardinals Gantin, Medina Estévez, and Ratzinger lamented careerism among some bishops who were ambitious for promotion to more prestigious and wealthier sees and acknowledged that the transfer of bishops marked a departure from traditional practice. Theologians, canonists, and church historians pointed to the need to reform the system of selecting bishops and especially to broaden the participation of the clergy and people.

Recognizing the limitations of the "Norms," the CLSA proposed, in its own *Procedures* of 1973, that a Diocesan Committee consisting of priests, religious, and laity should assess diocesan needs, determine the qualities desired in a bishop, and identify three priests likely to best serve the diocese. The names and accompanying recommendations would then be forwarded up the hierarchical chain, eventually reaching the Congregation for Bishops in Rome. The input of the laity, however, was limited to the initial work of the committee. Once the list left the committee and proceeded through clerical hands, it could be altered substantially.

In addition to proposals put forward by Huels and Gaillardetz and by Lafont, Voice of the Faithful in the Diocese of Bridgeport offered two proposals for reform of the process of making bishops. The first, building on the CLSA *Procedures*, urges that a Diocesan Committee, consisting of elected representatives of the clergy and people, should determine diocesan needs, the qualities desirable in a bishop, and identify the most qualified priests. The committee would send its report simultaneously to the Congregation for Bishops, the USCCB, the archbishop and provincial bishops, and all the faithful of the diocese. In this way the desires of the faithful expressed by their representatives would go directly to Rome. The second proposal calls for the election of a bishop by a diocesan synod composed of the archbishop, provincial bishops, and elected representatives of the clergy, religious, and laity. After considering the candidates whose qualifications were assessed by the Diocesan Committee, the synod would elect a bishop and the archbishop would communicate the results to the whole Church. Insistence on maintaining secrecy, fear of losing one's influence and patronage in making bishops, and dread of democracy are among the obstacles to the implementation of this proposal.

In this day and age when the implicit trust between bishops and people has been so eroded, it is imperative that all the faithful of the diocese should be free to elect a person whom they know to be worthy of the office. That is why Pope Leo the Great cautioned centuries ago: "The one whom the unanimous consent of the clergy and people demands should be preferred. . . . No one who is unwanted and unasked for should be ordained, lest the city either despise or hate the bishop whom they did not choose." The bishop should be elected for a fixed, and possibly renewable, term, and should serve the diocese for which he is elected, without expectation of being transferred elsewhere. Pope Celestine I's centuries-old admonition is still valid today: "The one who is to be head over all should be elected by all."[58]

Notes

1. "Norms for the Selection of Bishops," in Patrick Granfield, *Ecclesial Cybernetics: A Systems Analysis of Authority and Decision-Making in the Catholic Church with a Plea for Shared Responsibility* (New York: Macmillan, 1973), 261–67 (1972 version), and *The Choosing of Bishops*, ed. William W. Bassett (Hartford, CT: Canon Law

Society of America, 1971), 103–7 (1971 version); John Tracy Ellis, "The Appoint-
ment of Bishops and the Selection of Candidates in the United States since Vatican
II," in *Electing Our Own Bishops, Concilium* 137, ed. Peter Huizing and Knut Walf
(New York: Seabury Press, 1980), 82–83, and "The Selection of Bishops," *American
Benedictine Review* 35:2 (June 1984): 118.

2. Donald E. Heintschel, foreword to *Procedure for the Selection of Bishops in the
United States* (Hartford, CT: Canon Law Society of the United States, 1973) ii; Ladislas Orsy, SJ, "What the New Norms Say and Don't Say," *America*, September 12, 1972,
11–13; John F. Fahey, "Sorry, These Norms Won't Do," *America*, September 12, 1972,
113–14. Also see the comments of several authors in "Selection of Bishops—A Fol-
low-Up," *America*, October 14, 1972, 287–91; Raymond Goedert, "Selection of Bishops: A Canonical and Pastoral Critique of the New Norms," *PCLSA* (1972): 54–61.

3. Günter Biemer, "Election of Bishops as a New Desideratum in Church
Practice," in *Bishops and People*, ed. and trans. Leonard Swidler and Arlene Swidler
(Philadelphia: Westminster Press, 1970), 43–50; Richard Auwerda, "Becoming a
Bishop in the Netherlands since Vatican II," in Huizing and Walf, *Electing Our Own
Bishops*, 89–94; Muriel Bowen, "The Appointment of Bishops in Britain since Vati-
can II," in Huizing and Walf, *Electing Our Own Bishops*, 85–88; Hans Küng, "The
Freedom of the Election of the Bishop of Basel," in Huizing and Walf, *Electing Our
Own Bishops*, 94–98.

4. *The Second Synod of the Diocese of Bridgeport* (Bridgeport, CT: Roman Catholic Diocese of Bridgeport, 1972), 13, chap. 2, 26.

5. Bishop Leroy T. Mathiesen, letter to the editor, *National Catholic Reporter*,
June 16, 2006.

6. In this section I rely mainly on Thomas J. Reese, SJ, "The Selection of
Bishops," chap. 1 in *Archbishop: Inside the Power Structure of the American Catholic
Church* (San Francisco: Harper & Row, 1989), 1–52; and *A Flock of Shepherds: The
National Conference of Catholic Bishops* (Kansas City, MO: Sheed & Ward, 1992),
chap. 1; and *Inside the Vatican: The Politics and Organization of the Catholic Church*
(Cambridge, MA: Harvard University Press, 1996), 230–42; Ellis, "Appointment of
Bishops," 82–83; John T. Finnegan, "The Present Canonical Practice in the Catho-
lic Church," in Bassett, *Choosing of Bishops*, 85–102.

7. Reese, *Archbishop*, 1–9, 22–23.

8. Reese, *Archbishop*, 10–11; René Metz, "Papal Legates and the Appointment
of Bishops," *Jurist* 52 (1992): 259–94.

9. Reese, *Archbishop*, 30–36.

10. Reese, *Archbishop*, 35–36; John Tracy Ellis, letter to the editor, *America*, October 14, 1972, 289–90.

11. Reese, *Archbishop*, 36–46.

12. Reese, *Archbishop*, 12–17, 27–28; Ellis, "Appointment of Bishops," 83–84; J.
Michael Ritty and James A. Coriden, "Report to the CLSA Membership on the
Selection of Bishops," *CLSA Proceedings* 64 (2002): 336.

13. Reese, *Archbishop*, 15; Thomas J. Reese, SJ, "The Seattle Way of the Cross,"
America, September 20, 1986, 111–12; Timothy P. Schilling, "When Bishops Dis-

agree: Rome, Hunthausen and the Current Church Crisis," *Commonweal*, September 12, 2003, 15–22.

14. Reese, *Archbishop*, 11–12.

15. Metz, "Papal Legates," 260.

16. Ritty and Coriden, "Report," 336–45; James A. Coriden and J. Michael Ritty, "The Selection of Bishops," *CLSA* Proceedings 65 (2003): 66–76.

17. Richard Gaillardetz, "Mission and Ministry," in *Lay Ministry in the Catholic Church: Visioning Church Ministry through the Wisdom of the Past*, ed. Richard W. Miller II (Liguori, MO: Liguori), 49–66, esp. 63.

18. Bishop Thomas Gumbleton, address to the Southern Illinois Synod of the Laity (Belleville, IL: June 19, 2004), quoted in *Church Watch*, August–September 2004, 4–5.

19. Andrew Greeley, "Watch Out for the Ambitious Clerics in Purple," *National Catholic Reporter*, September 9, 1995; William Byron, SJ "Thinking Systemically: The Church in Crisis," *Origins* 32, no. 1 (May 16, 2002): 7; Peter Steinfels, *A People Adrift* (New York: Simon & Schuster, 2003), 314–15; Reese, *Inside the Vatican*, 241–42.

20. Ritty and Coriden, "Report," 336–37.

21. Stephen M. DiGiovanni, *The Catholic Church in Fairfield County, 1666–1961* (New Canaan, CT: William Mulvey, 1987), 235.

22. John Allen, "Ratzinger Weighs In on Careerism of Bishops," *National Catholic Reporter*, July 30, 1999; David Gibson, *The Coming Catholic Church: How the Faithful Are Shaping a New American Catholicism* (San Francisco: HarperCollins, 2003), 290.

23. John R. Quinn, *The Reform of the Papacy: The Costly Call to Christian Unity* (New York: Crossroad, 1999), 137; Gibson, *Church*, 297.

24. Siricius, *Epistolae et Decreta*, 10, chap. 5, par. 16, *PL* 13:1192, cited by William W. Bassett, "Subsidiarity, Order and Freedom in the Church," in *The Once and Future Church: A Communion of Freedom*, ed. James A. Coriden (Staten Island, NY: Alba House, 1971), 224, n. 20.

25. "Ordination of a Bishop," in *Rites of the Catholic Church*, 2 vols. (Collegeville, MN: Liturgical Press, 1990–1991), 2:71, art. 20; *Ceremonial of Bishops* (Collegeville, MN: Liturgical Press, 1989), 331.

26. Bernard Häring, *A Theology of Protest* (New York: Farrar, Straus & Giroux, 1970), 115–16; James Hennesey, SJ, "'To Chuse a Bishop': An American Way," *America*, September 2, 1972, 115–18, esp. 118; Granfield, *Cybernetics*, 247.

27. John Beal, "Toward a Democratic Church: The Canonical Heritage," in Eugene C. Bianchi and Rosemary Radford Ruether, *A Democratic Catholic Church: The Reconstruction of Roman Catholicism* (New York: Crossroad, 1992), 66–67. Also see Richard McBrien, "A Preliminary Ecclesiological Statement," in Bassett, *Choosing of Bishops*, 11–20.

28. Buckley, "Resources," 72; Gerard Mannion, "'A Haze of Fiction': Legitimation, Accountability, and Truthfulness," in *Governance, Accountability, and the Future of the Catholic Church*, ed. Francis Oakley and Bruce Russett (New York: Continuum, 2004), 173.

29. Andrew Greeley, "A Bad Day for the Bishops," *America*, March 22, 2004, 8–9, and *The Making of the Pope 2005* (New York: Little, Brown, 2005), 245–49.

30. Thomas P. Rausch, SJ, *Authority and Leadership in the Church: Past Directions and Future Possibilities* (Wilmington, DE: Michael Glazier, 1989), 146; James L. Heft, "Accountability and Governance in the Church: Theological Considerations," in Oakley and Russett, *Governance*, 130; Byron, "Thinking Systemically," 7; Reese, *Inside the Vatican*, 241–42.

31. Cited by Heft, "Accountability," 130.

32. Quinn, *Reform*, 117; John M. Huels, OSM., and Richard R. Gaillardetz, "The Selection of Bishops: Recovering the Tradition," *The Jurist* 59 (1999): 348.

33. Paul Lakeland, *The Liberation of the Laity: In Search of an Accountable Church* (New York: Continuum, 2003), 272; *NRB Report*, 143, D.

34. Manya A. Brachear, "New Bishop Faces Uncertain Welcome," *Chicago Tribune*, June 22, 2005, 1.

35. I want to thank Fr. Art Espelage, OFM, of the CLSA for sending me a copy of the *Provisional Plan*. The text (without Goedert's cover letter but with new preliminary remarks) is reprinted in Granfield, *Cybernetics*, 257–61.

36. *Procedure for the Selection of Bishops*. The Roman "Norms" are reprinted on pp. 4–5. Msgr. Thomas Green kindly sent me a copy of this text.

37. James A. Coriden, Thomas J. Green, and Donald E. Heintschel, eds., *The Code of Canon Law: A Text and Commentary* (Mahwah, NJ: Paulist Press, 1985), 322, n. 38; Thomas J. Green, "Critical Reflections on the Schema on the People of God," *Studia Canonica* 14 (1980): 235–322, esp. 269–72.

38. James Provost, "Selection of Bishops—Does Anybody Care?" *Chicago Studies* 18 (1979): 211–22, esp. 213–18; Ellis, "Selection of Bishops," 119, and "Appointment of Bishops," 82–83.

39. Norman Bolduc, "Report of the CLSA Committee on Selection of Bishops," *PCLSA* (1988): 299–304; Ritty and Coriden, "Report," 334–60; Coriden and Ritty, "Selection of Bishops," 65–91. I want to thank Dr. Ritty for sending me copies of these documents.

40. Reese, *Inside the Vatican*, 242.

41. *Report of the Church in America: Leadership Roundtable 2004 at The Wharton School*, 47, at www.nlrcm.org. Thomas J. Healey, "A Blueprint for Change: A New National Roundtable Offers Suggestions for Improving Church Management," *America*, September 26, 2005, 16.

42. Huels and Gaillardetz, "Selection of Bishops," 357–68.

43. Huels and Gaillardetz, "Selection of Bishops," 368–76.

44. Ritty and Coriden, "Report," 352; Coriden and Ritty, "Selection of Bishops," 82.

45. Ghislain Lafont, OSB, *Imagining the Catholic Church: Structured Communion in the Spirit*, trans. John J. Burkhard (Collegeville, MN: Liturgical Press, 2000), 169–76.

46. Gerard Bartelink, "The Use of the Words *Electio* and *Consensus* in the Church until about 600," in *Election and Consensus in the Church, Concilium* 77, ed. Giuseppe Alberigo and Anton Weiler (New York: Herder and Herder, 1972), 147–54.

47. See "The Selection of Candidates for the Office of Bishop: A Proposal by Voice of the Faithful in the Diocese of Bridgeport, April 29, 2006," at www.votfbpt.org.

48. James Hennesey, SJ, "'To Chuse a Bishop': An American Way," 117–18, describes the electoral procedures used in the American Episcopal Church, citing the directives of the diocese of Los Angeles.

49. Steinfels, *A People Adrift*, 348.

50. Granfield, *Cybernetics*, 247–50.

51. Avery Dulles, SJ, "The Papacy for a Global Church," *America*, July 15, 2000, 6–11.

52. Ladislas Orsy, SJ, "The Papacy for an Ecumenical Age: A Response to Avery Dulles," *America*, October 21, 2000, 9–15.

53. Provost, "Selection of Bishops," 215. See also Alois Müller, ed., *Democratization of the Church, Concilium* 63 (New York: Herder and Herder, 1971); James H. Provost and Knut Walf, *The Tabu of Democracy in the Church, Concilium* (London: SCM Press, 1992); Eugene C. Bianchi and Rosemary Radford Ruether, eds., *A Democratic Catholic Church: The Reconstruction of Roman Catholicism* (New York: Crossroad, 1992).

54. John L. Allen Jr., *Conclave: The Politics, Personalities and Process of the Next Papal Election* (New York: Doubleday Image, 2002); Greeley, *Making of the Pope*; Robert Blair Kaiser, *A Church in Search of Itself: Benedict XVI and the Battle for the Future* (New York: Alfred A. Knopf, 2006).

55. Alfons Auer, Günter Biemer, Karl August Fink, Herbert Haag, Hans Küng, Joseph Möller, Johannes Neumann, Joseph Ratzinger, Joseph Rief, Karl Hermann Schelkle, Max Seckler, and Peter Stockmeier, "Limited Term of Office for Resident Bishops?" in Swidler and Swidler, *Bishops and People*, 22–37; Bassett ("Subsidiarity," 263) suggests a term of no more than ten years.

56. Byron, "Thinking Systemically," 7; Lafont, *Imagining the Catholic Church*, 174, n. 26.

57. Lafont, *Imagining the Catholic Church*, 175.

58. Leo I, *Epistolae*, 14.5, *PL* 54:673; Celestine I, *Epistolae*, 4.5, *PL* 5,434–35.

"Is He Worthy?" 7

FROM THE EARLY CENTURIES UNTIL the present the question "Is he worthy?" has been vital to every episcopal election. Reform of the electoral process is necessary, but it will have little meaning if the bishops do not alter their manner of government so as to be more attentive and responsible to the people they serve. The willingness and ability of a candidate for the episcopal office to listen to his priests and people and to hold himself accountable to them is a significant measure of his "worthiness." The abject failure of the American bishops—indeed, of bishops in other countries—and of the popes and the curia to address the scandal of priestly sexual abuse in a pastoral manner makes abundantly clear the need to look closely at the qualities desirable in a bishop. If the bishop is again to be perceived as the worthy and trusted leader of the community, then he must be cut from a different mold from that of his predecessors.

The responsibilities of a bishop are daunting, as the Code of Canon Law makes clear: "The diocesan bishop is to rule the particular church committed to him with legislative, executive and judicial power in accord with the norm of law" (c. 391.1). He exercises these powers in person, but he may delegate the executive and judicial powers to subordinates (c. 391.2). This canon imposes an almost unbearable burden on a bishop as it entrusts him with absolute power over all the faithful of his diocese, clergy and people alike, without any real checks or balances. The bishop is made an emperor, a czar, an autocrat, with all the potential to become a tyrant. Canon 391 must be altered radically so that all the clergy and people of the diocese, who are making their journey to holiness under the bishop's leadership, will have an effective voice in all matters that affect their spiritual well-being.

In order to make that possible, several fundamental reforms ought to be carried out: (1) the bishop should know his people, and his diocese should be small enough for him to be able to do so; (2) in accordance with the principle "what touches all should be approved by all," the bishop should seek the counsel and consent of the faithful in all significant matters; (3) he must acknowledge that he is accountable to his people and, setting all secrecy aside, he must be transparent in his leadership; (4) as a disciple of Jesus, he should abandon forever the medieval pomp and pomposity surrounding the modern episcopate and adopt a simpler lifestyle; and (5) he ought to understand that the people he leads are his equals inasmuch as both he and they, by virtue of baptism, are equally disciples of Jesus. Let me elaborate on these points.

The Bishop as Shepherd

The evangelical image of the Good Shepherd is the one most often associated with the bishop, though in today's technological world it seems quite anachronistic. Jesus declared that "the sheep follow [the shepherd], because they recognize his voice. But they will not follow a stranger; they will run away from him because they do not recognize the voice of strangers." Saying, "I am the Good Shepherd, and I know mine, and mine know me" (Jn 10:1–18), Jesus reminds us that the Good Shepherd is prepared to leave the ninety-nine sheep to go in search of the one that is lost (Mt 18:10–14). Pope John Paul II's postsynodal exhortation, *Pastores Gregis*, emphasizes the bishop's role as shepherd of the flock.[1] A bishop who is a true shepherd will speak out, without fear, about the needs of the people entrusted to his care, even if that means putting his career in jeopardy and, indeed, laying down his life. From the martyrdom of St. Polycarp, bishop of Smyrna, in 155, to the assassination of Oscar Romero, archbishop of San Salvador, in 1980, the history of the Church is full of examples of such good shepherds.[2]

If the bishop is truly to be a shepherd, and not a stranger to the people he leads, the diocesan community must be small enough for him to know the members and for them to know him. This will require a radical restructuring that will entail an increase in the number of bishops and of dioceses. St. Ignatius of Antioch (d. ca. 107), the first person clearly identifiable as a bishop as we understand that term today, probably led a community of a few hundred, whom he knew quite well. Gathered about him were his principal collaborators, the presbyters and deacons. Aside from a much larger number of parishioners, the circumstance may have been comparable to an urban parish of half a century ago when the pastor was assisted by four or five curates.

Denied any real input into the appointment of their bishop, the local clergy and people today seldom, if ever, have any knowledge of the person being assigned to lead them. They have no opportunity to ask about his background; his prior experience, especially as a pastor; his involvement, if any, in handling cases of sexual abuse; his capacity for spiritual guidance; his willingness to listen both to priests and people and to collaborate with them; or his ability to delegate responsibility and to seek and to be guided by wise counsel. All of these issues go to the question "Is he worthy?" The current structure isolates the bishop from the people and shields him from hearing dissonant voices. If he lived side by side with them, visiting their homes, meeting them on the street, in the workplace, in shops, malls, and diners, he could speak more authoritatively about their needs, instead of issuing pronouncements formed in the abstract without any experiential foundation. In turn, the people would be willing to listen to him because of the personal bond they would have formed with him. He would not be a stranger to them as most bishops are today. Unknown and ignorant of life in his new diocese, a newly appointed bishop requires a year or more to become acquainted with the nature and needs of the diocese and with a tiny fraction of the people.

In earlier times the bishop was chosen from the community by the clergy and people who knew him just as he knew them. As a faithful servant, he usually remained in their midst until death. Just as Christ was described as the spouse of the Church, so the bishop was said to be wedded to his see. The ring given to him at his consecration symbolized that union, and his pastoral staff signified his role as shepherd and manifested his care for his flock. At a time when the model of the modern bishop often seems to be the corporate executive of the world of business, moving from company to company, these images clash with reality. Through circumstances often beyond his control, today's bishop has a lifestyle with little resemblance to that of a humble shepherd. The idea that the bishop is linked to his see by a matrimonial bond seems quaint. In such conditions, the meaning of the nonverbal signs that are intended to convey a sense of the bishop's commitment to his people, the staff and ring, is obscured. Rather than discard these valued images sanctioned by centuries of tradition, however, a more intimate personal bond between the bishop and his people must be created.

More bishops and smaller dioceses are needed. Today, dioceses are simply too large in population and too vast in area to allow a bishop with responsibility for the spiritual welfare of hundreds of thousands or millions of souls to claim seriously to be a shepherd who knows his sheep. The

Code of Canon Law tacitly acknowledged that fact by requiring a bishop personally to visit his diocese every year "either in its entirety or in part, in such a way that the entire diocese is visited at least every five years." He may assign the task to an auxiliary bishop or vicar general (c. 396), but in doing so he misses the opportunity to gain direct, personal knowledge of his people.

The United States is divided into thirty-four ecclesiastical provinces, each headed by an archbishop. There are some 281 active bishops serving a Catholic population approximating 64 million.[3] On average there is one bishop for every 227,758 people. The archbishops of New York, Philadelphia, Boston, Washington, D.C., Chicago, and Los Angeles, to cite only a few, are each responsible for millions of people whom they simply do not know. To take another example, the ecclesiastical province of Hartford, comprising the states of Connecticut and Rhode Island, is governed by an archbishop and the provincial bishops of Norwich, Bridgeport, and Providence. In the Diocese of Bridgeport, embracing all of Fairfield County, there are approximately 360,000 Catholics and at least four major cities: Stamford with a population of about 120,000; Norwalk, 84,000; Bridgeport, 139,000; and Danbury, 78,000. Other major population centers in the state include Hartford (124,000), New Haven (124,000), and Waterbury (108,000). The archbishop and three provincial bishops are personally unknown and usually invisible to the majority of the population.

Each of these cities ought to have a bishop, but one could argue that any diocese with over 2,000 members is simply too large for the bishop to truly know the people. As a consequence, instead of one bishop in each city, there might rather be several dioceses corresponding to important urban subdivisions, each with its own bishop. Each of the vicariates or deaneries into which many dioceses are subdivided could be established as a diocese. As the Church's diocesan structure is the outgrowth of historical development, it can be and needs to be changed. One might object that, as the diocesan bureaucracy is already extensive and complex, the multiplication of dioceses would require the creation of additional administrative apparatuses in each of the new sees; however, that is not a sufficient reason for not increasing the number of dioceses so as to make the bishop more accessible to the people. A decentralization of administration ought to reflect more clearly the actual needs of local communities. A restoration of small faith communities would breathe new life into the Church.[4]

The present practice is to assign auxiliary bishops to outlying territories in an archdiocese or diocese, but if the bishop is truly a sign of the unity of the community, auxiliaries ought to be made bishops in their own right. An auxiliary bishop is an anomaly because he cannot be bishop, in the proper sense, of the diocese where he serves so long as the governing bishop is still alive. To get around this difficulty the papacy in the late thirteenth century devised the idea of titular bishops, that is, bishops holding title to sees no longer in existence, most of them now in Islamic lands. Thus, when an auxiliary is ordained he becomes titular bishop of some exotic place that he has likely never heard of and which he probably will never visit. Theoretically he is obliged to pray several times a year for the people of his titular see. Not only are there many auxiliary or titular bishops assisting diocesan bishops, but also the throng of archbishops and bishops serving in the papal curia and diplomatic service are also titular bishops. This is a grave perversion of the concept of bishop as the spiritual leader of a community. A bishop assigned to a fictitious diocese can hardly be described as shepherd of a nonexistent flock, and his use of the pastoral staff and ring is an abnormality. The existence of more than one bishop in a diocese, even if one is a titular bishop of a defunct diocese or a coadjutor bishop, contradicts the principle of unity of the local church symbolized in its bishop. Henceforth, the Church should rid itself of the embarrassment of auxiliary and titular bishops assigned to dead dioceses. All bishops should be residential, that is, responsible for a diocesan community, and the title of bishop (or archbishop) should not be given as an honor (as in the case of the many curial archbishops and bishops) without diocesan responsibility. Priests of the diocese can carry out the functions currently entrusted to auxiliary bishops.[5]

Counsel and Consent

A bishop who wishes to truly lead his people and give voice to their needs will recognize his obligation to ask their counsel and consent whenever he contemplates any important action. Their good advice may save him from serious missteps and their consent will assure him that his faithful people are committed to following his lead. In returning to this ancient tradition, the bishop will enable both clergy and laity to participate more fully in the life of the Church in accordance with their baptismal responsibilities. Bishops might attend to these ancient words: "Plans fail when there is no counsel, but they succeed when counselors are many" (Proverbs 15:22). Writing to his priests and deacons around AD 250, St. Cyprian, bishop of Carthage, said: "From the beginning of my episcopate I determined to do nothing on my own private judgment without your counsel and the consent of the people."[6] Counsel and consent are thus Christian virtues as well as two of the foundational principles of modern democratic government.

As we have seen, it was a commonplace saying that a bishop could not be elected without the consent of the clergy and people. From the earliest times, moreover, the Christian community has expressed its consent in liturgical responses, such as the simple "amen," and in the recitation of the Nicene Creed; but as Kleinheyer points out, the liturgy is not the place to express dissent.[7] Most bishops, after taking counsel with some priests and some people, have acted on the assumption that they had the tacit or implicit consent of the larger community. Vatican II acknowledged the importance of the consent of the faithful in doctrinal matters when it affirmed that "the whole body of the faithful . . . cannot err in matters of belief. This characteristic is shown in the supernatural appreciation of the faith (*sensus fidei*) of the whole people, when, 'from the bishops to the last of the faithful,' they manifest a universal consent in matters of faith and morals" (*LG* 12). The authenticity of Church teachings and the validity of Church laws are confirmed by their reception by the faithful, who give implicit or explicit consent. Many Catholics did not receive Paul VI's 1968 encyclical *Humanae Vitae* as authentic and by ignoring it or acting against it withheld their consent.[8]

The Second Vatican Council acknowledged the right of the faithful to make known their needs to their pastors (*LG* 37; Code of Canon Law, c. 212.3). However, structures to enable the faithful to do so, giving their counsel or explicit consent, are lacking entirely or are inadequate. The council's emphasis on collegiality and Paul VI's decision to convene regular synods of bishops failed to loosen the stranglehold of the papal curia on all phases of Catholic life. As William Bassett points out, "The ancient order of the Church where frequent councils gathered the clergy and laity in mutual consultation and support, an authentic *sensus ecclesiae*, is today virtually nonexistent." Emphasizing the need to develop "new strategies . . . to give the laity a meaningful voice in Church affairs," John Lynch remarks: "Despite the efforts of Vatican II, the Church still appears to be a pyramid with all power flowing from the top down. Authority whose purpose is to serve must be open to those who are being served."[9]

As the number of the faithful runs into many thousands, mechanisms to obtain counsel and consent are needed. Elected representatives of the people from the parishes, as well as representatives of the priests, deacons, and religious, can give counsel and consent in the name of the entire body. This characteristic mode of democratic action has its basis in a principle of Roman law incorporated into the canonical tradition of the Church: "what touches all should be approved by all"—"*quod omnes tangit, ab omnibus debet approbari*" (Code of Canon Law, c. 119.3).[10]

The most effective means of achieving this goal is to establish elected, representative councils on every level of Church government. In order to encourage the lay faithful to assume their rightful place in the Church, the SecondVatican Council recommended the formation of a Diocesan Pastoral Council (CD 27). According to the Code of Canon Law, the council, whose members are appointed by the bishop for a fixed term and have only a consultative vote, should meet at least once a year; and the bishop alone determines whether its acts should be made public (cc. 511–14). A Diocesan Finance Council, consisting of at least three persons expert in finance and civil law and appointed by the bishop for a term of five years, is responsible for preparing an annual budget and reviewing the annual accounting of income and expenses drawn up by the diocesan financial officer. The Finance Council also advises the bishop on investments and the appointment or removal of the finance officer and must give or withhold consent to the bishop on the alienation of property (cc. 492–94, 1277, 1292). The bishop also establishes the norms for pastoral and finance councils in each parish; the members of these councils possess only a consultative vote (cc. 536–37).[11]

With these and other organisms in mind the National Review Board recommended the following:

> The bishops should trust and learn to make greater use of those consultative and deliberative bodies established by canon law to assist them in the pastoral care and governance of their dioceses. These bodies should be filled with faithful lay persons and priests who are talented, responsible, and dedicated to the Church, but who are also capable of offering, and who are expected to offer, truly independent counsel to the bishop.[12]

These councils ought to be established in such a way that the voice of the laity may be heard in a constructive manner.Written constitutions and bylaws for each body, ratified by the people, should regulate times of meetings, agenda, publication of minutes, and so forth. The members, serving for a fixed term, should be elected by the faithful, not appointed by the bishop or the pastor, as that vitiates their independence and raises the issue of cronyism. Bernard Häring comments that church leaders, who think themselves responsible only to God, need to be open to healthy dialogue and ought to seek "deliberate training for constructive criticism."[13] Parish and diocesan councils must have real responsibilities and real authority in the use, maintenance, and administration of parish or diocesan property and finances, and should also reflect the concerns of the people in matters of liturgy, religious education, and sacramental life.

For many centuries bishops were accustomed to holding diocesan synods or councils, and the bishops of a province often gathered in council under the presidency of the archbishop.[14] The ancient canons required the frequent convocation of diocesan and provincial synods. The Council of Trent, for example, stipulated that diocesan synods should be held annually and provincial councils every three years (sess. 24, "On Reformation," chap. 2). The councils usually enacted canons or decrees, the stuff that provided the foundation for centuries of canonical collections and on which the modern Code of Canon Law rests. Councils also provided an opportunity for the bishops to reach consensus on matters of belief and practice, to admonish and correct one another, and in severe cases, to depose errant bishops. During the first millennium the conciliar tradition was paramount. The first eight ecumenical councils from Nicaea I in 325 to Constantinople IV in 869 exhibited a final, determinative authority, but the subsequent schism between East and West disrupted that ancient tradition. Whereas the Orthodox churches continue to affirm that an ecumenical council is the final authority, the Western Church has fallen under the domination of the papal monarchy. The Great Western Schism of the late fourteenth century brought forth a conciliar challenge to papalism, but since the proclamation of papal infallibility by Vatican I, papal ascendancy in the Western Church has been strengthened.

As a faint echo of ancient custom, the 1917 Code of Canon Law required the convocation of diocesan synods every ten years (c. 356) and provincial councils every twenty years (c. 283). Although Vatican II was hopeful that synods and councils might "flourish with renewed vigor" (*CD* 36), the 1983 code departed even further from tradition by stipulating that provincial councils should be held whenever a majority of the provincial bishops determined that the moment was opportune (cc. 439–46, esp. 440). The decision to convene a diocesan synod rests with the bishop, after seeking the advice of the Priests' Council. Acknowledging the place of the laity in the Church, the synod should include not only clergy and religious, but also laypeople "chosen by the pastoral council in a manner and number to be determined by the diocesan bishop." If there is no pastoral council, the bishop will determine the manner of selection. He may also appoint additional clergy, religious, or laity. The members, however, have only a consultative vote and the bishop is the sole legislator who alone can authorize publication of the synod's decisions (cc. 460–68).[15]

In the United States early in the nineteenth century, John England, bishop of Charleston, South Carolina, drew up a constitution for his diocese, providing for an annual convention that was composed of two houses, one of priests and the other of the elected representatives of the laity. None of his contemporaries imitated his example, however, and his plan died with him. Lamenting the failure of the bishops to cooperate or pursue a common agenda, England urged the frequent convocation of councils, whose decrees would be subject to papal approval. He also proposed that "no affair of general importance to the American Church be undertaken unless after deliberation in Council" (art. 3).[16] As Gerald Fogarty makes clear, diocesan synods and provincial and plenary councils were held at various times in the late eighteenth and nineteenth centuries. Aside from the First Synod of Baltimore in 1791, nine provincial councils of Baltimore were held approximately every three years until 1858; a tenth council was held in 1869. After several other ecclesiastical provinces were established, three plenary councils (attended by bishops of all the provinces) were convened with papal authorization in 1852, 1866, and 1884.[17] Following the Second Vatican Council some bishops convened diocesan synods, attended by priests, deacons, nuns, and laymen and laywomen, but this practice has fallen into disuse.

A return to the conciliar tradition is essential if a vibrant Catholic Christian community is to exist. Commenting that "never has the credibility of the American hierarchy been lower and never have the laity's demands for accountability from their church leaders been higher," Fogarty suggests that the revival of provincial councils might help to alleviate the crisis.[18] However, future councils cannot be mere clerical bodies. Rather, the voice of the great majority of the faithful, the laity, must be heard. It is necessary to regularly convoke diocesan synods and provincial councils, in which not just the bishops but the elected representatives of priests, deacons, religious men and women, and laymen and laywomen, in proportion to their numbers, are actively involved. At present, canon law permits priests and laity to be summoned to various particular councils (plenary, provincial, diocesan) but they have "only a consultative vote" (c. 443.1–5; LG 62).

In like manner, the triennial synods of bishops convened in Rome and any future ecumenical or general council should also include elected representatives of these groups. Councils, rather than mere consultative bodies, whose decisions can be ignored at will by the pastor, the bishop, the archbishop, or the pope, should have deliberative authority to render final decisions on all matters of doctrine and discipline. The nonordained must share equally in all deliberations because the faith concerns all the people, not just the pope and the bishops. Pope Innocent III made that point when he summoned bishops, abbots, priors, superiors of religious orders, representatives of chapters of canons, and ambassadors of secular rulers and city-states to the Fourth Lateran Council of 1215 to deliberate concerning "the common state of all the faithful." As Brian Tierney points out, the council was "the greatest representative assembly that the Western world had ever seen." Thus, he concluded, "Representation and consent . . . are not alien to the tradition of the church"; nor would the implementation of these practices "be a revolutionary departure but a recovery of a lost part of the church's own early tradition."[19]

Accountability and Transparency

The convocation of councils at fixed intervals is a principal means of holding bishops accountable for their actions and might have averted some of the difficulties that have beset the Church in recent times. The crisis of priestly sexual abuse made manifest for the whole world to see that the bishops have little sense of accountability to the people they serve. In their desire to avoid scandal and possible lawsuits, bishops transferred guilty priests from parish to parish without alerting anyone to the potential danger. As a consequence, a greater scandal than they could have imagined has occurred and the very idea of priesthood as a holy and noble calling has suffered untold damage. Putting the good of the institutional Church above all else, the bishops failed to grasp that their first responsibility as true shepherds is to protect the sheep, especially the most defenseless among them. Their failure, according to Peter Steinfels, was not so much a matter of ill will; rather, they did not understand the magnitude and significance of the problem, and failed to act decisively in attempting to resolve it. Nor did they provide a thorough explanation to the faithful of what had happened, why, and what was being done about it.[20]

More than a decade after the crisis of sexual abuse was first exposed, the bishops met in Dallas in June 2002 to adopt the Charter for the Protection of Children and Young People and the "Norms" to enforce it. In Washington in November they accepted the "Norms" as reviewed by the Vatican after discussion by a joint Vatican-USCCB committee. The bishops often spoke at their conferences about the need for accountability and transparency. Though they expressed their determination to prevent priests from preying on the flock in the future, they were woefully negligent in acknowledging their own responsibility for this tragedy. Gathered in Washington, they adopted a tepid statement promising to correct one another in a fraternal spirit in the future, but they steadfastly avoided pointing the finger at any of their members for having allowed the wolves to run free among the flock.[21] The National Review Board commented that the "absence of fraternal correction compounded the lack of episcopal accountability and further fueled the present crisis." With a view to the future, the board stated: "The bishops and other church leaders must listen to and be responsive to the concerns of the laity. To accomplish this, the hierarchy must act with less secrecy, more transparency and a greater openness to the gifts that all members of the church bring to her." [22]

Two areas in which greater accountability and transparency are needed are (1) the publication of documents in chancery archives related to priestly sexual abuse and (2) the oversight of parish and diocesan finances. Although the bishops paid lip service to transparency, many of them are still resistant to the publication of documents that will likely reveal the extent of their complicity and that of their subordinates in the crime of sexual abuse of children. The court-ordered publication of some of those documents in Boston confirmed the faithful's suspicions about the negligence of Cardinal Law and his former auxiliaries in this respect. The investigation by a grand jury in Philadelphia laid bare a sordid policy of cover-up by the late Cardinal John Krol and his recently retired successor, Cardinal Bevilacqua. [23] The Diocese of Bridgeport, Connecticut, has opposed in court efforts to compel the publication of documents showing the handling of priest predators by the late Bishop Walter W. Curtis and his successor, Edward M. Egan, now cardinal archbishop of New York. The *Connecticut Post* (September 26, 2004) editorialized: "By keeping the records sealed, the church continues to cast doubt and shame on itself. It's time to come clean." Commenting on the response of Cardinal Roger Mahony to priestly sexual abuse in the archdiocese of Los Angeles, the *New York Times* (October 14, 2005) headed an editorial "The Stonewalling Shepherd." [24] Instead of persisting in an attempt to conceal past wrongdoing, bishops, like everyone else, must take responsibility for their actions. Their past failures have done untold harm to the Church and destroyed the implicit trust of the faithful. The legal arguments aside, it is morally imperative that this material be published. That will be painful for everyone but it is necessary to clear the air and to begin the process of renewing the Church. Msgr. William Fay, general secretary of the USCCB, suggested "that this moment will not pass from view until every stone that is hiding some secret has been overturned to let the daylight shine on that spot. Such a thing is happening now, and the more it is resisted, the longer and more painful it will be. This is not a day to hide from the truth, but to embrace it." [25]

The faithful are right to insist that their bishops provide a full and detailed financial accounting. In their pastoral letter on stewardship of May 1993 the American bishops declared: "Sound business practice . . . requires several things: pastors and parish staff must be open, consultative, collegial and accountable in the conduct of affairs . . . [and] lay Catholics ought to have an active role in the oversight of the stewardship of pastoral leaders and administrators at the diocesan level."[26] With little explanation of the source of the funds and the impact on other diocesan programs, however, bishops have expended vast sums of money in settlements for survivors of priestly sexual abuse. In addition, as Francis Butler of FADICA (Foundations and Donors Interested in Catholic Activities) notes, there are numerous instances of bad investments, "million-dollar embezzlements by pastors," and the misappropriation of diocesan funds by financial officers and bishops. When stringent controls are lacking and large sums of money are easily accessible, the temptation to steal is very great. Archbishop Rembert Weakland of Milwaukee, for example, using diocesan resources, allowed himself to be blackmailed in the amount of $450,000 by a former lover. A priest in the diocese of Santa Rosa, California, accused of embezzling from his parish, charged that Bishop Patrick Ziemann demanded sexual favors in return for concealing the embezzlement. Oftentimes financial improprieties are ignored or covered up.[27] Particularly disturbing is the case of a pastor in Darien, Connecticut, who reportedly diverted $1,400,000 to his personal use; when the diocese of Bridgeport failed to act in a timely manner, the associate pastor and parish bookkeeper hired a private investigator, who turned up initial evidence of wrongdoing. Aside from removing the pastor and ordering an audit, Bishop William E. Lori's response was to reprimand the associate pastor.[28]

Although canon law and the Accounting Practices Committee of the USCCB provide guidelines for financial accountability, individual bishops, as Butler points out, "consistently ignore" them. Among other inadequacies he notes that procedures for financial accountability vary throughout the country's dioceses. Bishops generally lack the training and financial acumen necessary to effectively manage the multimillion-dollar corporations that are today's dioceses, and most pastors are similarly ill equipped. Furthermore, the training and qualifications of diocesan finance officers vary widely, and the meager compensation offered is unlikely to attract the most qualified people. The failure of diocesan and parish finance councils to discover and to halt financial manipulation makes clear their ineffectual character. Perhaps viewing their position as honorary, as Butler suggested, the members neglected to ask the demanding questions that might have averted theft and fraud.[29]

Butler recommends the following: (1) compliance by every diocese with the USCCB's financial standards; (2) accreditation of compliance for the benefit of potential donors; (3) publication of complete annual financial audits of every diocese and parish; (4) strengthening diocesan and parish finance councils and clear definition of their responsibilities; (5) explanation of diocesan and parish financial decisions in public forums; (6) development of a national financial planning process; and (7) serious examination of fund-raising.[30]

The Leadership Roundtable commended the archdiocese of Boston in 2006 for its "comprehensive, consolidated, audited and reader friendly financial" report.[31] Emphasizing the faithful's right to know, Cardinal McCarrick observed: "The church is supposed to be a family and you can't have a family if only half the people know what you're doing. . . . The sunshine should come in." Charles Zech, the economist, notes that "Catholics who believe they have an input into Church decision-making processes at both the parish and diocesan levels, and who consider the Church to be accountable and transparent with its finances, contribute more."[32]

Nevertheless, old habits die hard. Men who have lived their lives in secrecy and shadow are uncomfortable when the light of openness and honesty is turned on them. The ideal of transparency trumpeted by the bishops in the wake of the scandal of priestly sexual abuse is not something they wish to bring to reality. The essential business of the meeting of the USCCB in Washington in November 2005, for example, was carried out behind closed doors, to the exclusion of the press and the public. In an editorial entitled "The Disappearing Bishops," the *National Catholic Reporter* (November 25, 2005) reflected on the shrinking of the USCCB as the outcome of the Vatican's efforts during the pontificate of John Paul II to curtail the power and influence of national episcopal conferences. *NCR* commented that the bishops "are withdrawing from the national stage and from any meaningful engagement with Rome. . . . What we witnessed in Washington this month . . . was one of the sadder and maybe one of the final chapters in the devolution of the U.S. bishops as a national body. . . . Our bishops have nothing to say to us. And they know it."

Reacting to the bishops' apparent preference for closed-door sessions in their recent annual meetings, Russell Shaw declared: "More and more, the attitude appears to be that the church's business is the bishops' business and no one else's." As the price of leadership, he argued, bishops must take public stands and the flak that accompanies them. In language reminiscent of the ancient principle "what touches all ought to be approved by all," he remarked: "Where decisions have an impact on everyone, does not everyone have a need and right to know what is going on? In the church, this appears to be a necessary corollary of the fundamental equality of all the members."[33]

If the bishops are ever to recapture the trust and credibility so foolishly thrown away, they must abandon the old ways of secrecy and intimidation and adopt a new management style that is honest and open and allows all the faithful, priests, deacons, religious, and laymen and laywomen alike, to bring their gifts to the table. *Lumen Gentium* 37 and the Code of Canon Law (c. 212.3) both stress the right and the duty of the faithful to make known their views on matters pertaining to the good of the Church; but the failure of the pope and the bishops to develop effective instruments for real dialogue with the faithful and to stifle opinions they do not wish to hear has, in the judgment of the canonist John Beal, reduced those statements to "hollow rhetoric."[34]

The Virtue of Simplicity

The pomp of Catholic ritual often enhances the solemnity and the splendor of the liturgical celebration, but Catholics are increasingly put off by the pomp and circumstance surrounding bishops, vestiges of an aristocratic society long gone. Entirely alien to the essence of Christianity, this pretentiousness seeks to perpetuate false ranks and hierarchies. Such forms of address as Your Holiness, Your Eminence, Your Excellency, Most Reverend, Very Reverend, Right Reverend, and Reverend are out of place in Christ's Church.[35] They are a reflection of the Old Regime when bishops ranked among the nobility and cardinals were spoken of as princes of the Church. That anyone should be described as a prince of the Church is indeed an anomaly. Titles suggest a certain status and authority, but if one is to be truly revered, truly excellent, truly eminent, or truly holy, he must earn that by his works rather than by his incumbency of an ecclesiastical office. As John Paul II notes: "The Bishop's governance . . . will be pastorally effective . . . only if it rests on a moral authority bestowed by his life of holiness" (*PG* 43). In earlier times Leo I identified himself simply as bishop of Rome, and his contemporary, St. Patrick, the apostle of Ireland, described himself as "a sinner," "the least of all the faithful," and, finally, a bishop.[36]

The American bishops of the nineteenth and early twentieth centuries were known as builders because they erected churches, schools, and other necessary structures, but they also built mansions thought to befit their exalted status. While some bishops today are known for their simplicity of life, others have emulated the lifestyle of the rich and powerful. At a time when the Church has incurred vast expense because of the scandal of sexual abuse and when parishes and schools are being closed, the faithful have been dismayed, indeed outraged, on learning that some bishops were still splurging on episcopal mansions and other extravagances. As one example, Bishop William Murphy of Rockville Centre, Long Island, spent lavishly on renovating a former convent for his personal use. A few episcopal mansions have been sold because of the increasingly precarious status of diocesan finances.[37]

The pomp surrounding bishops also is reflected in the dress that they affect in public. The *Ceremonial for Bishops* describes the choir dress of a bishop as follows:

> A purple cassock with purple sash of silk having silk fringes at both ends (but not tassels); a rochet of linen or similar fabric; a purple mozzetta (but without the small hood); over the mozzetta the pectoral cross, held in place by a cord of interwoven green and gold; a purple skullcap; a purple biretta with tuft. When the purple cassock is worn, purple stockings are also worn, but are optional with the black cassock with piping. A purple *cappa magna*, without ermine, may be used only within the diocese and then only on the most solemn festivals. The bishop wears ordinary black shoes, without buckles.

On nonliturgical occasions the bishop wears "a black cassock with red-silk stitching, red buttonholes and buttons, . . . [a] purple silk sash, with silk fringes at both ends; pectoral cross . . . purple skullcap and *collare* (rabat). Use of purple stockings is optional." A green cord may be worn with the bishop's black plush hat. Only on very solemn occasions should he wear a purple cloak of watered silk. Cardinals wear red garments, rather than purple, all of watered silk. Red cords, "interwoven with gold strands," adorn a cardinal's pectoral cross and the tassels of his plush hat.[38]

Until 1870 bishops were accustomed to wearing a green, flat, wide-brimmed hat with a low crown, with twelve green tassels (six on each side). The hat for cardinals was red. Like a feudal lord, the bishop, ennobled by his elevation to this office, also has a coat of arms with a pious motto specially designed by an expert in heraldry and often displayed in the diocesan newspaper or website.

Fr. Willard Jabusch, composer of liturgical music, describes the grand style affected by two American cardinals, George Mundelein and Samuel Stritch, both archbishops of Chicago. Mundelein, the self-anointed "Prince of the West," whose license plate bore the number one, erected a mansion for himself modeled on Mount Vernon. As a young seminarian Jabusch was called upon to carry Stritch's twenty-foot-long train of scarlet watered silk; the cardinal wore an ermine mantle and a ring and pectoral cross, both encrusted with emeralds and diamonds. In 1969 Paul VI ordered the cardinals to cut back on the length of their trains; in place of the traditional hat, they now receive a red biretta and skullcap. Jabusch concludes that young Catholics today "find episcopal costumes and regalia curious and antique."[39]

Recalling gospel admonitions against ostentation and careerism, Bernard Häring observes that in earlier times popes and bishops, with palatial residences, sumptuous clothing, and jewelry, mistakenly imitated the majestic lifestyle of secular monarchs. "Why," he asks, "is the church today so unwilling to adjust to the modest style and titles of modern democratic leaders? Why all the insistence on outmoded vestments, titles and promotions?"[40] Centuries ago, St. Bernard of Clairvaux, addressing his former protégé, Pope Eugene III (1145–1153), remarked that St. Peter "is known never to have gone in procession adorned with either jewels or silks, covered with gold, carried on a white horse, attended by a knight or surrounded by clamoring servants. . . . In this finery you are the successor, not of Peter, but of Constantine."[41]

In his homily opening of the synod of bishops on September 30, 2001, Pope John Paul II reminded them that, if they are to serve the poor, defend the least among the faithful, and protest against the "unacceptable gap between luxury and misery," they must, if their "word is to be credible . . . give proof of conduct detached from private interests and attentive towards the weaker ones."[42] In his postsynodal exhortation he affirmed that "the bishop who wishes to be an authentic witness and minister of the Gospel of hope must be a *vir pauper* [a poor man]. . . . The Bishop's decision to carry out his ministry in poverty contributes decisively to making the Church the 'home of the poor'" (*PG* 22).

Taking up the pope's theme, Bishop Nestor Ngoy Katahwa of Kolwezi in the Congo bluntly declared:

> With our title of "princes of the church," we are led to cultivating the search for human honors and privileges, while the King, in reference to whom we are princes, finds his glorification on the cross. . . . We are more at ease with the powerful and the rich than with the poor and the oppressed. And the fact that we maintain sole legislative, executive and judicial powers is a temptation for us to act like dictators, more so inasmuch as our mandate has no limitations.[43]

One who is worthy, then, of the episcopal office will assume a lifestyle consonant with the values of the gospel and will abandon the antiquated dress of earlier times in favor of simpler attire more appropriate to this day and age.

A Hierarchical Church or a Discipleship of Equals?

Perhaps the most essential reform of the episcopacy is not administrative or structural but psychological, namely, the abandonment of the concept of a hierarchical church and the recovery of a sense of the discipleship of equals.[44] In the wake of Vatican I and the restorationist policies of John Paul II we have been bombarded with the notion that the Church, by divine institution, is hierarchical, and that the democratic ideals of the secular world have no application to the Church. That contradicts the Second Vatican Council's description of the Church as the People of God and its encouragement of both episcopal collegiality and greater participation in the life of the Church by all the faithful, ordinary priests and laity alike. Reflecting an earlier ecclesiology that Yves Congar calls *hierarchology*, the restorationists insistently repeat the mantra "the Church is not a democracy" and demand that everyone give unquestioned obedience to the hierarchy and the magisterium. They understand the magisterium to be the pope.[45]

The "modern imperial papacy," as Francis Oakley describes it, is founded on the absolutist tradition of the Roman Empire and was developed in the nineteenth and twentieth centuries as a reaction to the growth of democratic government and fear of the popular will.[46] Pius IX not only condemned liberty of conscience and denied that anyone outside the Catholic Church could be saved, but he also induced the First Vatican Council to proclaim the doctrine of papal infallibility. This doctrine has since been used to curtail theological speculation unacceptable to the Congregation for the Doctrine of the Faith and to encourage what has become known as *creeping infallibility*. Repeating Gratian's idea that the Church was divided into two classes (C. 7, XII, 1), Leo XIII stressed that the pastors, the first class, are responsible for teaching, governing, and legislating; the laity, the second class, "has the duty of submitting, of obeying, of following the laws, and of showing honor." The popular mind gave succinct expression to this idea by declaring that laypeople were obliged to "pay, pray, and obey." In 1906 Pius X, now St. Pius X, emphasized that the Church is "an unequal society" consisting of "two categories of persons, the shepherd and the flock." The former have the right and authority to promote and guide while the "sole duty" of the multitude, "as a docile flock," is to follow the lead of their pastors. For his part, Pius XII in 1945 denied that the community of the faithful could ever be the final authority: "There does not exist in the Church founded by Christ, a popular tribunal or a judicial power deriving from the people." In 1964 Paul VI summed up the position of his predecessors: "The Church is not a democratic association established by human will." In 1968 he added: "The Church is hierarchical and an organic unity; it is not democratic in the sense that the community itself enjoys the priority of faith or authority over those whom the Spirit has placed at the head of the Church."[47] When John Paul II suggested to some American bishops in September 2004 that "better structures of participation, consultation, and shared responsibilities" were needed, he emphasized that this should be recognized as an "intrinsic requirement of the exercise of episcopal authority and a necessary means of strengthening that authority." But he was equally emphatic in saying that this "should not be misunderstood as a concession to a secular 'democratic' model of governance."[48]

Existing in historical time and place, the Catholic Church, while divine, also exhibits the characteristics of other human institutions. The message of freedom and equality, the abolition of distinctions between men and women, between slaves and free people, was enunciated loud and clear in the gospels and epistles. However, as the Church grew and added members, the simplicity of the earliest days gave way to more complex structures and ways of being and doing. Church leaders at first imitated the administrative configuration of the Jewish synagogue, but in time as the Christian community became less Jewish and more Gentile, the administrative apparatus of the Roman Empire provided the model for ecclesiastical governance. The popes took over the trappings of the imperial court and bishops attempted to emulate their splendor. From time to time bishops and popes cozied up to divine-right monarchs and dictators whose conduct was the antithesis of the Christian message of love of God and of neighbor. The vast majority of the People of God were steadily excluded from any meaningful role in the administration of the Church. Although pastors have some responsibility and enjoy the privileges of the clerical state, many priests are treated as children by their bishops.

In its present structure the Church is not a democracy, but, as Brian Tierney notes, neither was it founded as "an absolute dictatorship." During the first millennium the responsibility for maintaining the true faith rested with the community of all the faithful. According to Tierney, "The first popes did not even claim the powers that modern ones take for granted. They did not exercise jurisdiction over the whole church; it did not occur to anyone that they were infallible; they did not appoint bishops; they did not summon general councils."[49] Both Tierney and Oakley have stressed that until comparatively recent times the Church was a constitutional body in which the voices of popes, bishops, councils, and faithful were heard. The decree *Haec Sancta* promulgated by the Council of Constance emphatically declares that final authority in the Church rests with a general council representing the Catholic Church militant, in other words, with the People of God. Although supporters of the papal monarchy dispute that statement, *Lumen Gentium*, in its description of the Church, gives priority to the People of God (chap. 2) over the hierarchy (chap. 3). In the words of St. Paul, all power comes from God (Rom. 13:1), and the implication of

Lumen Gentium seems to be that God has bestowed power and authority first on the People of God, who in turn confer it on the hierarchy. In that sense the People of God do possess final authority. In times past bishops were held accountable to church councils and could be deposed by them, just as the Council of Constance removed three popes who had caused the Great Western Schism.

The imperial mode of government to which Catholics have been subjected in modern times is in direct opposition to the words of Jesus. Speaking of the dictatorial and abusive rulers of his own time, Jesus said, "You know that the rulers of the Gentiles lord it over them and the great ones make their authority over them felt. But it shall not be so among you. Rather whoever wishes to be great among you shall be your servant. Whoever wishes to be first among you shall be your slave" (Mt 20:25–26; Lk 22:25–26). In other words Christians are called upon to be servants of one another and not to seek domination over others. The idea that there are two classes of citizens in the Church, the hierarchs who command and the docile multitude who render blind obedience, disrupts the unity of the Church as Christ's Body.

The unity of the Church does not require uniformity as some hierarchs would insist, but rather permits diversity based on the variety of gifts that each person brings to the service of the whole. While acknowledging the human necessity for leadership, the Church can and should conduct its affairs according to democratic principles, so that the voices of the great majority of Catholics, who are not ordained to specific offices, can be heard. The principle "what touches all should be approved by all"—"*Quod omnes tangit, ab omnibus debet approbari*" can appropriately serve as a guide for the development of future structures of Church government. Only by ruling with the consent of the governed will the bishops regain the trust and respect that have been lost.

We need to recapture the ideal of equality. Despite our differences as men and women, adults and children, our disparate physical prowess or lack thereof, intelligence, education, wealth or poverty, we are all God's children and are equal in God's sight. St. Paul reminds us: "For through faith you are all children of God in Christ Jesus. For all of you who were baptized into Christ have clothed yourselves with Christ. There is neither Jew nor Greek; there is neither bond nor free; there is neither male nor female. For you are all one in Christ Jesus" (Gal. 3:28).

As Christ's faithful ones we are all equally his disciples and he is our only true teacher. With St. Paul we can recognize that different ministries are necessary for the well-being of the community, but the exercise of a given ministry should not exalt one person above another or endow one with a privileged status denied to the others. In what John Beal calls "a stunning reversal" of the idea that the Church consists of two classes, the Second Vatican Council declared:"If by the will of Christ some are made teachers, dispensers of the mysteries and shepherds on behalf of others, yet all share a true equality with regard to the dignity and to the activity common to all the faithful for the building up of the Body of Christ" (*LG* 32).[50] In Gregory the Great's phrase we are all called to be "servants of the servants of God."

Recapitulation

To sum up, if the bishops are again to enjoy the confidence and respect of the faithful, they must adopt a manner of leadership consonant with the core of the Christian message enunciated in the New Testament. If the concept of the bishop as a shepherd is not to be mere pious jargon, the bishop must actively seek to know his people by living closely in their midst. He must value their wisdom and lived experience and seek their counsel and consent in all that touches the faith and the Christian life. In exercising his direction, he will be accountable to the people and open and transparent in his dealings with them. Discarding titles and vesture more suited to a bygone age of kings and princes, he must adopt a style indicative of his task as the servant of God and of God's people. He must understand that, while it is given to him to lead and to teach, he nevertheless stands on an equal footing with the faithful as disciples of Jesus. If he comprehends that, the faithful may indeed proclaim, "He is worthy!"

Notes

1. See the text at www.vatican.va/holy_father/john_paul_ii/apost_exhortations.

2. See "The Martyrdom of Polycarp," in Cyril C. Richardson, *Early Christian Fathers* (New York: Macmillan, 1970), 141–58; Robert S. Pelton, CSC, ed., *Monsignor Romero: A Bishop for the Third Millennium* (South Bend, IN: University of Notre Dame Press, 2004).

3. P. J. Kenedy, ed., *The Official Catholic Directory Anno Domini 2004* (Denver: National Register, 2004); see www.usccb.org/dioceses and the websites for specific dioceses.

4. Patrick Granfield, "Legitimation and Bureaucratisation of Ecclesial Power," in *Power in the Church. Concilium* 197, ed. James H. Provost and Knut Walf (Edinburgh: T. & T. Clark, 1988), 86–93.

5. Code of Canon Law, cc. 403–11; Thomas C. Anslow, CM, "Titular Bishops as an Institution according to the *Annuario Pontificio*," *The Jurist* 58 (1998): 124–51; John M. Huels, OSM, and Richard R. Gaillardetz, "The Selection of Bishops: Recovering the Tradition," *Jurist* 59 (1999): 360.

6. Cyprian, *Epistolae*, 5.4, *CSEL* 3:512; G. W. Clarke, trans., *Letters of St. Cyprian of Carthage*, 4 vols., Ancient Christian Writers 43, 44, 46, 47 (New York: Newman Press, 1984–1989), 1:89, ep. 14; Patrick Granfield, "Concilium and Consensus: Decision-Making in Cyprian," *Jurist* 35 (1975): 397–408.

7. Gerald Bartelink, "The Use of the Words *Electio* and *Consensus* in the Church until about 600," in *Election and Consensus in the Church, Concilium 77*, ed. Giuseppe Alberigo and Anton Weiler (New York: Herder and Herder, 1972), 147–54; Bruno Kleinheyer, "Consensus," in Alberigo and Weiler, *Election and Consensus*, 27–30.

8. Yves Congar, "Reception as an Ecclesiological Reality," in Alberigo and Weiler, *Election and Consensus*, 43–68; Weiler, "Nicholas of Cusa," in Alberigo and Weiler, *Election and Consensus*, 98–99; James A. Coriden, *The Canonical Doctrine of Reception* (Southampton, MA: Association for the Rights of Catholics in the Church, n.d.).

9. William W. Bassett, "Subsidiarity, Order and Freedom in the Church," in *The Once and Future Church: A Communion of Freedom*, ed. James A. Coriden (Staten Island, NY: Alba House, 1971), 217; John Lynch, "Power in the Church: An Historico-Critical Survey," in Provost and Walf, ed., *Power in the Church*, 13–21, esp. 21.

10. Yves Congar, "Quod Omnes Tangit, ab Omnibus Tractari et Approbari Debet," *Revue historique de droit français et étranger* 36 (1958): 210–59.

11. Barbara Anne Cusack, "The Internal Ordering of Particular Churches [cc. 460–572]," in *New Commentary on the Code of Canon Law*, ed. John P. Beal, James A. Coriden, and Thomas J. Green (New York: Paulist Press, 2000), 645–52, 666–71, 708–11.

12. *A Report on the Crisis in the Catholic Church in the United States. The National Review Board for the Protection of Children and Young People Established by the United States Conference of Catholic Bishops* (Washington, DC: USCCB 2004), 143, D.

13. Bernard Häring, *A Theology of Protest* (New York: Farrar, Straus & Giroux, 1970), 105–14.

14. Francis Dvornik, "Origins of Episcopal Synods," in Coriden, *Once and Future Church*, 25–56; Eric W. Kemp, *Counsel and Consent: Aspects of the Government of the Church as Exemplified in the History of the English Provincial Synods* (London: SPCK, 1961).

15. John G. Johnson, "Groupings of Particular Churches [cc. 431–459]," in Beal, Coriden, and Green, *New Commentary*, 577–88; Cusack, "The Internal Ordering of Particular Churches," in Beal, Coriden, and Green, *New Commentary*, 610–22.

16. "Bishop England's Constitution," and "Report on the State of the Church in the U.S.," in "Papers Relating to the Church in America from the Folios of the Irish College at Rome," *Records of the American Catholic Historical Society* 8 (1897): 454–59, 460, 462; James Hennesey, SJ, "'To Chuse a Bishop': An American Way," *America*, September 2, 1972, 117; Leonard Swidler, *Toward a Catholic Constitution* (New York: Crossroad, 1996), 118–22; Trisco, "Democratic Influence," in Alberigo and Weiler, *Election and Consensus*, 135–36.

17. Gerald P. Fogarty, SJ, "Episcopal Governance in the American Church," in *Governance, Accountability, and the Future of the Catholic Church*, ed. Francis Oakley and Bruce Russett (New York: Continuum, 2004), 103–18.

18. Fogarty, "Episcopal Governance," 117–18.

19. Brian Tierney, "Collegiality in the Middle Ages," in *Historical Problems of Church Renewal, Concilium* 7, ed. Roger Aubert and Anton G. Weiler (Glen Rock, NJ: Paulist Press, 1965), 5–14, esp. 11–12, and "Church Law and Alternative Structures: A Medieval Perspective," in Oakley and Russett, *Governance*, 49–61, esp. 61.

20. Peter Steinfels, *A People Adrift* (New York: Simon & Schuster, 2003), 307–14.

21. For the charter and the "Norms" see the Office of Child and Youth Protection section of www.usccb.org. See their Statement of Episcopal Commitment, November 2002, at www.usccb.org/statements. David Gibson, *The Coming Catholic Church: How the Faithful Are Shaping a New American Catholicism* (San Francisco: HarperCollins, 2003), 21–34, 273–79.

22. *NRB Report*, 139, 143, D, 144, F.

23. Investigative Staff of the *Boston Globe*, *Betrayal: The Crisis in the Catholic Church* (Boston: Boston Globe, 2002); Ralph Cipriano, "Grand Jury Findings," *National Catholic Reporter*, October 7, 2005; Michael Newall, "Shining Light on a Cover-Up," *National Catholic Reporter*, April 28, 2006.

24. Gibson, *Church*, 298, 307–11.

25. Cited by Gibson, *Church*, 307–9.

26. *Stewardship: A Disciple's Response* (Washington, DC: USCCB, 1993), 34–35.

27. Francis Butler, "Financial Accountability: Reflections on Giving and Church Leadership," in Oakley and Russett, *Governance*, 153–60, esp. 153–54.

28. Alison Leigh Cowan, "Auditors Say Priest Took $1.4 Million before Ouster," *New York Times*, July 29, 2006; see www.stamfordadvocate.com/scn-fayarchive.

29. Butler, "Financial Accountability," 154–59.

30. See his proposals in *Report of the Church in America: Leadership Roundtable*, 32–33, at www.nlrcm.org. Also see Butler, "Financial Accountability," 160.

31. Geoffrey Boisi quoted in *The Tidings*, July 7, 2006.

32. Cardinal McCarrick cited by Gibson, *Church*, 307; Charles Zech in *Report of the Church in America: Leadership Roundtable*, 33, at www.nlrcm.org.

33. Russell Shaw, "Is This Transparency?" *America*, May 16, 2005, 11–13.

34. John Beal, "It Shall Not Be So Among You! Crisis in the Church, Crisis in Church Law," in Oakley and Russett, *Governance*, 88–102, esp. 91.

35. Bassett, "Subsidiarity," 225, n. 24, comments that French aristocratic usage provided the title *monsignor*; Urban VIII in 1630 gave cardinals the title *eminence*; and after 1929 Pius XI gave bishops the title *excellency*, thus giving them equal status with Italian senators. Gibson, *Church*, 301.

36. See Patrick's *Confessio* and *Epistola*, in *St. Patrick: His Writings and Muirchu's Life* (Totowa, NJ: Rowman & Littlefield, 1978), 23, 35, 41, 55.

37. Jimmy Breslin, "LI Bishop's Mansion: Biggest Waste of Money, Bar Nun," *Newsday*, October 8, 2002; Gibson, *Church*, 298–301; Ralph Cipriano, "Lavish Spending in an Archdiocese Skips Inner City," *National Catholic Reporter*, June 19, 1998.

38. *Ceremonial of Bishops* (Collegeville, MN: Liturgical Press, 1989), 35, 331–32, app. 1; James-Charles Noonan Jr. *The Church Visible: The Ceremonial Life and Protocol of the Roman Catholic Church* (New York: Viking Penguin, 1996), pt. 4, "Vesture and Insignia."

39. Willard F. Jabusch, "Lord of the Ring," *Commonweal*, September 27, 2002, 31; Paul VI, *Motu Proprio, Dress and Insignia of Cardinals, Bishops, and Lesser Prelates*, March 31, 1969.

40. Häring, *A Theology of Protest*, 109.

41. St. Bernard of Clairvaux, *De Consideratione*, PL 182:776, bk. 4, chap. 3.6; *Five Books on Consideration*, trans. John D. Anderson and Elizabeth T. Kennan (Kalamazoo, MI: Cistercian Publications, 1976), 117.

42. See www.vatican.va/holy_father/john_paul_ii/homilies/2001.

43. John L. Allen Jr. reported Bishop Katahwa's comments in the *National Catholic Reporter*, October 12, 2001.

44. Elisabeth Schüssler-Fiorenza, *In Memory of Her* (New York: Crossroad, 1984), 104, and "A Discipleship of Equals: Ekklesial Democracy and Patriarchy in Biblical Perspective," in Eugene C. Bianchi and Rosemary Radford Ruether, *A Democratic Catholic Church: The Reconstruction of Roman Catholicism* (New York: Crossroad, 1992), 17–33.

45. Yves Congar, *Lay People in the Church: A Study for a Theology of Laity* (Westminster, MD: Newman Press, 1965), 45.

46. Francis Oakley, "Constitutionalism in the Church?" in Oakley and Russett, *Governance*, 76–87, esp. 77.

47. Vatican I, *Pastor Aeternus* (1870); Pius IX, *Quanta Curia* (1864), *Quanta Conficiamur* (1863); Pius X, *Vehementer Nos* (1906); Paul VI, *Ecclesiam Suam* (1964), excerpted in *Rome Has Spoken: A Guide to Forgotten Papal Statements and How They Have Changed through the Centuries*, ed. Maureen Fiedler and Linda Rabben (New York: Crossroad, 1998), 15, 23, 48, 56, 94–95. See Patrick Granfield, *Ecclesial Cybernetics: A Systems Analysis of Authority and Decision-Making in the Catholic Church with a Plea for Shared Responsibility* (New York: Macmillan, 1973), 173–74 and 185–86 for citations of Leo XIII; *Acta Sanctae Sedis* 21 (1888): 322; Pius X, *Acta Sanctae Sedis* 39 (1906): 8; Pius XII, *Acta Apostolicae Sedis* 37 (1945): 261; and Paul VI, *The Pope Speaks* 13 (1968): 38.

48. See www.vatican.va/holy_father/john_paul_ii/speeches/2004; Tom Rachman, "Pope Talks with U.S. Bishops about Scandal," *Austin American-Statesman*, September 11, 2004.

49. Brian Tierney, "Church Law and Alternative Structures: A Medieval Perspective," in Oakley and Russett, *Governance* 50.

50. Beal, "It Shall Not Be So Among You," 91–92.

Epilogue

Re-Membering a Dis-Membered Church

IN THE PRECEDING PAGES I have attempted to outline the history of the election of bishops by the clergy and people of the diocese. The thought that the clergy and people should do this today may seem preposterous to those inured to the idea that the pope freely appoints the bishops. Popular election of bishops, as I have demonstrated, is hallowed by usage from the earliest times, by canons enacted by Church councils, and by repeated papal affirmation. Sadly, however, the history of episcopal elections is marked by a progressive disenfranchisement of the laity and the rank and file of the clergy. The Church, the Body of Christ, has been dis-membered as ordinary clergy and laypeople have been denied the right to proclaim that one among them is worthy to be their bishop.

Speaking of the Church, St. Paul compares it to the human body composed of many members whose individual gifts are essential to the unity and health of the whole:

> As a body is one though it has many parts, and all the parts of the body though many are one body, so also Christ. For in one Spirit we were all baptized into one body, whether Jews or Greeks, slaves or free persons, and we were all given to drink of one Spirit. Now the body is not a single part, but many. . . . But as it is there are many parts, yet one body. The eye cannot say to the hand, "I do not need you," nor again the head to the feet, "I do not need you." . . . But God has so constructed the body as to give greater honor to a part that is without it, so that there may be no division in the body, but that the parts may have the same concern for one another. If one part suffers, all the parts suffer with it; if one part is honored, all the parts share its joy. Now you are Christ's body, and individually parts of it. (1 Cor. 12:30)

In earlier times the participation of the metropolitan bishop, the provincial bishops, the priests, and the people in episcopal elections reflected the Pauline image of the Church as Christ's Body. The Church is one under the headship of Christ and all its members are dependent on one another and responsible for sharing their gifts for the good of the whole. And yet, although St. Paul emphasizes that one part of the Body cannot say to another, "I do not need you," that is exactly what has happened. A progressive dismissal of various elements considered unnecessary by the hierarchy characterizes the history of episcopal elections. The uneducated were told, "We do not need you," presumably because of their ignorance and their tendency toward rowdy behavior. Women were told, "We do not need you," no doubt because, as Gratian puts it in the *Decretum* (C. 33, q. 5, c. 13), they were not made in God's image. The rank and file of priests and deacons were told, "We do not need you," probably because noble blood did not course through their veins. The laity in general were told, "We do not need you," surely because their function was to listen and obey. The exclusion of all these members of Christ's Body has led many to wrongly identify the Church with the hierarchy. The rest have been cast aside, cut off, disenfranchised, dis-membered. The Body of Christ has been mutilated.

If the unity and health of the Body of Christ are to be restored, it is essential that the Church take up again the ancient tradition of the popular election of bishops. The restoration to the clergy and people of their baptismal right to elect their own bishops is a necessary step toward re-membering our dis-membered Church. By taking that step we will be helping to make Christ's Body, the Church, whole and entire again.

Select Bibliography

Sources

A Report on the Crisis in the Catholic Church in the United States. The National Review Board for the Protection of Children and Young People Established by the United States Conference of Catholic Bishops. Washington, DC: USCCB 2004.

Andrieu, Michel. *Le Pontifical romain au moyen âge.* 4 vols. Vatican City: Bibliotheca Apostolica Vaticana, 1938–1941.

———. *Les Ordines Romani du haut moyen âge.* 4 vols. Louvain: Spicilegium Sacrum Lovaniense, 1931–1957.

Barry, Colman. *Readings in Church History.* Rev. ed. 3 vols. in 1. Westminster, MD: Christian Classics, 1985.

Beal, John P., James A. Coriden, and Thomas J. Green, eds. *New Commentary on the Code of Canon Law.* New York: Paulist Press, 2000.

Bradshaw, Paul F. *Ordination Rites of the Ancient Churches of East and West.* New York: Pueblo, 1990.

Clarke, G. W., trans. *The Letters of St. Cyprian of Carthage.* 4 vols. Ancient Christian Writers 43, 44, 46, 47. New York: Newman Press, 1984–1989.

Ehler, Sidney Z., and John B. Morrall. *Church and State through the Centuries.* Westminster, MD: Newman Press, 1954.

Flannery, Austin, OP, ed. *Vatican Council II: The Conciliar and Post-Conciliar Documents.* 2 vols. Northport, NY: Costello Publishing, 1996.

John Paul II. *Pastores Gregis: Post-Synodal Apostolic Exhortation.* Vatican City: Libreria Editrice Vaticana, 2003.

Lora, Ermino. *Enchiridion dei Concordati: Due Secoli di Storia dei Rapporti Chiesa-Stato.* Bologna: EDB, 2003.

Mercati, Angelo. *Raccolta di Concordati in materie ecclesiastiche tra la Santa Sede e la autorità civili.* Vatican City, 1954.

"Norms for the Selection of Bishops (1971)." In Bassett, *The Choosing of Bishops,* 103–7.

Procedure for the Selection of Bishops in the United States. A Suggested Implementation of Present Papal Norms. Hartford, CT: Canon Law Society of America, 1973.

Report of the Church in America: Leadership Roundtable 2004 at the Wharton School. www.nlrcm.org.

Tanner, Norman. *Decrees of the Ecumenical Councils.* London: Sheed & Ward; Washington, DC: Georgetown University Press, 1990.

Tierney, Brian. *The Crisis of Church and State.* Englewood Cliffs, NJ: Prentice Hall, 1964.

Modern Works

Alberigo, Giuseppe, and Anton Weiler, eds. *Election and Consensus in the Church. Concilium* 77. New York: Herder and Herder, 1972.

Aubert, Roger, and Anton G. Weiler, eds. *Historical Problems of Church Renewal. Concilium* 7. Glen Rock, NJ: Paulist Press, 1965.

Bartelink, Gerard. "The Use of the Words *Electio* and *Consensus* in the Church (until about 600)." In Alberigo and Weiler, *Election and Consensus,* 147–54.

Bassett, William W., ed. *The Choosing of Bishops.* Hartford, CT: Canon Law Society of America, 1971.

———. "Subsidiarity, Order and Freedom in the Church." In Coriden, *The Once and Future Church,* 205–65.

Beal, John. "It Shall Not Be So Among You! Crisis in the Church, Crisis in Church Law." In Oakley and Russett, *Governance,* 88–102.

Bellitto, Christopher. *The General Councils: A History of the Twenty-One Church Councils from Nicaea to Vatican II.* Mahwah, NJ: Paulist Press, 2002.

Benson, Robert Louis. *The Bishop-Elect: A Study in Medieval Ecclesiastical Office.* Princeton, NJ: Princeton University Press, 1968.

Bianchi, Eugene C., and Rosemary Radford Ruether. *A Democratic Catholic Church: The Reconstruction of Roman Catholicism.* New York: Crossroad, 1992.

Biemer, Günter. "Election of Bishops as a New Desideratum in Church Practice." In Swidler and Swidler, *Bishops and People,* 38–53.

Bokenkotter, Thomas. *A Concise History of the Catholic Church.* Rev. ed. New York: Doubleday Image Books, 1990.

Buckley, Michael J., SJ. *Papal Primacy and the Episcopate: Towards a Relational Understanding.* New York: Crossroad 1998.

———. "Resources for Reform from the First Millenium." In Pope, *Common Calling,* 71–86.

Butler, Francis. "Financial Accountability: Reflections on Giving and Church Leadership." In Oakley and Russett, *Governance,* 153–60.

Cardman, Francine. "Myth, History and the Beginnings of the Church." In Oakley and Russett, *Governance,* 33–48.

Congar, Yves. *Lay People in the Church: A Study for a Theology of Laity.* Westminster, MD: Newman Press, 1965.

Coppa, Frank, ed. *Controversial Concordats: The Vatican's Relations with Napoleon, Mussolini, and Hitler.* Washington, DC: Catholic University of America Press, 1999.

Coriden, James A., ed. *The Once and Future Church: A Communion of Freedom.* Staten Island, NY: Alba House, 1971.

————. *Who Decides for the Church? Studies in Co-Responsibility.* Hartford: Canon Law Society of America, 1971.

Coriden, James A., and J. Michael Ritty. "The Selection of Bishops." *CLSA* Proceedings 65 (2003): 65–91.

Eidenschink, John. *The Election of Bishops in the Letters of Gregory the Great.* Washington, DC: Catholic University of America Press, 1945.

Ellis, John Tracy. "The Appointment of Bishops and the Selection of Candidates in the United States since Vatican II." In Huizing and Walf, *Electing Our Own Bishops,* 81–84.

————. "The Selection of Bishops." *American Benedictine Review* 35:2 (June 1984): 111–27.

Fogarty, Gerald, SJ. "Episcopal Governance in the American Church." In Oakley and Russett, *Governance,* 103–20.

Funk, Francis Xavier. *A Manual of Church History.* Translated by P. Perciballi and W. H. Kent. 2 vols. London: Burns, Oates and Washbourne, 1938.

Gaudemet, Jean. "Bishops: From Election to Nomination." In Huizing and Walf, *Electing Our Own Bishops,* 10–15.

————. "The Choice of Bishops: A Tortuous History." In *From Life to Law. Concilium,* edited by James Provost and Knut Walf, 59–65. Maryknoll, NY: Orbis Books, 1996.

Gibson, David. *The Coming Catholic Church: How the Faithful Are Shaping a New American Catholicism.* San Francisco: HarperCollins, 2003.

Granfield, Patrick. *Ecclesial Cybernetics: A Systems Analysis of Authority and Decision-Making in the Catholic Church with a Plea for Shared Responsibility.* New York: Macmillan, 1973.

————. "Episcopal Elections in Cyprian: Clerical and Lay Participation." *Theological Studies* 37 (1976): 41–52.

————. *The Limits of the Papacy: Authority and Autonomy in the Church.* New York: Crossroad, 1987.

Guilday, Peter. *A History of the Councils of Baltimore.* New York: Arno Press and the New York Times, 1969.

Heft, James L. "Accountability and Governance in the Church: Theological Considerations." In Oakley and Russett, *Governance,* 121–35.

Hennesey, James, SJ. *American Catholics: A History of the Roman Catholic Community in the United States.* New York: Oxford University Press, 1981.

Huels, John M., OSM, and Richard R. Gaillardetz. "The Selection of Bishops: Recovering the Tradition." *Jurist* 59 (1999): 348–76.

Huizing, Peter, and Knut Walf, eds. *Electing Our Own Bishops. Concilium* 137. New York: Seabury Press, 1980.

Klauser, Theodor. *A Short History of the Western Liturgy: An Account and Some Reflections.* Oxford: Oxford University Press, 1979.

Kleinheyer, Bruno. "Consensus in the Liturgy." In Alberigo and Walter, *Election and Consensus,* 27–30.

Kölmel, Wilhelm. "Episcopal Elections and Political Manipulation." In Alberigo and Weiler, *Election and Consensus*, 69–78.

Lécuyer, Joseph. "The Bishop and the People in the Rite of Episcopal Consecration." In Huizing and Walf, *Electing Our Own Bishops*, 44–47.

Legrand, Hervé-Marie. "Theology and the Election of Bishops in the Early Church." In Alberigo and Weiler, *Election and Consensus*, 31–42.

Lynch, John E. "Co-Responsibility in the First Five Centuries: Presbyteral Colleges and the Election of Bishops." In Coriden, *Who Decides for the Church?* 14–53.

McBrien, Richard. *Lives of the Popes: The Pontiffs from St. Peter to John Paul II.* San Francisco: HarperSanFrancisco, 1997.

McMillan, Sharon L. *Episcopal Ordination and Ecclesial Consensus.* Collegeville, MN: Liturgical Press, 2005.

Metz, René. "Papal Legates and the Appointment of Bishops." *Jurist* 52 (1992): 259–84.

Miller Richard W., II, ed. *Lay Ministry in the Catholic Church: Visioning Church Ministry through the Wisdom of the Past.* Liguori, MO: Liguori, 2005.

Oakley, Francis. *The Conciliarist Tradition: Constitutionalism in the Catholic Church, 1300–1870.* Oxford: Oxford University Press, 2003.

Oakley, Francis, and Bruce Russett, eds. *Governance, Accountability, and the Future of the Catholic Church.* New York: Continuum, 2004.

O'Meara, Thomas F. "Emergence and Decline of Popular Voice in the Selection of Bishops." In Bassett, *The Choosing of Bishops*, 21–32.

Pope, Stephen J., ed. *Common Calling: The Laity and Governance of the Catholic Church.* Washington, DC: Georgetown University Press, 2004.

Provost, James H., and Knut Walf. *Power in the Church. Concilium* 197. Edinburgh: T & T. Clark, 1988.

Quinn, John R. *The Reform of the Papacy: The Costly Call to Christian Unity.* New York: Crossroad, 1999.

Reese, Thomas J., SJ. *Archbishop. Inside the Power Structure of the American Catholic Church.* San Francisco: Harper & Row, 1989.

———. *A Flock of Shepherds. The National Conference of Catholic Bishops.* Kansas City, MO: Sheed & Ward, 1992.

———. *Inside the Vatican. The Politics and Organization of the Catholic Church.* Cambridge, MA: Harvard University Press, 1996.

Ritty, J. Michael, and James A. Coriden. "Report to the CLSA Membership on the Selection of Bishops." *CLSA Proceedings* 64 (2002): 334–60.

Rosmini, Antonio. *The Five Wounds of the Church.* Translated by Denis Cleary. Leominster, MA: Fowler Wright Books, 1987.

Schimmelpfennig, Bernhard. "The Principle of the *Sanior Pars* in the Election of Bishops during the Middle Ages." In Huizing and Walf, *Electing Our Own Bishops*, 19–23.

Steinfels, Peter. *A People Adrift.* New York: Simon & Schuster, 2003.

Stockmeier, Peter. "The Election of Bishops by Clergy and People in the Early Church." In Huizing and Walf, *Electing Our Own Bishops*, 3–9.

Sullivan, Francis A., SJ. *From Apostles to Bishops: The Development of the Episcopacy in the Early Church.* New York: Newman Press, 2001.

———. "St. Cyprian on the Role of the Laity in Decision Making in the Early Church." In Pope, *Common Calling,* 39–50.

Swidler, Leonard. *Toward a Catholic Constitution.* New York: Crossroad, 1996.

Swidler, Leonard, and Arlene Swidler, eds. and trans. *Bishops and People.* Philadelphia: Westminster Press, 1970.

Tierney, Brian. "Church Law and Alternative Structures: A Medieval Perspective." In Oakley and Russett, *Governance,* 49–61.

———. *The Foundations of the Conciliar Theory: The Contribution of the Medieval Canonists from Gratian to the Great Schism.* Cambridge: Cambridge University Press, 1955.

Trisco, Robert. "Bishops and their Priests in the United States." In *The Catholic Priest in the United States: Historical Investigations,* edited by John Tracy Ellis, 111–292. Collegeville, MN: Saint John's University Press, 1971.

———. "The Debate on the Election of Bishops in the Council of Trent." *Jurist* 34 (1974): 257–91.

———. "Democratic Influence on the Election of Bishops and Pastors and on the Administration of Dioceses and Parishes in the U.S.A." In Alberigo and Weiler, *Election and Consensus,* 131–39.

———. "The Variety of Procedures in Modern History." In Bassett, *The Choosing of Bishops,* 33–60.

Ullmann, Walter. "The Election of the Bishops and the Kings of France in the Ninth and Tenth Centuries." In Alberigo and Weiler, *Election and Consensus,* 79–86.

Weiler, Anton G. "Nicholas of Cusa on the Reform of the Church." In Alberigo and Weiler, *Election and Consensus,* 94–103.

Index

accountability, 2, 104, 130, 161, 162–66
Agapetus I, pope, 38
Alexander II, pope, 54, 55
Alexander III, pope, 67
Alexander VI, pope, 79
Alexander VIII, pope, 90
Alexandria, patriarch of, 19
Alfonso X, king of Castile, 70
Allen, John, 145
Ambrose, bishop of Milan, 20, 31
Anicetus, pope, 13
Anselm, archbishop of Canterbury, 58–59
Antioch, 11, 12, 13, 19, 30, 154
apostles, 2, 3, 7–8, 9, 10, 11, 12, 13, 16,
    22, 28, 107, 109
Apostolic Canons, 22, 23, 24, 25, 26
Apostolic Constitutions, 22, 23, 28
apostolic delegate, 105, 106, 122, 134, 135
apostolic succession, 11, 86
archbishop. *See* metropolitan
Arian heresy, 18, 38, 41
Arles, metropolitan of, 42
Athanasius, bishop of Alexandria, 18,
    26, 31
Augsburg (1566), Diet of, 90
Augustine, bishop of Hippo, 20, 21, 24,
    29, 50, 146
Augustine, bishop of Canterbury, 42
Avignon Papacy, 65, 74, 75

Baltimore, archdiocese of, 101, 122, 128,
    161; Eighth Provincial Council (1855),
    102; First Synod of (1791), 161; ple-
    nary and provincial councils, 161;
    Second Plenary Council (1866), 103;
    Third Plenary Council (1884), 105
Banks, Robert, bishop of
    Green Bay, 127
Bardstown, diocese of, 101
Barnabas, 8, 11
Bassett, William, 158
Beal, John, 130, 171
Belleville, diocese of, 128, 131
Benedict XV, pope, 107
Benedict XVI, pope, x, 18, 145. *See also*
    Ratzinger, Joseph
Benson, Robert, 33
Bernard of Clairvaux, 168
Bevilacqua, Cardinal Anthony, archbishop
    of Philadelphia, 127, 163
Bishops: administration of church prop-
    erty, 25; appointments, American gov-
    ernment influence on, 125; authority,
    absolute, of, 153; auxiliary bishops,
    124–25, 156–57; coadjutor bishops,
    125; coat of arms of, 167; confer-
    ences of, 3, 109, 119, 131, 138, 145,
    162, 165; consecration of, 14, 19, 49,
    50, 58, 68, 72–73, 80, 86, 89, 92, 93,

109, 110, 155; deposition of, 26, 60,
68, 74; dress of, 1, 51, 72–73, 81, 167,
168; elections of, in early texts, 14,
17; elections in the Byzantine empire,
37–30, 59; elections in the Christian
Roman Empire, 17–20; elections in
the Latin West, 40–45; elections, papal
pronouncements on, 26–29; feudal
princes, 51–53; legislation on, conciliar, 21–26; lifestyle of, 167–68; liturgy
for making a bishop, 28–29, 48–50,
71–73, 80, 82, 108–11, 112; mansions
of, 131, 166–67; ministry of, 15, 16,
24–26, 40, 68, 92, 168, 172; miter, 1,
29, 71, 72, 73, 110; nomination of,
royal, 37–60; office of, 1–5, 12–14; ordination of, 2, 9, 14, 15, 18, 19, 22, 23,
24, 28, 31, 32, 40, 41, 42, 44, 48, 50, 51,
52, 57, 58, 59, 60, 66, 71, 80, 86, 90,
108, 109, 110, 111, 113; papal reserva-
tion of appointments, 73–75, 76, 77,
78; poverty of, 168; provincial, 16, 23,
25, 26, 27, 30, 31, 32, 38, 40, 43, 44,
46, 49, 50, 57, 58, 59, 66, 68, 71, 72,
80, 86, 92, 94, 96, 103, 104, 105, 106,
111, 112, 120, 123, 135, 136, 137,
141, 142, 143, 146, 147, 148, 156,
160, 161, 178; qualifications of, 9, 16,
22, 47, 73, 87, 88, 119, 133, 135, 138,
145, 146, 148, 164; resignation of,
3, 74, 76, 87, 93, 109, 122, 123, 131,
140, 145, 146; ring, 12, 29, 44–45, 50,
52, 56, 57, 58, 59, 60, 71, 72, 73, 110,
129, 155, 157, 167; shepherd, 1, 3, 10,
23, 41, 45, 49, 58, 73, 88, 97, 154–57,
162, 163, 169, 172; spiritual adultery,
73, 129; staff (crosier), 1, 44–45, 50, 52,
56, 57, 58, 59, 60, 71, 72, 73, 110, 155,
157; term of office, 132, 145, 146,
148; titles of, 166; titular bishops, 157;
transfer of, 5, 11, 22, 24, 46, 48, 51,
56, 60, 73, 74, 76, 78, 103, 112, 127–
29, 131, 132, 147, 148, 162; virtue of
simplicity, 166–68; worthiness of, 5,
15, 16, 18, 19, 20, 22, 24, 30, 32, 40,

41, 43, 46, 47, 49, 50, 59, 67, 69, 70,
72, 77, 80, 92, 94, 95, 103, 105, 106,
109, 123, 131, 134, 145, 148, 153–72.
See also hierarchy
Body of Christ, xii, 3, 31, 88, 123, 136,
144, 171–72, 177–78
Boniface I, pope, 26–27
Boniface VIII, pope, 73
Boniface, bishop, 45
Boston, archdiocese of, 101, 122, 144,
156, 163, 165
Bourges (1438), Pragmatic Sanction of,
78
Braxton, Edward, bishop of Belleville,
131
Bridgeport, diocese of, 31, 127, 128, 156,
163, 164; Second Synod of (1971), 122
Buckley, Michael, SJ, 130
Burke, Raymond, archbishop of
St. Louis, 127
Butler, Francis, 164–65
Byron, William, SJ, 126, 130–31, 146, 147
Byzantine empire, 37–40, 51, 59

Caecilianus, bishop of Carthage, 25–26
Callistus I, pope, 14, 129
Callistus II, pope, 57, 58
Calvin, John, 86
Canon Law Society of America, xi, 120,
121, 122, 126, 142; Procedure for the
Selection of Bishops in the United
States, 132–36, 139, 140, 144, 147,
148
canons of cathedral chapters, x, 65–67,
69, 70, 71, 72, 73, 77, 78, 79, 81, 86,
87, 88, 89, 95, 96, 98, 101, 102, 103,
105, 107, 108, 111, 112, 121
Canterbury, archbishops of, 42, 58–59,
67–68
CARA (Center for Applied Research on
the Apostolate), 126
cardinals, 78, 87, 88, 124, 129, 145, 147,
166, 167; College of, x, 5, 54, 55, 60,
65, 67, 70, 75, 76, 78, 138
Cardman, Francine, 7

Carolingian Empire, 45–47
Carroll, John, bishop of Baltimore, 100–101, 112
Catherine of Siena, St., 75
Catholic Emancipation, 96
Celestine I, pope, 27, 31, 41, 43, 49, 77, 148
Celestine V, pope, 145
Ceremonial for Bishops, 129, 167
Charlemagne, emperor, 37, 46–47, 57, 60
Charles VII, king of France, 78
Charles the Bald, emperor, 47
Charter for the Protection of Children and Young People, 128, 162
Chicago, archdiocese of, 127, 156
Chlothar II, king of the Franks, 43
Christus Dominus, 2–3, 108, 109, 159
Church: classes in, 169; hierarchical church, 168–72; property, 25, 41, 47, 50, 57, 58, 68, 91, 93, 108; territorial structure, 29–31; unequal society, 169; widowed, 23, 67, 69, 73, 129
Civil Constitution of the Clergy, 92, 112
Clement IV, pope, 70
Clement VII, pope, 75
Clement VIII, pope, 89
Clement XIV, pope, 100
Clement of Rome, First Letter of, 11–12, 13, 145
Clovis, king of the Franks, 42
Code of Canon Law (1917), x, 5, 98, 106, 107–8; (1983), 121, 128, 147, 153, 156, 158, 159, 160, 166
Collegiality, ix, 2, 3, 120, 158, 169
Committee, Diocesan, for the Selection of Candidates for the Office of Bishop, 132–36, 139–41, 142, 148
conciliarism, 65, 76–78, 86, 91, 111, 160
Concilium Germanicum (743), 45
concordats, 97, 107, 108, 112, 125, 130; Austria-Hungary (1855), 94; Bavaria (1817), 94; Bologna (1516), 79, 94; Fontainebleau (1813), 96; France (1801), 93–94, 99, 112; Germany (1933), 99, 100, 112; Hanover (1824),

95; Holy Roman Empire (1784), 91; London (1107), 59, 68; Poland, 92; Portugal, 92, 94; Prussia (1821), 95; Sardinia-Piedmont, 91–92; Spain, 91–92, 94; Spain (1941), 112; Spain (1953), 100, 112; Sutri (1111), 57; Two Sicilies (1818), 92, 94; Upper Rhineland, 95; Vienna (1448), 78–79; Worms (1122), 57–58, 60
congé d'elire, 47
Congregation for Bishops, 120, 121, 123, 124, 128, 141, 143, 147, 148
Congregation for Divine Worship, 128
Congregation for the Doctrine of the Faith, 128, 169
Connecticut Post, 163
Congar, Yves, 169
Conroy, George, bishop of Ardagh, 104
Consistorial Congregation, 106
Constans, emperor, 21
Constantine, emperor, 18, 26, 168
Constantinople, 19, 27, 37, 38, 39, 46. *See also* councils
Constitution of Lothar (824), 51, 52
Constitution on the Sacred Liturgy, 109
consultors, diocesan, 102, 103, 105, 106, 107, 121, 123, 124, 131
Cooke, Cardinal Terence, archbishop of New York, 124, 127
Coriden, James, 137
Cornelius I, pope, 14, 16
Corinth, church of, 11–12, 13, 145
Corrigan, Patrick, priest of Hoboken, 104, 106
council, diocesan finance and pastoral, 159
councils: Ancyra (314), 21, 24; Antioch (341), 21, 23, 24, 25, 26; Arles (314), 21, 23, 24, 26; Basel (1431), 76–77, 78, 79; Braga (572), 43–44, 59; Carthage (419), 21, 22, 23, 23, 25, 26; Chalcedon (451), 21, 23, 30, 73; Constance (1414–18), 76, 78, 81, 170, 171; Constantinople I (381), 21, 25, 30, 32; Constantinople IV (869), 39, 160; ecumenical, 2, 21, 25, 30, 43, 66, 160, 161;

Fismes (881), 47; Jerusalem (51 AD), 8, 11; Laodicea (343–81), 21, 22, 23; Lateran I (1123), 58, 60; Lateran II (1139), 66; Lateran III (1179), 67; Lateran IV (1215), 69–70, 81, 161–62; Lateran V (1512–17), 79–80, 82; Lyon II (1274), 70–71; Nicaea I (325), 21, 22, 23, 24, 30, 38, 49, 160; Nicaea II (787), 39; Paris (614), 43; Pisa (1409), 76; provincial, 21, 25, 30, 43, 88, 97, 102, 111, 146, 160, 161; Rheims, (1049), 53; Rome (313), 26; Sardica (343/344), 21, 22, 23, 24, 26; Toledo IV (633), 44, 59; Trent (1545–63), 85–89, 111, 159; Tyre (336), 26; Vatican I (1869–70), 83. 160, 169; Vatican II (1962–65), ix, 54, 83, 108–9, 112, 119, 120, 123, 124, 158, 160, 161, 169, 171. See also synods
counsel and consent, 154, 157–62, 172
Curtis, Walter W., bishop of Bridgeport, 122, 163
Cyprian, bishop of Carthage, 15–17, 28, 31, 86–87, 157

Dailey, Thomas, bishop of Brooklyn, 127
Damasus, bishop of Rome, 26
Den Bosch, diocese of, 122
The Didache, 14, 31
discipleship of equals, 168–72
Donatists, 26
Dulles, Cardinal Avery, SJ, 144
Durand, Guillaume, bishop of Mende, Pontifical of, 71–72, 80, 81

Edes, Ella B., 104
Egan, Cardinal Edward, archbishop of New York, 127, 163
Egypt, 14, 17, 30
Election of a Bishop, Proposal for the, 142–47
Ellis, John Tracy, 124, 125
England, 42, 58, 68, 75, 86, 96, 101
England, John, bishop of Charleston, 101, 160–61
Epiphanius, patriarch of Constantinople, 38

Eugene III, pope, 168
Eugene IV, pope, 76–77
Eusebius, bishop of Caesarea, 13, 18

Fabian, pope, 18
FADICA (Foundations and Donors Interested in Catholic Activities), 164
Fahey, John F., 120
Fay, Msgr. William, 163
Febronius, Justin (Johan Nikolaus von Hontheim, auxiliary bishop of Trier), 91, 111
Felix, bishop of Aptonga, 25
Ferdinand and Isabella, king and queen of Spain, 79
Fogarty, Gerald, SJ, 161
Formosus, pope, 51
Formularies of Marculf, 43
France, 59, 66, 78, 79, 90, 92–93, 98–99, 112. See also Gallicanism
Francis I, king of France, 79
Franco, Francisco, 100
Franklin, Benjamin, 100
Frederick II, emperor, 67
Frederick III, emperor 78
Freiburg, diocese of, 121
Fulbert, bishop of Chartres, 53
Funk, Francis X., 17

Gaillardetz, Richard, 126, 130, 136–37, 148
Gallicanism, 90–91, 93, 94, 111
Gantin, Cardinal Bernard, 24, 74, 128, 129, 147
Gaul, Merovingian, 42–43
George, Cardinal Francis, archbishop of Chicago, 127, 131
Germany, 37, 45, 46, 47, 53, 56, 58, 79, 91, 112, 121, 125, 130
Germanus, bishop of Auxerre, 19–20
Goedert, Raymond, 132
Granfield, Patrick, 9, 16, 130, 144, 145
Gratian, 66, 169, 178
Greeley, Andrew, 126, 130, 145
Green, Thomas, 132

Gregory I, the Great, pope, 40–41, 59, 139, 172
Gregory II, pope, 38, 45
Gregory VII, pope, 31, 54–56, 60, 71, 91
Gregory X, pope, 70, 75
Gregory XVI, pope, 97
Gregory, bishop of Tours, 42–43, 59
Gregory, Wilton, archbishop of Atlanta, 128, 131
Gregory of Nazianzus, 19
Guise, Charles de, Cardinal of Lorraine, 87
Gumbleton, Thomas, auxiliary bishop of Detroit, 126

Haarlem, canons of, 121
Haec Sancta, 76, 78, 170
Häring, Bernard, 130, 159, 168
Hartford, archdiocese of, 156
Heft, James, 130
Heintschel, Donald E., 120
Hennesey, James, SJ, 7, 130
Henry III, emperor, 53
Henry IV, emperor, 55–56
Henry V, emperor, 56–58
Henry I, king of England, 59
Henry II, king of England, 67–68
Henry VIII, king of England, 86
Hickey, Cardinal James, 127
hierarchology, 169
hierarchy, 87, 96, 112, 122, 123, 129, 130, 143, 161, 163, 169, 170, 171, 178
Hincmar, bishop of Rheims, 47
Hippolytus of Rome, *Apostolic Tradition*, 14, 28, 31
Hitler, Adolf, 99
Hosius, bishop of Córdoba, 24
Huels, John, 130, 136–37, 148
Hugh of Fleury, 59
Hughes, Alfred, archbishop of New Orleans, 128
Humbert of Silva Candida, Cardinal, 53
Hunthausen, Raymond, archbishop of Seattle, 125

Ignatius, bishop of Antioch, 12, 154

Index of Prohibited Books, 91, 97
infallibility, papal, 85, 98, 112, 160, 169
Innocent II, pope, 66
Innocent III, pope, 67, 68, 69, 161
Innocent IV, pope, 70
Innocent VI, pope, 75
Innocent VIII, pope, 79
Innocent XI, pope, 90
Innocent XII, pope, 90
Inquisition, Holy Office of the, 97
investiture: canonical, 107; lay, 52, 53, 54–56; war of investitures, 56–60
Ireland, 41, 95, 96
Irenaeus, bishop of Lyons, 13
Irene, Byzantine empress, 39
Isidore, archbishop of Seville, 44–45, 79
Italy, 37, 38, 40, 45, 46, 54, 55, 58, 97, 98, 99, 112, 130

Jabusch, Willard, 167
Jefferson City, diocese of, 126
Jerome, 17
Jerusalem, 8, 11, 70
John X, pope, 52
John XII, pope, 52
John XXIII, pope, 85
John, king of England, 68
John Chrysostom, bishop of Constantinople, 19
John Paul II, pope, 3, 4, 23, 67, 85, 122, 125–26, 146, 147, 165, 166, 168, 169; *Pastores Gregis*, 2, 154
Joseph II, emperor, 91, 97
Julius II, pope, 79
Jus regale, 52, 59, 90
Jus spolii, 52
Justinian, Byzantine emperor, 38

Kaiser, Robert Blair, xii, 145
Katahwa, Nestor Ngoy, bishop of Kolwezi, 168
Kenrick, Peter, archbishop of St. Louis, 103
Klauser, Theodor, 29
Kleinheyer, Bruno, 158
Knoxville, diocese of, 127

Komonchak, Joseph, 131
Krol, Cardinal John, archbishop of Philadelphia, 163
Küng, Hans, 146

Lafont, Ghislain, proposal of, 137–39, 147, 148
Laínez, Diego, Jesuit general, 87
Lakeland, Paul, 131
Langton, Stephen, archbishop of Canterbury, 68
Lateran Treaty of 1929, 99, 112
Law, Cardinal Bernard, archbishop of Boston, 122, 127, 146, 163
Leadership Roundtable, 135–36, 165
Legrand, Henri, 27, 107
Leitner, Louis, 102
Leo I, the Great, pope, 27, 31, 43, 77, 87, 148, 166
Leo III, Byzantine emperor, 38
Leo III, pope, 46
Leo IX, pope, 53
Leo X, pope, 79–80
Leo XIII, pope, 86, 99, 169
liberalism, papal condemnation of, 96–98, 112
licentia eligendi, 47
Linus, pope, 13
Lombards, 37, 45
London, 42, 59, 68, 100
Lori, William E., bishop of Bridgeport, 127, 164
Louis XI, king of France, 78
Louis XIV, king of France, 90, 111
Louis XVIII, king of France, 94
Louis the Pious, emperor, 51
Los Angeles, archdiocese of, 127, 156
Lothar, king of the Franks, 51
Lumen Gentium, xi, 2–3, 108, 130, 158, 166, 170–71, 172
Luther, Martin, 80, 85–86
Luxembourg, 125
Lynch, John, 158

Mahony, Cardinal Roger, archbishop of

Los Angeles, 127, 163
Magna Charta, 68
Mannion, Gerard, 130
Marsiglio of Padua, Defensor Pacis, 74–75
Martin V, pope, 76
Martin, bishop of Braga, 43
Martin, bishop of Tours, 19–20, 42
Mathiesen, Leroy T., bishop of Amarillo, 122
Matthias, election of, 8–9, 15, 144
Maximilian II, Holy Roman Emperor, 90
Mazzuchelli, Samuel, OP, 102
McCarrick, Cardinal Theodore, archbishop of Washington, 127, 165
McCormack, John, bishop of Manchester, 128
McGlynn, Edward, 105
McHugh, James, bishop of Rockville Centre, 128
McMillan, Sharon, 2, 8, 48, 50, 71, 80, 89, 110
McNally, Robert, SJ, 80
Medeiros, Humberto, archbishop of Boston, 127
Medina Estévez, Cardinal Jorge, 128, 129, 147
Menas, patriarch of Constantinople, 38
metropolitan (archbishop), 23, 24, 25, 26, 27, 28, 29, 30, 32, 38, 39, 40, 42, 43, 44, 45, 46, 47, 48, 49, 50, 53, 54, 57, 58, 59, 66, 71, 72, 77, 80, 81, 82, 87, 89, 91, 92, 93, 94, 97, 101, 106, 110, 111, 113, 120, 136, 137, 139, 141, 178
ministry in the early Church, 8–12
Missale Francorum, 49
Mundelein, Cardinal George, archbishop of Chicago, 167
Murphy, William, bishop of Rockville Centre, 127–28, 167
Mussolini, Benito, 99
Myers, John, archbishop of Newark, 127

Napoleon, emperor, 92–94, 112
Napoleon III, emperor, 98

National Association of Laity, 125
National Catholic Reporter, 165
National Conference of Catholic Bishops (NCCB), 123, 133, 134–35. *See also* USCCB
National Review Board, 4–5, 131, 159, 162–63
Netherlands, 121, 131, 146
New York, archdiocese, 30, 101, 104, 105, 122, 123, 124, 127, 156
New York Times, 163
Nicene Creed, 158
Nicholas I, pope, 47, 51
Nicholas II, pope, 54
Nicholas V, pope, 78
Nicholas of Cusa, *The Catholic Concordance*, 77–78
Niederauer, George, archbishop of San Francisco, 131
Norms for the Selection of Bishops, 119–21, 132, 135, 146, 147
Norwich, diocese of, 156
nuncio, papal, 120, 122, 123, 124, 131

Oakley, Francis, 76, 169, 170
O'Connell, Anthony, bishop of Palm Beach, 126–27
O'Connor, Cardinal John, archbishop of New York, 124, 127
O'Malley, Cardinal Sean, archbishop of Boston, 127
O'Reilly, Bernard, bishop of Hartford, 102
Ordination of a Bishop, 109–11, 112
Ordo Romanus XXXIV, 48
Organic Articles of 1802, 94
Origen of Alexandria, 17
Orsy, Ladislas, SJ, 40, 120, 144
Ostrogoths, 40, 41
Otto I, emperor, 52
Otto IV, emperor, 67

Palladius, bishop to the Scots, 41
Papal States, 46, 98
Paris, archdiocese of, 121

Paschal II, pope, 56–57
patriarchates, 19, 30, 38, 39
Patrick bishop, apostle of Ireland, 41–42, 166
Paul III, pope, 86
Paul VI, pope, 3, 109, 119, 138, 146, 167, 169; *Humanae Vitae*, 158
Paul, St., 8, 9, 11, 13, 170, 171, 177–78
Pelagian heresy, 41
People of God, 108, 109, 112, 119, 120, 130, 133, 136, 137, 169, 170, 171
Pepin, king of the Franks, 45
Peries, George, 105–6
Peter, St., 8, 53, 72, 110, 168; First Letter of, 10, 13
Philadelphia, archdiocese, 101, 127, 156
Philip Augustus, king of France, 66
Philip II, king of Spain, 90
Photian Schism, 39
Pius II, pope, 76, 78
Pius VI, pope, 91, 93, 101, 112
Pius VII, pope, 93, 94, 95, 112
Pius IX, pope, 96, 98, 99, 112
Pius X, pope, 99, 169
Pius XI, pope, 99
Pius XII, pope, 100, 122, 169
Polycarp, bishop of Smyrna, 12, 13, 154
Pontian, bishop of Rome, 14
Pontifical, 71, 72, 109, 110, 111; Magdalen College, 68; Roman (1485), 80–82, 89; Roman (1595), 89; Romano-Germanic, 49–50
popes, 13, 14, 16, 18, 25–27, 28, 31, 38, 40, 41, 43, 45, 46, 47, 49, 50, 51, 52, 53, 54, 56, 57, 59, 60, 66, 67, 68, 69, 70, 71, 75, 76–77, 79–80, 86, 87, 89, 91, 93, 94, 95, 96, 97, 98, 99, 100, 107, 122, 129, 139, 145, 148, 160, 161, 168, 169, 172; election of, 14–15, 26, 50–52, 53, 54, 65, 67, 70, 75, 79. *See also* John Paul II, Paul VI
presbyter, 9–14, 20, 22, 23, 25, 28, 31, 49, 55, 72, 86, 145, 154
Priests' Council, 135, 136, 138, 139, 140, 141, 160

Priests' Senate, 122, 133, 134, 135
Propaganda, Congregation for the Propagation of the Faith, 96, 101, 102, 103, 105, 106
Providence, diocese of, 156
Provisors, Statutes of (1351, 1390), 75
Provost, James, 135, 144
Prussia, 95, 98
Pseaume, Nicholas, bishop of Verdun, 87
Punctation of Ems, 91

Quinn, John, archbishop of San Francisco, 129, 131
Quod omnes tangit ab omnibus debet approbari, 27, 33, 154, 158, 165, 171

Ratzinger, Cardinal Joseph, 128–29, 146, 147. *See also* Benedict XVI
Rausch, Thomas, SJ, 130
Ravenna, 38, 40
Reese, Thomas, SJ, 27, 100, 122, 125, 126, 135, 146, 147
reform, pleas for, 130–32
Ricci, Scipio, bishop of Pistoia, 91
Rigali, Justin, archbishop of Philadelphia, 127
Ritty, Michael, 137
Roberts, William, 93
Rome, church of, 12–13, 14, 15, 16, 17, 26, 27, 29, 30
Romero, Oscar, archbishop of San Salvador, 154
Roosevelt, Franklin D., president of the United States, 125
Rosmini, Antonio, *The Five Wounds of the Church*, 97, 112
Rotterdam, diocese of, 122
Ruini, Cardinal Camillo, papal vicar for Rome, 129

San Francisco, archdiocese of, 131
Santa Fe, archdiocese of, 122
Schism, Great Western, 65, 75, 81, 160, 171
secrecy, 97, 99, 103, 104, 106, 112, 120, 136, 137, 145, 146, 148, 154, 163, 165–66
Selection of a Bishop, Proposal for the, 139–41
sensus ecclesiae, 158
sensus fidei, 158
sensus fidelium, 136
Sergius III, pope, 51
Seven, the, election of, 9, 28, 31
sexual abuse crisis, ix, xi, 2, 4, 128, 144, 146, 153, 155, 162, 163, 164, 165, 166
Shaw, Russell, 165
Sheehan, Cardinal Lawrence, archbishop of Baltimore, 128
Sheil, Bernard, auxiliary bishop of Chicago, 125
Shepherd of Hermas, 13
Siete Partidas, 70
simony, 24, 44, 48, 53, 56–58, 60, 76, 77, 79, 101, 146
Siricius, bishop of Rome, 26
Sixtus IV, pope, 79
Spain, 17, 37, 41, 43–45, 59, 70, 79, 90, 92, 94, 100, 112, 130
Spalding, John Lancaster, bishop of Peoria, 105
Spellman, Cardinal Francis, archbishop of New York, 122, 123
Speyer, diocese of, 121
St. Louis, archdiocese of, 122
Statuta antiqua Ecclesiae, 42
Steinfels, Peter, 126, 143, 162
Stephen II, bishop of Rome, 45
Stephen III, bishop of Rome, 50
Stephen VI, bishop of Rome, 51
Stritch, Cardinal Samuel, archbishop of Chicago, 167
subsidiarity, 120, 136, 143
Switzerland, 121, 125
Symmachus, bishop of Rome, 40
Symons, Keith, bishop of Palm Beach, 127
synod, diocesan, for the election of a bishop, 142–43; of Bishops (2001), 168; on the Eucharist, 4; Roman, triennial, 161

synods, diocesan and provincial, ix, 2, 3, 21, 24, 25, 26, 30, 38, 39, 43, 44, 56, 59, 60, 78, 88, 94, 103, 111, 121, 142, 148, 158, 160, 161; Brixen (1080), 56; Frankfort (794), 46; Herstal (779), 46; Meaux (845), 47; Numidia (312), 26; Pistoia (1786), 91; Rome (499), 40; Rome (769) 50; Rome (825), 52; Rome (861), 51; Rome (896), 51; Rome (963), 52; Rome (1059) 54; Rome (1075), 55; Rome (1112), 57; Sutri (1046), 53; Thionville (844), 47; Valence (845), 47; Worms (1076), 55. *See also* councils
Syria, 14, 30

Talleyrand, bishop of Autun, 93
Terna, 96, 105, 112, 121, 135, 136, 137
Theodoric, Ostrogothic king, 40
Theodosius II, emperor, 26–27
Thomas à Becket, archbishop of Canterbury, 67–68
Tierney, Brian, 162, 170
Timothy, First Epistle to, 9–10, 22, 48, 130
Titus, Epistle to, 9–10, 22
transparency, 2, 122, 137, 141, 162–65
Trisco, Robert, 96, 100
Tübingen, University of, 146

Urban II, pope, 56
Urban VI, pope, 75
United States, church in the, 100–107, 156, 160–61

USCCB (United States Conference of Catholic Bishops), 123, 133, 134–35, 141, 143, 148, 162, 163, 164, 165; Committee on the Selection of Bishops, 123

Valentinian I, Roman emperor, 26
Valerius, bishop of Hippo, 20
Vatican Council for the Public Affairs of the Church, 119
Vienna (1815), Congress of, 94
Voice of the Faithful: in Bridgeport, xi, 132, 140, 148; in San Francisco, 131; in Wellesley, xi

Washington, D.C., archdiocese of, 125, 156
Weakland, Rembert, archbishop of Milwaukee, 164
Weiler, Anton, 77
Wheeler, William, priest of St. Louis, 103
Wigger, Winand, bishop of Newark, 104
William the Conqueror, king of England, 58
William II, king of England, 58
Wiseman, Nicholas, archbishop of Westminster, 96
women, ordination of, 134, 147

York, diocese of, 42

Zech, Charles, 165
Ziemann, Patrick, bishop of Santa Rosa, 164

About the Author

Joseph F. O'Callaghan, professor emeritus of Medieval History and former director of the Center for Medieval Studies at Fordham University, is also past president of the American Catholic Historical Association.

His primary academic interest lies in the history of medieval kingship and parliaments with particular attention to medieval Spain. His publications include *Reconquest and Crusade in Medieval Spain* (2003); *Alfonso X and the Cantigas de Santa Maria: A Poetic Biography* (1998); *The Learned King: The Reign of Alfonso X of Castile* (1993); *The Cortes of Castile-León, 1188–1350* (1989); *A History of Medieval Spain* (1975). Many of his articles have been collected in *Alfonso X, the Cortes, and Government in Medieval Spain* (1998), and *The Spanish Military Order of Calatrava and its Affiliates* (1975). He also translated *The Autobiography of St. Ignatius Loyola* (1992) and *The Latin Chronicle of the Kings of Castile* (2002). A life-long interest in family history led to the publication of *The O'Callaghan Family of County Cork* (2005).

Long active in his parish as a lector, eucharistic minister, member of the Parish Council, the RCIA team, and the Liturgy Committee, he also collaborated with his wife, Anne, now deceased, in presenting educational programs to catechists in the diocese of Bridgeport, Connecticut. For many years he has lived in Norwalk with his wife and their four children.